MW01485531

# WHIRLWIND

Plainspoken
Books

# WHIRLWIND

## My Life Reporting the News

### BILL KURTIS

UNIVERSITY PRESS OF KANSAS

Published by Plainspoken Books,
an imprint of the University Press of Kansas (Lawrence, Kansas 66045), which was
organized by the Kansas Board of Regents and is operated and funded by
Emporia State University, Fort Hays State University, Kansas State University,
Pittsburg State University, the University of Kansas, and Wichita State University.

Library of Congress Cataloging-in-Publication Data
Names: Kurtis, Bill, author
Title: Whirlwind : my life reporting the news / Bill Kurtis.
Description: Lawrence : University Press of Kansas, 2025. | Includes index.
Identifiers: LCCN 2025001982 (print) | LCCN 2025001983 (ebook) |
ISBN 9780700640041 cloth | ISBN 9780700640058 ebook |
ISBN 9780700640065 audio
Subjects: LCSH: Kurtis, Bill | Journalists—United States—Biography |
BISAC: BIOGRAPHY & AUTOBIOGRAPHY / Personal Memoirs |
HISTORY / United States / 20th Century | LCGFT: Autobiographies Classification:
LCC PN4874.K86 A36 2025 (print) | LCC PN4874.K86 (ebook) LC record available
at https://lccn.loc.gov/2025001982.
LC ebook record available at https://lccn.loc.gov/2025001983.

British Library Cataloguing-in-Publication Data is available.
EU Authorised Representative Details: Easy Access System Europe
Mustamäe tee 50, 10621 Tallinn, Estonia | gpsr.requests@easproject.com

Printed in the United States of America
10 9 8 7 6 5 4 3 2
The paper used in this publication is acid free and meets the minimum requirements
of the American National Standard for Permanence of Paper for Printed Library
Materials Z39.48-1992.

Cover Design: Karl Janssen
Cover Photo: Bill Kurtis, circa 1982, in the newsroom,
reflecting on his final broadcast as anchorman for the
Channel 2 News, WBBM-TV Chicago. Courtesy of Kurtis Productions.

I'd like to dedicate this book to the men and women of the television news business. Whatever I experienced, they were also there, creating a visual history. For the most part our work disappeared like smoke in a breeze, seen once by thousands of people and then never seen again. I hope this book plays a small part to revive what has been lost on the airwaves.

# Contents

A photo gallery follows page 106.

# Preface
## Whirlwind

It seems only fitting that my whirlwind of a career started with a tornado.

It was the biggest tornado Kansas had ever seen that spun around my priorities, threw me into a life of journalism, and blew me toward the Windy City, where my very first story would be covering the trial of the century. And it only got wilder from there. Thinking about all the biggest moments in my life still makes my head spin.

From where I'm standing now, coming up on almost six decades of this journey, the skies behind me look "clear for takeoff." A story of great moments in America's recent history, told through the eyes of a newsman who always seemed to be in the right place at the right time. But believe me, in the moment, on the ground, it was anything but that. My journey is filled with questions and uncertainty and lots of running on instinct. It was usually a coin flip whether it was my choices or divine guidance that most would call luck that got me into a high-profile, high-stakes situation or a moment of national chaos and calamity. But those moments never lasted long, and I quickly found myself thrown up, spun around, and tossed on to the next thing.

I look a lot of risks to get here, from turning down an offer for steady, honest work as a lawyer for a job in the growing new field of television news to figuring out how to sneak a story out of a communist country to deciding whether to risk my serious reputation as a journalist to take a part in some comedy movie called *Anchorman*.

I also rarely knew the importance of where I was at the time. I seldom saw myself as sitting on the inside of a major moment in history—especially at the beginning of my story. I was working my first job, trying to impress my bosses, build a career for myself, and make ends meet. I would be getting up every morning and going to work just like everyone else. It didn't really occur to me that while everyone else would be going to banks and law firms and department stores, I would be going to a courthouse to sit within spitting distance of Charles Manson and then reporting what I had seen to the world. Only after the fact, sometimes *years* after the fact, did I realize that I was watching history unfold.

But time passed; today's news was written into the history books. My life's journey was given structure. The lessons and chance opportunities I was offered in my childhood pointed me in the direction my life would take me. A double education in journalism and the law turned out to be the perfect combination for my first big story, the trial of Richard Speck, and for my second big story, the trial of the Chicago Seven, and for my third big story, the trial of Charles Manson. Helter Skelter is right. I had a lifetime of experience in the first few years of my career. I had good instincts, strong skills, the right friends, and plenty of luck, and I ended up at a pioneering local television station hoping to show that TV news could be real journalism. We ended up doing just that as I broke the truth about Agent Orange and became the first American to return to Vietnam after the war.

Only now is the storm of life that I'm still caught in starting to come into focus. I suppose that's what time does. It gives us perspective and context. It smooths the rough edges. Events become memories, and memories become stories. Time can tame the whirlwind into a pleasant summer breeze.

So yes, it seems only fitting that my whirlwind of a career started with a tornado. An unexpected, deadly twister on a late-summer day in Kansas that started my wild journey.

# WHIRLWIND

ONE

# The Topeka Tornado

Three years of law school is a long time, and graduation deserves a celebration. Mine was limited to pouring a glass of champagne in the backyard of Washburn University's married housing near the campus of Washburn University School of Law in Topeka, Kansas. A single evening was about all the time we had. My wife, Helen, was still teaching second grade and caring for our six-month-old daughter, Mary Kristin. After two years as part-time weatherman at the only television station in town, WIBW-TV, I was filling on-air slots where needed.

It may be hard to believe, but even after three years of law school, I was still trying to make up my mind about what to do for the rest of my life. Broadcasting seemed a natural choice, having started when I was sixteen at a small radio station in Independence, Kansas—KIND. At twenty-six, I had ten years' experience in radio and television, but that just made the choice harder when compared with a career as a lawyer. After all, I had just spent three years preparing to carry a briefcase and learning to say, "Yes, your honor." Maybe the image of Perry Mason motivated me to accept a job with a two-man law firm in Wichita, Kansas. Trial work. Personal injury practice. Good lawyers to learn from—John Frank and Pat Kelly. But the agonizing decision between broadcasting and law wouldn't go away, even as I sipped the champagne and symbolically broke the glass in the plastic garbage can. After all, this was a forever choice—I'd better love it.

We were still adjusting to the slow pace of summer. The days were growing longer and warmer, the responsibilities of the school year fell away, and vacation plans arrived on the horizon. In Kansas, this also meant waiting for the inevitable growling skies to descend to the ground. The unstable transition from spring to summer always brought notable cause for concern.

Topeka had 127,000 people, four radio stations, and two newspapers. Santa Fe employed 2,400. Some of the largest grain elevators in the world stood along the Union Pacific tracks in North Topeka. On a hazy day, they looked almost like skyscrapers.

Forbes Air Force Base was home to the 313th Troop Carrier Wing. Many of their C-130s were already flying to Vietnam. It was June 1966.

The wheat harvest had started in the southern counties, slowed a bit by rain. The weather in Topeka was mostly cloudy with an occasional thunderstorm predicted. A pretty typical day.

Washburn was all leafed out, its oak trees and sugar maples high-lighting the meandering walkways across campus. It was an oasis in the steamy Kansas summers. The stately old buildings reeked of education, making you just want to go inside and study.

Graduation from law school was one thing, but even with a job already lined up, I still had to pass the bar. So after the champagne, I plowed immediately into some catch-up. Around 4:00 p.m., I was in a tax review class in the basement of the law school, Carnegie Hall, one of the oldest of the original buildings on campus. It was a beautiful gray structure full of memories and tradition, with columns in front and the smell of law books when you entered. In one corner near the front door stood a clutch of walking canes that belonged to seniors. They were symbolic of the school's founder, Ichabod Washburn, an abolitionist from the 1860s. His likeness, a lean man dressed in a black cutaway frock coat with an Abe Lincoln top hat, was widely regarded as one of the weirdest mascots in America. It was perfect for an arrogant senior law student to say, "Yeah, I made it and you didn't."

But my mind wasn't on taxes. I was going to fill in for news director Tom Parmley on the 6:00 p.m. news at WIBW-TV. Tom wanted to leave early for vacation.

Ask any person that Wednesday late afternoon, and I'd bet no one had a clue about what was coming. Our minds were on the daily routine. But across the state, as is often the case in Kansas, a lot was happening farther west. Overnight, Hays got five inches of rain that produced flash floods. Great Bend got golf-ball-sized hail.

I thought we'd probably lead my newscast with the weather, as usual. A low-pressure system carrying warm, tropical air was coming up from Oklahoma across southeast Kansas. And some forecasters thought severe thunderstorms could develop in the northeast.

Since my weatherman days, I'd thought I could smell a severe thunderstorm coming, and I had the feeling.

I had come to learn that weather reports in farm country are different than city weathercasts. Out in the big coastal cities, folks want to know if their weekend will be affected by rain. But in the Great Plains, weather is success or failure. Too much rain means crops are washed out. Not enough can mean a shriveling field of heartbreak.

At the station, we were limited to watching the teletype wire from the National Weather Bureau's radar, the only one available to us. There was no Doppler radar at the time or the million-dollar setups big-city weather departments would develop.

We took severe weather seriously and set up our own warning system. Storm spotters took position on the western edge of Topeka, in the direct path of the weather flow. I imagined Londoners watching the skies for Luftwaffe fighters and bombers in World War II. That was how seriously we took it.

As I scoured the wires for top stories, the conditions were closer to the possibility of a severe thunderstorm. The US Weather Bureau had issued a tornado *watch* for portions of south-central and eastern Kansas. That meant be on the watch for tornadoes. It's the warning we take in but don't act on.

The ad hoc team that did act on the tornado watch was getting into place, however. Spotters were heading toward the western city limits. Nineteen-year-old Rick Douglas was trying to get to the highest point around for better visibility. Burnett's Mound was so perfectly sited at the southwest edge of the city that the legend had grown that it would protect the city if any tornado approached.

Twenty-nine-year-old Dave Hathaway, in his fifth year as a highway patrolman, reported for the 3-to-10 shift. He was assigned to a section of southwest Topeka that was full of suburban homes, quiet neighborhoods. Should be an easy night.

Further into the city's core, forty-eight-year-old Mary Hatke was walking on Kansas Avenue in the heart of downtown and was aware of the atmosphere. The air was still. No birds singing. No leaves fluttering. Even the sunlight seemed strange. It just didn't look right.

A squall line of thunderstorms had developed and was advancing toward Topeka. The temperature was 75 degrees, and the air was thick and unstable.

The Volunteer Emergency Services Team (VEST) was alerted and deployed. It was a group of citizens band radio volunteers who today would be called storm chasers. Generally, they took a position, monitored the clouds, reported the information, and stayed at their post until the danger had passed.

Despite the preparations, I had no expectations of anything more serious than the usual warnings. Decades of false reports had left a tinge of not wanting to be the boy who cried wolf. But we went through the motions just in case.

One thing jumped off the teletype—a report from Manhattan that high winds had taken a roof off a garage and the squall line was heading for Topeka. Years later, I would learn that it was a tornado and had also damaged some buildings on the campus of Kansas State University, sixty miles west. But at the time, the information did not confirm a tornado.

At 6:00 in Topeka, the sun was out, but the light quickly changed to a sickly yellowish green. People were looking up at the boiling clouds and listening to thunder in the distance.

Spotter John Meinholdt pulled his Ranchero up to the summit of Burnett's Mound, the hill on the southwest edge of the city, and radioed in that a major storm was approaching from the southwest, bearing 210 to 260 degrees. A radio volunteer spotter relayed the message to the weather bureau. At 6:50, it issued a bulletin on the weather wire: "Heavy thunderstorms moving into the western edge of the Topeka area. Could produce hail and strong wind gusts up to 80 mph."

By this time, my newscast was over, but General Manager Charlie Ross held me in the studio to give the all clear. We waited. Time seemed to be holding too. This was the broadcaster's moment, perched beneath a wave that was getting ready to break over us. How had I wound up here? What had led me to the news desk that night, to the dead center of the action? Would the next words I uttered mean life and death for thousands, or would the moment pass, as it had countless times before? Did lawyers feel like this waiting for a verdict?

Richard Garrett, meteorologist in charge of Topeka's weather bureau, was a legendary figure who had helped form the network of spotters, media, and civil defense. It was a different era of storm chasing. Those on the ground had only radios, what they could see in the sky, and their instincts. They had none of the moment-by-moment information that came with the advent of satellites, internet, and cell phones. We felt those same limits in our studio. Radar-indicated tornadoes were years away. We were working nearly blind. We needed that first sighting.

Then, a call from Lester Osburn, twenty miles southwest of Topeka. He phoned the emergency operator and reported that two tornadoes had merged into one large white twister on the ground, "boiling like an A-bomb mushroom."

It was the first sighting of the tornado.

Then a report came in from Ed Rutherford, our veteran cameraman. Years later in Chicago, we called him street-smart, low-key; he'd been through it all. He was a reconnaissance cameraman in the air force. Ed had a two-way radio, and when he called in that he'd just seen a tornado on the ground passing his house and heading northeast toward the city, it was my absolute truth. I needed no further confirmation. But it was only one sighting, and I expected it to lift back into the cloud.

WIBW radio's general manager, Jerry Holley, broke into the Kansas City–Minnesota baseball game with a warning.

Inside the main studio, I was suited up, ready to go on camera. The director, Don Franzen, was at the center of a studio crew waiting for the word to pull the trigger on what we did for a living: broadcast information. Small, routine actions were suddenly of enormous importance. Our hope that the tornado watch would expire peacefully was quickly fading. The information coming from the news desk would mean life or death, and we all sensed it. There could be no mistakes.

Charlie Ross was there gathering reports, some as small as a few words from engineers, cameramen, and salespeople who walked into the studio, drawn to the center of activity. Was it real? they asked. Should they go home?

From the station's location at the northwest corner of Topeka, no one in the building had actually seen it. We were reacting to two-way radios, highway patrol communication. For a moment, I felt like a young Ronald Reagan creating a baseball play-by-play by reading a ticker tape of the action.

There was one important clue that sent a shiver through me: the faces. Everyone seemed to believe what I did—that this was the one. After we heard Rutherford's call-in, blood drained away, leaving facial features changed by a mixture of fear, dread, and the burden of responsibility to act in the face of great danger, realizing that perhaps no other broadcasters had faced this moment—at least none that we knew. There was quiet in the studio, a fear of disturbing the void when time slows to a trickle but, for those in the moment, knowing that time was moving dangerously close to a decision point.

At 7:01, we broke into the CBS program, *Lost in Space*, on TV. Maybe it was the feeling that it really couldn't be happening while knowing that we had to give a warning—"Tornado on the ground, heading for the city"— words that none of us had ever dreamed we'd be saying.

Charlie's decision to break into programming was the beginning of twenty-four hours of straight coverage.

We were still waiting for the second confirmed sighting, so we were repeating that we were still only in a tornado watch, adding information as best we could. The exact time is hazy, but I remember going into anchor mode. It's not as easy as we make it look. I would describe it as an extremely intense focus. There is no script. Your brain becomes a computer, having to separate the noise and clutter coming at you, most of which is unconfirmed, from the facts, then mentally build those facts into a timeline. Sometimes you are not only the final filter but also the most accurate. No one else was following every scene that aired, every damage report. Did you actually see the tornado?

Then, in a single crystallizing moment, a short burst came in from Rutherford, still on the scene—"The Embassy and Huntington Apartments have been wiped out." That was it for me. No hearsay. No rumor. It was a veteran's eyes on the beast. He knew what he was doing.

The white tornado was on the far side of Burnett's Mound and now big enough to wipe out a giant apartment complex on the city side. I mentally drew a line between the two points and saw an arrow pointing right into the center of the Kansas capital, cutting through everything that makes a city a city where families raise their children and send them to school down the street, where they can run a few blocks for extra milk and on Sundays go to church. It was a living, breathing community. To me, it was the beating heart of Topeka.

These images flashed like a lightning bolt. So did the realization that the next words I would say would have to turn the *watch* into a full-scale *warning*. These words would move my community to action, to basements, to shelters. I thought, *This must be what hysteria feels like.* Would profanity work, or breaking down in tears?

Instead, I said from the gut and from the heart with emphasis, "For God's sake, take cover." Though I didn't realize it at the time, those words would be etched into the history of that moment. In his account of the tornado, *And Hell Followed with It*, Bonar Menninger later wrote, "With those five words, Kurtis had crossed a line between the objective and the personal. In its effect, he might as well have been reaching through the TV and grabbing viewers by the lapels."

While the tornado was blasting its way into neighborhoods and shopping malls as if buildings had been placed in its path for maximum damage, the staff inside the WIBW studio were in shock but working their jobs. The dreaded announcement had been made that broke the tension and pointed us back to reality—to do our jobs. I remember standing in front of a hand-drawn weather map with a plastic sheet over it and a flow of people bringing information or trying to help. Charlie Ross had assumed the reins, Don Franzen was directing, Tom Scott filled in as floor director helping to funnel information to me, Darrel Witham was in master control with Elmer Gunderson, and Max McDowell and Ron Ulm were in the newsroom. General manager Thad Sandstrom was in a meeting downtown. Paul Winders, Ralph Thompson, Al Austin, Ron Douglas, Bill Woodruff, and George Logan helped WIBW become the key means of communication for first responders and our listeners. Roger Bailey and Roger Wilson manned WIBW radio to reach 105 Kansas counties. They were the only source for hours for the Kansas families across the state worried about loved ones in the capital.

Outside the studio and across town, the tornado brought a scene of chaos and destruction—one that we in the studio wouldn't fully understand until hours later. At 7:02, the weather bureau hit the sirens and nineteen alarms came to life, starting low, then steadily building to blare their full warning.

One Kansas state trooper called in, reporting funnel-type clouds only miles southwest of the Mound. "I'm about a mile or so south on Wanamaker Road, and it's coming directly at me. Five, six, or seven miles."

It was building speed and size. People were beginning to get the warning; outside, they were running toward shelters.

Patrolman Hathaway pulled over under the I-470 overpass. It was raining heavily. He put out flares to stop traffic and turn cars around.

Washburn geology professor Al Stallard watched from outside his house and estimated that the tornado was half a mile wide—black—churning along the ground hitting trees and grinding them into the mixer. It dropped up and down as it moved along the ground.

A pony farm was directly below Burnett's Mound at the end of Fairlawn Road. Ray White had 250 Shetland ponies grazing. The ponies were lifted off the ground and carried off or slammed back down, crushed, impaled, decapitated, disemboweled by tree branches, fence posts, barbed wire.

Rick Douglas was making the final climb to the top of the ridge when hail, gravel, and trees began hitting his car. He started back down, the tornado chasing him and pushing the car around.

Hathaway was watching and described the sound for Menninger as "a freight train full of angry bees." He told the dispatcher the tornado was on the Mound.

Both Douglas and Hathaway saw a house lifted off its foundation some two hundred feet, as if it were riding a geyser. And then it exploded.

The I-470 underpass was getting crowded. Hathaway was there. Douglas had taken shelter there, and the Tuttle family was trying to get away when they realized they'd better take cover. Harold Tuttle was a highway patrolman. He had also been stationed at Schofield Barracks on December 7, 1941. In the car, he had two grandchildren and Virginia, his wife. When they reached the underpass, they saw Hathaway and said, "It's too late." They got out and began running up the embankment.

The tornado was nearly at the water tank on the side of Burnett's Mound. That meant for half a mile, the winds were shredding everything—not blowing it down but shredding.

Douglas grabbed a concrete bridge pillar as the wind ripped his jacket off.

Virginia Tuttle felt like she was beginning to slip away. Slowly she was pulled out from under the underpass and into the air. She was flying. So was Douglas. It was 7:14.

The tornado was 5,000 feet tall with 200-mile-an-hour winds, traveling northeast at 32 miles an hour. It was slipping down the north side of the Mound into County Fair Estates. Inside the homes of the subdivision were stories of mayhem, houses coming apart, people hit by debris or trying to keep from blowing away. Author Bonar may have been quoting Sue Goodin, huddling with fifty others in the basement shelter of the clubhouse at the Huntington Apartments, describing the sound as "The buffalo were returning, riding the wind. Ten thousand hoofbeats pounding the ceiling above in a thundering, clattering stampede."

From a church parking lot, *Topeka Daily Capital* photographer Perry Riddle shot the tornado coming over the Mound. Perry and I would wind up in Chicago and on the street at the Democratic National Convention in 1968, and we'd just point at each other as if to say, "Hey, how 'bout that tornado?"

Perry, a disciple of his famous mentor, Rich Clarkson, got the iconic shots of both events.

At the law school, review class was still going on, and Leon Taylor stood outside watching what he at first thought were birds flying around a dark, shapeless cloud coming across the golf course on campus. Then he realized those specks were pieces of houses and he went inside.

Across campus, our neighbors rushed to our little apartment in student housing, grabbed Helen and Mary Kristin, and drove to the basement of the science building to take shelter. Helen was a twenty-six-year-old teacher whose monthly income helped pay my way through law school. We'd started dating in high school, rounding all the usual bases. She was homecoming queen; I was the quarterback. We both loved performing in theater. I always told Helen that I'd call if it was ever more than a tornado watch, but when the time actually came that June evening, I was busy. I don't think she ever forgave me.

After the tornado, there was no electricity, no telephones, and no Washburn. For a long time, we didn't know what had happened to the law school.

Judge Newton Vickers walked into the studio two hours after the tornado went through and said with an ashen face, "Washburn's gone." Carnegie Hall, MacVicar Chapel, Rice Hall, Thomas Women's Gymnasium, Crane Observatory, Boswell Hall. All demolished.

Rick Douglas emerged cut, battered, and covered in mud. He was taken to the hospital by a stranger who waved off Rick's objections to putting his bloody body in a new car. It was like that. Everyone was helping everyone.

It wasn't the end when the tornado finally lifted off the ground northeast of town. It was only the beginning. People emerged from their shelters to a blue sky, the crisp air that follows a storm, and a silence so unique that some thought the tornado had taken away their hearing. At any other time, it would have been a beautiful new world, but the scene didn't say that. They had entered a city without power or telephone access. Houses were reduced to haystacks of debris if they hadn't disappeared entirely. Washburn University was virtually leveled—not a single building remained standing, and most were wiped out completely. The trees, yes, the trees were broken statues, stripped bare of leaves and limbs, among the piles of sandstone and splintered roofs and glass, big blocks of debris looking like the discovery of an artifact in the Roman Forum. In the twenty-two-mile path of wreckage, seventeen people lay dead and five hundred were injured. Eight hundred homes were gone, and the storm left behind nearly $200 million in damage (almost $2 billion in 2025 dollars). At the time it was the most destructive tornado the country had ever seen, and it still ranks among the worst on record. Kansans looked upon this new beginning wrought by a maelstrom of destruction, loss, and heartbreak as Kansans do: with unwavering resolve, hard work, and deep compassion. Today, the tall trees, peaceful grounds, and resplendent buildings of Washburn University, rebuilt from nothing, stand as a beautiful monument to being a Kansan.

And what of the people for whom time stopped on June 8, 1966? Their families have heard the stories, but the real horror for those in the direct path is permanently incised within.

Years later, I was giving a speech in Emporia, Kansas, at the dedication of a refurbished Madonna of the Trail statue marking the start of the Santa Fe Trail. It was near 100 degrees, but a crowd sat in the sun listening to my speech. At the end, I walked over to ask why—why had they come out here in the blazing heat? Why didn't they move into the shade? They said, almost in unison, "We were watching the tornado coverage and wanted to thank you."

It's been like that for sixty years. Lives saved by *five words spoken in five seconds.*

As for so many Kansans, the Topeka Tornado opened a new beginning in my life. For months, I had been agonizing between a career in law and a career in television. Law was a time-honored tradition with centuries of pedigree, while television journalism was still in its infancy, inventing itself as it went along. But now, in the wake of the tornado, the potential of television news showed itself. It could save lives. If it could do that in 1966, what potential did it have for the future? From a maelstrom of tragedy, I was given the privilege of seeing into the future. That one decision was life-changing. I could feel the wind at my back.

I sent a videotape to five stations around the country: Miami, New York, Los Angeles, Chicago, and Kansas City. Within three months, I received an offer from WBBM-TV in Chicago, owned by CBS Television. Helen, Mary Kristin, and I loaded up the Nash Rambler, hitched on a U-Haul trailer, and headed off. We were leaving the home we knew, still a demolished shadow of what it had once been, for the brave unknown.

As we departed, most of the folks left in the tornado's wake worked to rebuild their lives and return to something safe and comfortable. But for me, the whirlwind of my life was only starting to spin.

# TWO

# Learning Lessons and Chasing Dreams

The singularly terrifying, exhilarating moment spent covering the Topeka Tornado pointed me in the direction my life would take. Without that storm, I may have been a small-town trial lawyer practicing somewhere in the Midwest. Not a bad life, though certainly less exciting. But even before that storm shook up my priorities, smacked me with perspective, and sent me sailing toward Chicago, life was laying the groundwork for my career as a broadcaster. When I took my family to Chicago in the summer of 1966, I left behind the expansive prairies and rolling hills of Kansas that I had known since I was a small boy. Kansas is my home. It is a part of who I am. The winds that blow through wheat fields and big bluestem brought my grandparents in from the East, pushed my parents together, and shaped the person I became and the life I led. The years spent in the fields and small towns offered me lessons and experiences that, in hindsight, seem to fit perfectly in the narrative of my life: mismatched passions for football and theater, an after-school job at the local radio station, my service in the US Marine Corps, and even my time studying to be a lawyer. I needed it all to get where I was going, even if I didn't know where that was.

My parents, William A. Kuretich (who changed our name to Kurtis when I was ten) and Wilma Mary Horton met at Emporia State University Teachers College in Emporia, Kansas. My father played football—quite well, actually—and he and my mother liked to dance in a ballroom that has been preserved for over eighty years. The dance floor is worn smooth as glass and still remains as the launchpad for romance. I visited the college several years ago and walked into the ballroom, where I conjured up the sweet clarinet of Benny Goodman and watched long-forgotten reflections of twirling coeds in the wall mirrors like time capsules looking back at me as if saying, "OK, kid, let's see what *you've* got." I imagined my parents' smiles, not knowing what lay ahead. Students at a time when the cruelties of the Great Depression were everywhere except here, where for a few minutes they could hold each other safely and let the storms blow past.

My dad was a confident, curious, and uncomplicated man. After graduation, he followed a career of military service. By the time I was born in Pensacola, Florida, he was an instructor for naval aviators at the Naval Air Station there. Between periods of overseas service and meeting the flight-time requirements to maintain proficiency in the cockpit, he was barely present during my earliest years. His father was a full-blooded Croatian who had arrived in the United States around 1914 with a wave of Eastern Europeans seeking jobs, avoiding conscription, fleeing persecution, and the host of other reasons people venture halfway across the world. He followed the path of many Croatians before him who first began arriving on the flat prairies of central Kansas in the 1870s with Russian Mennonites. The Turkey red wheat these immigrants carried with them eventually transformed Kansas into the breadbasket of the world.

My grandfather journeyed from Croatia to Ellis Island to Hope, Kansas. Shortly after he arrived, a young woman hopped off the train in Hope, having unknowingly followed in his footsteps from Croatia to Hope. She was a stout, hardworking peasant's daughter who started the town creamery. Their marriage was made in heaven's idea of paradise—a life of heavy labor and abundant love in Kansas. In the morning, dairy farmers would deliver fresh milk to Grandma Tabb's storefront in the two-block town, where Grandma Tabb unloaded it and poured it into buckets for the day's product. Another pour into a cream separator to remove the butterfat by centrifugal force, then a third pour to pasteurize it. In a matter of minutes, straight raw cream became ice cream and thick, delicious drinks.

Like most farmers, Granddad chose farming because he loved the land. He loved watching the miracle of first shoots breaking the soil, the smell of the earth when the sun winked through clouds in the morning, and watching a breech calf being born and sometimes having to pull the small legs by hand when the calf got hung up inside. For farmers, it's worth the risk of supporting a family on what they produce from the land. It's a hard but simple life that my immigrant grandparents embraced.

Granddad and Grandma Kuretich planted a family tree that grew like the deep-rooted prairie plants that could be burned, stomped by buffalo, and withered by drought and still come back in the spring. They survived dust and depression, fought wars, and fed the nation with their hands in the soil. During it all, they held on to a dream. They passed that dream on to their children, and it filtered down to me in holiday-table talk that bridged the generations: "You can be anything you want to be." That gave me license to dream about a life of anything *but* farming.

Wilma was a farm girl from Wayside, Kansas, a little railroad town by the side of the tracks that, how do I say it, never reached its true potential. The population remained under two hundred souls for more than a century. To say the little rural gem of Wayside is like something out of *Little House on the Prairie* is actually more accurate than you might think. My grandmother's one-room schoolhouse and the tiny post office (only sixty-four square feet) were moved a few miles west of town to became part of the Little House on the Prairie Museum. The museum, which my parents started, is still thriving. But after Wayside's post office was shut down and memorialized, the lights were pretty much turned off for the town.

Wilma's father, my Granddad Bert, had come to this part of southeast Kansas from Pennsylvania in 1921 seeking oil. Granddad Bert married Lillian Jones, the local schoolmarm who taught six or more grades in the one-room schoolhouse with a portrait of Abraham Lincoln on the wall and a pull-down map that showed fewer than fifty countries. Five days a week, Lillian would walk to school, a trip of several miles down dirt roads, across fields and prairies, and under the wide-open Kansas skies.

This is the world of my earliest memories. I was born in 1940 in Pensacola, Florida, where my father was busy teaching wannabe navy pilots. When I was born in late September, he sensed that his work was for more than reserve training. He was proved right less than three months later, when the attack on Pearl Harbor changed everything for our family, our country, and the world. Less than a year after Pearl Harbor, my mother and I headed for Kansas to wait out the war. My recollections from my time in Wayside, living with the Hortons on the "home place," are now based almost entirely on Kodak prints and home movies, but I remember the warm, loving, spacious farmhouse where there was no lack of stimulus. My mother and I lived with her parents, four sisters, and brother, and as the first grandchild, I was everyone's focus. My mother suspected that my learning to walk was delayed because I was constantly being held by one of my aunts.

The Great Depression was on the downslope, and though the ag markets were growing to support the war, the mental trauma of the death-grip economy was still impressed on most people's memories, especially Grandad Bert's. He always looked old to me. I don't remember a single smile on his taut, hardened face. What I do remember is a balding white head with stern eyes ready to criticize if you were late to work or when he was leaning forward to drop tobacco spit in a Folger's coffee can. If ever a photograph captured a life's moment in time, it is Granddad with a thumb in a suspender stretched over a work shirt buttoned to the neck, waiting until the picture-taking with his round-faced grandson was over and he could get back to work. He was what work looked like—work that took all day and all night, work that answered the call of whatever was needed until the day he died.

I learned from my grandparents to look to the skies and to worship the rain, which was always good news in Kansas. It was the equalizer that kept farmers pulling the same load, watching the same skies, and rolling the dice one season more to see if God would provide enough moisture to coax a livelihood from the earth. Who you were or where you were from didn't make much difference when the skies gave everyone the same opportunity. But you still had to apply your individual talents and do the crushing hard work to harvest a life. That proved to be a definitive theme throughout my life that has served me well—should we wait for God to answer our prayers, or does he grant us the opportunity to answer them ourselves? Looking back on a life of opportunities given, chances taken, and a fair share of dumb luck, I'm tempted to believe the latter.

As the war years dragged on, Granddad continued to rule the farm operation and was too busy to think much about what was going on in Germany and Japan. But my mother would read me letters from my father, which had been stripped to the basics by censors. He wrote to us about his work directing a large squadron of Marine and navy pilots during the Battle of Okinawa, for which he received a Bronze Star.

I didn't understand most of his description of ordering eight Corsairs with five-hundred-pound bombs on each plane for a strike near Yona-baru. That was what dads did, I figured. I was lucky to have my own excitement to keep me busy.

The annual highlight of life on that Kansas farm was always wheat harvest. I can still see the dinosaur-shaped threshing machine driven by a fifty-foot fan belt on its side, screeching a noise that could be heard a mile away as a cutter sliced the stalks. The cut wheat was bundled up by a team of young, muscular men and laid on a wide hopper, where it was shaken until the kernels dropped out and the chaff blew away, covering anyone who stood below. From there, the wheat went for the fourteen-mile drive to Independence to be stored in rounded silos that reached so high into the sky, I thought these were the skyscrapers I heard so much about. I was too young to join the team as a water boy, but I sure wanted to.

The work was hard, but there were few complaints. Part of the reason was lunch. The phrase "An army fights on its stomach" is also true for a thresher crew. When the lunch bell rang, the twenty men working in the field happily drove to the house, where a blue-and-white-checked table-cloth covered picnic tables set up end to end on the porch. My mother and her sisters were waiting with fried chicken, green beans with ham, German potato salad, and a variety of pies—cherry, peach, banana, rhu-barb, chocolate, wild plum, and persimmon. And that was only the first course. The men arrived, some washing and some not, with wheat dust still caked on their faces. They didn't talk much other than to celebrate a new dish of ham smothered in peaches arriving or deviled eggs stacked high. Iced tea added the sound of ice chipped from the block of ice that had arrived by horse-drawn wagon. The only complaints were that many of the dishes never made it past the halfway point of the table. I've never seen a photograph of the thresher table, but the impression was so in-tense to a toddler that it has stayed with me for the length of a lifetime.


Dad stayed with the Marines after World War II and didn't come back to Kansas to retire until 1956. Mom and I saw a lot more of him than we had during the war years and followed him to his posts back in Florida, Vir-ginia, North Carolina, California, and elsewhere. Still, I think my mother was afraid I'd escape my childhood without spending real time with my father and that I'd reached a point where she could no longer comfortably control me. Her instincts were right. I was filling the void left by the traveling career military man with my own activities. Thankfully, since I had spent my high school years in the idyllic sanctuary of Independence, Kansas, those activities turned out to be theater, football, and working at the local radio station. Hardly the behavior of a fatherless ne'er-do-well.

When Dad was home, he was a firm presence, but his mind was always in the sky. For aviation Marines, their love of flying makes the military regimentation of life on base an irritant. Terra firma is just a holding pattern until the next takeoff. And let's face it, the peacetime military is little more than a holding pattern compared to war. He was a reasonable man who didn't push me toward a military career. He just wanted me to follow what appealed to me. Like most fathers, he filled the role as head of the family, but my mother was his executive officer. She was the one who got things done. A pioneer woman from birth, she was strong, independent, loving, and no-nonsense. The threat of that strong presence (and an occasional whack) inspired me to try to please her where I could, mostly through achievement. Bringing awards home was one way to curry her favor, or at least I thought it was. I'm told that highly successful people are driven by insecurity that comes from seeking love and affirmation. My mother seemed to hold back in showering us with love, afraid that it would "go to our heads," as she would say. Looking back, I realize that the Depression-era mentality never left my family. There's no time to be frivolous. Do your job and do it well. Help others, but mind your own business. What effect did it have on me? I think a fear of offending stayed with me all my life. You could call it an avoidance of confrontation. Maybe that's just the Kansan in me, but in times of mistakes or failures, I tried to find reasons to blame myself rather than accuse someone else first.

When Dad retired as a brigadier general, USMC, in 1956 and finally joined us in Independence for good, the adjustment to civilian life was more difficult than he'd thought it would be. He left a role on national and international levels, where defending the country fell directly to him, to suddenly find himself alone in a field watching a herd of cattle. No one called him anymore. The few years between his retirement and my leaving for college were something of a last chance for him to discover who I had become and for me to learn who he really was. He would lead a series of mentors who would shape this period of my life. I was now a full-fledged teenager, and my mother decided to implement her plan to have me work for my dad. It was summer, and Dad was working his oil interests between Independence and Wayside. Every morning, I'd pack a sack lunch and drive to meet him at the highway where Wayside met US 75.

Those mornings were as cool as it would get all day. Winter wheat was coming up short and thick and green, giving the vast fields a suburban-front-lawn look. There was earth and there was the sky, one against the other in plein air beauty. Urbanites didn't appreciate the simplicity. They desired trees and mountains instead of flat land and empty sky. But for those who know Kansas, it's the most beautiful sight on God's green earth. To a teenager, it was like being alone at the beginning of the world.

But something was wrong on one particular morning. There was an obstacle in the highway half a mile ahead, a mass of twisted metal. I pulled over and ran to what used to be a four-door sedan. A windshield was shattered, the radiator was steaming with antifreeze, and a family of four lay inside. The driver was bleeding from the head, and thick matter was coming from his nose and mouth. Away in the ditch, another mass of mangled steel lay hissing. Only a child's crying broke the silence of the prairie and seemed to trigger reality into motion.

I was alone for a moment, but soon a few farmers who had heard the violent crash from the country store were running toward me.

"It's the young Defenbaugh!" one yelled. "Can you call an ambulance? You'll have to run to the store."

I took off.

The small town of Wayside suddenly came to life. Women were on the run to the crash. Children wanted to see.

After I got the ambulance on its way, I returned to the scene, amazed at the contrast with what I had seen just minutes before and the horror caught in a metal cage. Behind the bodies being slowly lifted from the wrenched metal and the screams of the small children inside were the worried faces of the townspeople. They had never seen anything like this either.

My father was already at an oil well, waiting for me to help him pull the pipes from a five-hundred-foot well to insert a new valve. When I finally arrived, he wondered why I was late. I told him what had happened, being first on the scene and doing what I could, which wasn't much.

My father's stoic reaction has never left me. His quiet realism showed me that there's no escaping the tragedy of life, whether on a battlefield or on a lonely country road. Any hope he and my mother had that raising a son in rural Kansas would shield him from the tragedy and horrors of the world was gone. The important reaction is to be prepared to help others in harm's way, and that requires composure. Don't waste time on hysterics—it clouds your brain. When faced with tragedy or hardship, square your shoulders, quiet your mind, bear down, and face it.

I didn't know it then, but moments like this would seem to chase me through life. Moments of sudden, unexpected chaos and tragedy in which I was expected to keep a cool head. Many times in my career, I have been faced with the wreckage but not paralyzed, felt the seconds ticking away as I sprang into action with no time to think or feel. I would often think about that morning on an isolated Kansas highway with a breeze that kept on blowing even when the world ended for young Defenbaugh.

Despite my father's intermittent absences during my childhood, those years did not suffer from a lack of strong male role models. The first in my life was Kayo Emmot, head football coach for the Independence High Bulldogs.

You wouldn't say Walter "Kayo" Emmot was an imposing figure at first meeting. He was shorter than you'd expect. His face was full and Irish beneath the buzz cut. That you would expect; it fit the brand of football coach. Everything about Kayo said football, from the way he dressed to the way he carried his beloved clipboard to the whistle swinging from his neck to the sound of cleats on pavement when he came in from practice.

In the corridors of Independence High School, he was a kind, charming teacher. But when he stepped onto the practice field, there was nothing normal about him. I've never seen anyone so focused, so motivated, so dominating of his surroundings. He powerfully transferred that concentration of purpose to his players. For the ninety minutes he held us captive every afternoon, Coach would do more than impart the principles of a game; he would create a structure for young men to follow throughout

life. I'm not even sure he thought about it that way. He was concentrating on building winning teams. And win we did. My senior season was
the first of six consecutive undefeated seasons—a state record that still
stands.

Though I didn't know it at the time, my education on the gridiron
would be a source of almost daily inspiration during my life as a broadcaster. Teamwork requires clear communication of a common purpose.
Leadership by example is always more effective than leadership by dom-
ination. Preparation and sacrifice are necessary ingredients for success.
And perhaps most important of all, have a clear focus on what you want
and execute your strategy to get there with determination and passion.

I dare say that for many of us, and certainly for me, Coach Emmot
was the first father figure we encountered as we transitioned out of the
family nest. Coaches and teachers hold a different place in our lives than
parents. Theirs is a family we choose to be a part of, not one we're born
into. Their perspective is different. Their respect and praise and lessons
are different. My time on the team was a sobering, no-nonsense splash of
reality that the world wasn't designed just for precious little high school
students. Coach was drill sergeant and kindly mentor, hard as nails and
warm as a grandparent's hug. You did what you were told, motivated by
equal parts respect and fear. Everyone on the field relied on everyone else,
and letting anyone down was a fate worse than death. If you didn't want
to be at practice, go where you'd rather be. But don't waste the coach's
time. And God help the player who exhibited an attitude.

I think his value was as a model of what a man could be—not the
physical, aggressive, screaming example he could have been but the singularly focused, motivated example he chose to be. His idea of a man was
one slow to show emotion, devoted to teamwork, extremely concentrated
on success, and endlessly committed and caring. So at the end of each
season, after the two-a-day practices, after the stomach-churning games,
after the chill fall nights under the dim glow of a Depression-era stadium,
every Bulldog who played for Coach knew the truth behind Kayo Emmot's success: he loved us. And we loved him.

I sometimes wonder if Kayo knew a fraction of the myriad lessons
he offered to the hundreds of boys he coached. And not just during the
forty-nine consecutively won games he coached but in each and every
encounter with his young men, both on the field and off.

I wish the football part of my story had a happier ending. It's a credit to Kayo that I got as much out of being coached by him as I did since my time on the field was so limited.

It was our second game of my senior year, late September 1957. Fort Scott was tough. I was playing quarterback and linebacker on defense when early in the first quarter, a Fort Scott halfback came straight at me. I dipped low to tackle him about waist high. His speed rocked me back on my heels. I did not see two of my own teammates also joining in the tackle. They landed on my shoulders, and I was crushed straight down under their weight. I don't think I felt anything, but the compression fractured a vertebra. Defying the indignity of being rolled off the field on a gurney, I stiffened up and walked to the sideline. A doctor had jumped over the fence and stopped me. He quickly discovered a muscle mass that had begun protective swelling around the injury. We drove to Mercy Hospital in Independence, where I would stay for a week. Then two weeks in bed at home followed by three months of walking in a metal back brace. Season over. The end of a dream. The hardest part was hobbling into Coach Emmot's gym office and telling him about my injury. Had Coach not stopped me, I would have tried to finish the season. The football addiction had caused me to suspend my reasoning abilities.

After I healed from the back injury and graduated from high school, I enrolled at Independence Community College to prove that I could still play football. But during my freshman year, I sustained yet another injury, a compound fracture of the index finger on my throwing hand. God was now being very specific—give up this sport. It's a dead end. It isn't where you're meant to be.


Sure enough, God or fate or the winds of history had pushed me away from my hopes of a future on the football field. However, my other extracurricular addiction proved to be much more fruitful.

On my sixteenth birthday in 1956, I picked up a work permit at the Kansas Department of Labor, applied for a Social Security card, and walked a half block to the only radio station in town, KIND: "Kind words for southeast Kansas."

My audition was before Nelson Rupard, the general manager and owner of the station. Mr. Rupard was in his midfifties at the time, a generous, kind, and deeply talented broadcaster. By the time I came on, he faced serious financial debt trying to keep KIND on the air and make a living at the same time. It wasn't easy operating the only radio station in a small Kansas town and having to sell commercials to the same local businesses week after week. It was quite the coup when a group of young men came on board at $1.35 an hour. We part-timers got the benefit of hands-on broadcasting experience in small-town Kansas, and he got the benefit of keeping his station on the air with low-wage talent.

I still don't know exactly why Mr. Rupard hired me. Maybe it was that breakthrough experience announcing over the public address system at George Washington High School when Dad was mustering out of the Marines in Washington, DC. Or maybe it was having won a disc-jockey contest at a radio station several years before when we were living in Fairfax, Virginia. Or maybe it was my uncommonly deep voice and the generic midwestern accent that's so common on the airwaves. Whatever combination of experience, talent, and sheer dumb luck landed me the job, it set me on a path toward the rest of my life. Nelson Rupard gave me the opportunity to learn the art and science of the trade, to make every mistake to be made and to learn from it. He also helped me find my voice—quite literally. I knew my voice was different, but he showed me that it needed exercise and training in the same way a gymnast never stops stretching. Speakers and singers are the same as they maintain the flexibility of the muscle within their throat. The voice is a gift, Mr. Rupard told me. It must be cared for. So I never smoked or drank to excess. I never strained my delivery, except for my broadcasts of Little League baseball games during the summer on KIND.

So while my classmates were filling grocery bags at the A&P and blasting seltzer water into tall soda glasses, some unseen force of history seemed to have guided me to exactly the right person at exactly the right place at exactly the right time. I started working weekends and holidays, picking up every shift I could find. And I never stopped.

One Sunday morning, a stranger peeked into the control-room window. I had just ripped the Associated Press hourly list of top stories off the wire and was getting ready to read them on the air. But the sight of a farmer-preacher with a worn, dog-eared Bible under his arm presented a more pressing need. He was an Okie through and through, with a face that was weathered and serious and hair that hadn't seen more than a finger sweep for weeks. He wore blue jeans and a short denim jacket and held a sweat-stained Stetson under his arm. The barely white shirt had a frayed, unbuttoned collar and a string tie, cowboy style. He looked like something the tornado had left behind. But what cut through all of that was a passion for the Lord. His penetrating, unblinking blue eyes told me that he had found God and believed he'd been chosen to tell the world about it. For a hundred dollars to rent the studio for an hour, Nelson Rupard allowed him to do just that.

He knocked at the window, and I motioned him into the studio to his right. It was also the record library where I developed my fondness for Count Basie, Duke Ellington, and Woody Herman, war-era classics that even at the time were starting to become oldies, eclipsed by the new sound of a young southerner named Elvis Presley. As I greeted the preacher, the smell of Bull Durham chewing tobacco and a powerful handshake assaulted my senses. He gripped my hand like an adult bear would hold a salmon he'd just picked out of a mountain stream. It was his unusual accent that made me pause before starting to set up the mic. It was a mix between Irish, Scots, old deep southern, and Ozark hillbilly. Something that could fit the profile of a mountain man, homesteader, or dirt farmer one step away from throwing everything he owned onto a Model T pickup and heading for California. In other words, it was pure American.

I assumed the role of engineer and pointed an index finger at him from the control room. Start.

His first words were a little shaky, like an old Ford needing a crank, but it wasn't long before he worked up some speed and the scriptures were flowing rapidly from memory. I turned the level down a bit before he blew out the old cardioid mic, my favorite. I didn't know how he would last the hour without a written script and the usual breaks that preachers use, but he did. And in his closing moment, he turned his attention toward me.

"And we pray for the young man behind the control-room window who set up my microphone this morning. I could see the glory of God in his eyes. He's making it possible for me to come to you and is worthy of your blessing in the form of a check or cash to this radio station, addressed to me."

Mr. Rupard always listened to every second of the day's broadcast; at least that's what I always imagined. Whenever I was on the air, he'd walk out of his apartment, connected to the station and only a fifty-foot walk from the control room, just to remind me he was there. If we had made a mistake, we knew it when he slammed the door behind him on his way down the hall. I came to dread that sound. It meant we were in for an ass-chewing.

But on this occasion, after the preacher had left the studio and continued on his holy mission, Mr. Rupard came into the booth, knelt beside me, and whispered,

"I want to apologize for your surprise guest this morning. When I saw the 'Reverend' in front of his name on the request last week, I thought since it's Sunday morning, he would be good for the programming schedule. You got everything but communion."

Then, with his pipe clutched between his teeth, he turned with one final knowing, mischievous, proud look and returned to his lair. I was left with an empty studio to break down, in broadcasting parlance, and felt the lingering presence of Jesus in the air.

Even after at the end of a storied career in broadcasting, Nelson Rupard was the best mentor I ever had. He had a profound respect for radio and its service to the listening public. It came through in his steel concentration and attention to detail. That respect for the craft stayed with me through sixty years of broadcasting. To him, it was a true profession of service that carried the burden of responsibility for doing more than entertain. We could change the lives of our listeners, our community, and our nation. I have carried his vision of broadcasting, and the reverence that came with it, ever since.

# THREE

# Finding My Way

In the fall of 1958, the era of history that would define my journalistic career was just beginning. The Supreme Court ordered the all-white Central High School in Little Rock, Arkansas, to integrate, reminding us all of when President Eisenhower had sent the 101st Airborne to escort those nine Black students to class the year before. Meanwhile, the Cold War was in full swing. Nuclear testing at home and abroad was ramping up, the US and the USSR were launching rockets and satellites and dogs into space as fast as they could, Nikita Khrushchev had taken power in the Soviet Union, and Fidel Castro's forces were closing in on Havana. Everything was changing—and fast. Hell, even the Brooklyn Dodgers had moved to Los Angeles. At the same time, I was enrolling at the University of Kansas, where in-state tuition was less than $300.

After my football dreams were quashed during my freshman season at Independence Community College, I thought I would embrace the big-time university life and go with the flow.

Unfortunately, going with the flow landed me in jail my first semester. Soon after arriving on campus, I pledged the Sigma Nu Fraternity, housed in a former governor's mansion, a glorious Georgian masterpiece. The pledges were initiated over the course of several weeks. One exercise was for the upperclassmen to take pledges in pairs out into the Kansas night and drop us on an isolated gravel road. "You're alone; you have no light, no map; and you have to get back to the house by sunrise. Have a nice night."

Well, at least there was no physical beating or hard drinking, which at the time we thought would have been a better choice. My partner and I walked until we saw a single light hanging high in the yard of a farm. It reflected against a porch with nothing else visible in the ink-black darkness surrounding the house. When we approached the door to ask for help, a dog exploded his warning. A farmer appeared at an upstairs window. "Yes?" We explained our situation and asked which way Lawrence was, and by the grace of God, he had the mercy to offer to drive us back to campus. When we walked under the Corinthian columns and through the front door of the fraternity house, the few seniors awake couldn't believe it. Slowly the pledge class limped in. After a quick head count, I could say, "All present and accounted for."

A few weeks passed, and it was our turn—for revenge. A fellow pledge was something of an electrical engineer. His hobby was building radios. After sourcing some stadium-grade speakers, he devised a scheme to get back at our elder tormentors. As the person with radio experience, the already iconic voice, and the authority as pledge class president, I was chosen to be the voice of our pirate radio broadcast. One night well after midnight, we backed a car up to the house, opened the trunk to reveal the massive speakers, and got ready to wake up the sleeping darlings inside. With just a few words into the mic, we discovered that the speakers were more powerful than we could have imagined. I don't think it lasted long, but it was long enough for a young mother who had just put her child to bed to be awakened by the boom. She called the police. The engineer and I were taken to the county jail for the remainder of the night. There were two inmates already in the cell, vagrants, we presumed. All it took to ensure that I'd be a law-abiding citizen for the rest of my life was one of these fellow inmates, a hulking vagrant who spelled trouble, asking me in a voice like gravel, "Hey, kid, what are ya in for?"

The next day before a judge, we argued that our case hardly warranted expulsion, especially since we had already spent time inside. Paid our debt to society, as it were. Lucky for us, wiser heads prevailed, and the dean of students relaxed any further penalty. My first time in a courtroom, and I had triumphed. Little did I know that fate would soon be guiding me toward history and into some of the most iconic courtrooms of the century.

There was one bright light that first semester: I was asked to audition for an announcer's job at the classical music station on campus, KANU-FM. I joined the staff as one of just a few undergrads thanks to my time with Nelson Rupard. KANU was rarefied air, to say the least (no pun intended). This was FM radio at its best: a 100,000-watt station broadcasting highbrow classical selections and talk news to a small audience of university intellectuals. We called it an oasis of culture in a sea of country-music lovers. And we were ahead of our time. National Public Radio wasn't launched until 1970. The station's live recording studios were in an architectural wonder built especially for radio broadcasting. It had round acoustical walls to eliminate the echo in big spaces. The broadcaster's booth was up in a crow's nest overlooking several studios at once. And broadcasting long, elegant musical recordings rather than three-minute hits meant that we announcers could study while on the job. I honed my "classical music talk" and continued to develop the voice that would serve me well for decades to come.

We all worked under Glenn Price, one of the original seven who'd started the station in 1952 and an associate professor at KU. He was a quiet man whose kind instruction shielded the fragile talents and egos of those of us attempting to enter broadcasting while guiding us in the right direction. One day, Glenn asked if I'd like to help him with a remote broadcast from Hoch Auditorium, just a stone's throw from KANU. That Sunday afternoon, I entered the front of the auditorium, an enormous Gothic hall with 5,500 seats. Predating Allen Fieldhouse, it was the home of Jayhawk basketball, its floors graced by early legends of the game like Wilt Chamberlain. But that day, it was a concert hall, ready for the final recital of a renowned organist who was retiring from the music faculty.

At first, I couldn't see a broadcast booth until I saw Glenn waving to me from a square hole rather high along one wall. I found my way through a back corridor behind that wall and joined Glenn, who had connected our remote gear with the engineer at the station just in time for the applause welcoming the professor.

Glenn motioned for me to sit down in front of the microphone and whispered that I should introduce the first selection.

Still a little green and overwhelmed by our perch being too far off the ground for my liking, I assumed the position. I introduced the program and the first selection with Glenn standing right behind me. The professor entered and walked across to the organ, alone on the stage in the darkened hall. The first notes filled the cavernous space with precisely what you'd expect—a thunderous opening.

And then came something we didn't expect: a discordant blast, totally out of place with the romantic chord that had preceded it. We waited for it to resolve, but it never did.

Shocked, Glenn and I looked at the stage and saw the professor face down on the keys. While the organ still droned, I turned bewildered to Glenn, who was on the phone to the studio, and he motioned for me to come out of the chair. He stepped in to throw the broadcast back to KANU.

A few moments later, we learned that the professor had suffered a heart attack and died where he fell—on the keys. It was a moment neither of us would ever forget. Through it all, Glenn Price was quiet and in control, the model of what a broadcaster should be. That experience was a gift for my future. Glenn's calm demeanor and decisive action in the face of the unexpected have always stayed with me. He was the best teacher I had at KU and one of the best people I have ever known. Once again, it seemed that something was preparing me for my own encounters with chaos on the air, which would come only several years later.

Amid all the semester's excitement, my grades slipped. I decided to leave the fraternity to others and turn back to the old standby for a radio rescue once again.

Soon I landed my second radio job that year when a call came in from a friend from Independence, Merle Blair, who had worked his way into a sales manager's job at a station in Topeka, about a half hour away. KTOP-AM was hot as a firecracker among teens. Elvis Presley, Frankie Avalon, and Ricky Nelson were climbing the charts and changing the sound of America. My deep voice was more classical music than rock and roll, but in my zeal to taste all aspects of broadcasting, I accepted a job as a Top 40 disc jockey.

I can still remember the patter delivered at the speed of a teenager behind the wheel of a Corvette: "You're listening to K-TOP, color channel 1490, Topeka. Let's get some traffic reports from our sonoramic news cruiser number 9. A little bit later, we'll hear from J. Jazzmo Bop, a professor in the College of Knowledge, with his all-night serenade of the greatest hits in Topeka. This is Tony Kurtis, with a *K*, if I may."

The studio was in what looked like a barn, which served both as farmhouse and as hay storage. The hot, hot, hot Top 40 format was quite a change from the academic refinement of KANU. It also took me away from campus. The thirty-mile commute was tricky. I ran from my last class at noon to pick up a sack lunch from the cafeteria in my campus dorm and then raced to North Topeka to be on the air at 1:00 sharp. In six months, I was never late. I'd avoid the turnpike and instead take Highway 10, a narrow state highway through the wheat fields, to save the fifty-cent toll. Close calls? Yes, every day.

It would have been a dream job for most students or anyone else in radio, for that matter. But I was already looking beyond KTOP. Don't get me wrong—it could be fun. But it was mind-deadening. Same shift, 1:00 to 4:00. Same music every day. Same commercials. Same mindless small talk. After six months, it was either make a change or check into the Menninger Clinic, the best mental hospital in the country.

By my junior year, between KANU and a full course load, I didn't have time for much else. No campus politics, no athletics, no special clubs. There was one exception: debate. I was a senior with no experience. Good old Independence High School was too rural and too small to have debate. Most of the team members were freshmen and had competed through high school. More than once, I asked myself under my breath, "What the hell am I doing here?" I picked up some pointers pretty fast, enough to come in handy years later. It was a steep learning curve and a humbling experience for me, facing off against teenagers who could debate circles around me. Still, I worked hard and came to love it.

It was more than a random choice. Still waffling between broadcasting and studying law, I thought debate would be helpful either way.

I was studying broadcast journalism, but the program was still in its infancy. Without a full curriculum that would prepare me for the job market, I needed to work to fill in the gaps on my own with debate club and radio jobs. In the decades since, my ad hoc parallel curriculum is in practice at most journalism and broadcast schools around the country. The University of Missouri runs its own television station, as does Syracuse. There isn't a serious degree program that doesn't also have the "experience" phase. While I stumbled through finding a way to align my education with my passion, today's KU graduates from the William Allen White School of Journalism and Mass Communications are entering broadcasting better prepared than any I've seen. They learn on the same editing machines the stations use and have instructors who come from the business. They are ready to go from graduation straight to the street as reporters and editors.

By the time graduation rolled around, I still couldn't decide if broadcasting was my life's calling or just the thing I did to earn pocket money. Several weeks before donning my cap and gown, I decided to play it safe and go to law school. Why law school? I guess I was playing my cards right. What if I didn't like broadcasting in the real world? Even worse, what if I didn't do well in it? The law could be a second choice. A safe choice. Certainly the added education would help me regardless of where I'd land after that, since I'd applied myself more to my part-time gigs than coursework and my grades had suffered. In the recesses of my brain, I dreamed of doing both: covering the law on the air. Of course, there were only three reporters covering the Supreme Court in 1962, one for each network. What I thought was a fleeting notion, whipping by me like wheat chaff in the wind, came to be the defining feature of my first years in front of a camera. But that would come later.

For the time being, my career plans, along with those of the rest of the men in my class, were delayed for six months so I could fulfill a requirement for mandatory military service. I chose the Marine Corps Reserve plan to serve six months' active duty with a commitment of six more years in reserve status so I could get to law school as soon as I could. So it was back home to my work with Dad in Independence for a few weeks. I hoped to learn what I could about military life from the general and tune up my physical condition before flying off to Parris Island, South Carolina.

When I arrived at the Marine Corps Recruit Depot at Parris Island, South Carolina, it was still shrouded in infamy from the Ribbon Creek incident. In April 1956, a drill instructor had ordered his platoon to march into a tidal marsh carrying heavy packs and rifles at night. Six had drowned during this extremely dangerous and unorthodox exercise. So by June 1962, the entire training program had changed significantly and was still being closely watched. I was assigned to First Battalion, Platoon 152. I was older than most of the men who had come straight from high school graduation. There were some other college graduates, a fact of which we were usually proud, especially my bunkmate from Harvard. But any mention of college was soon forgotten.

The first night after our arrival, we were standing at attention in front of our bunks in the squad bay of an old wooden barracks from World War II. The drill instructors asked the college graduates to step forward. We proudly advanced, happy to be acknowledged and elevated above our younger colleagues. And then came the order: "Now, you maggots think you're so fucking hot shit, get up on that chin-up bar and don't come down till I tell you. Put your elbows over it." South Carolina's thick, steamy air seemed to make gravity stronger, pulling us off the bar one by one. I wasn't the first and I wasn't the last to fall, but I suffered the verbal pummeling that is probably still deep in my ear canal. The word "maggot" is still rattling around in there.

The daily routine was not unpleasant. Up at 5:00 a.m. In a few minutes, already under immediate and intense pressure, we were in our fatigues and on the tarmac for a one-mile run. Once a week, the base Marine band would add some patriotic inspiration from John Philip Sousa and all the rest. Then breakfast at the mess hall and off to instruction in the art of killing.

Many of us found our training more efficient than painful. My favorite drill instructor was Sgt. I. B. Tchakirides, a tall, mustached, rock-hard, straight-as-a-flagpole Greek American, always trailed by his two assistants. He was the kind of man you'd follow into battle. He should have been on a poster. He was a model Marine whom I admired greatly. That often happens during boot camp. You bond with your buddies who go through it with you and with the leaders who take you through it. That's leadership—real leadership. Maybe it's also a little Stockholm syndrome, but I try not to think about that. The training was so immersive, hands-on, and motivated by fear that I believe it was the most effective style of learning I've experienced. The fact that I qualified as "expert" with the M14, hitting perfect scores at 200, 300, and 500 yards, is more a testament to the education than to any innate skill I may have possessed.

One day, Tchakirides assigned his junior drill instructor the job of taking the platoon to the twenty-one-day inspection, also called Black Friday. At the three-week mark, we were feeling pretty good, pretty salty, pretty cocky. The twenty-one-day inspection was designed to take the chips off our shoulders so they could keep building the soldiers they wanted, unobstructed by ego. In other words, it was designed for us to fail.

We stood at the edge of the tarmac as the corporal walked down the line criticizing brass that wasn't shined enough, shoes that might not reflect his stern face. The corporal held a short, sawed-off broom handle to make his criticisms with a tap here and a whack there. No one escaped the critical judgment, which was leading to a planned, massive failure of the platoon. Then he came to me. I was staring straight ahead as ordered, hands at my side, knuckles along the seams of my trousers, stiff as possible when the assistant drill instructor started hitting me in the stomach with the broomstick. He wanted me to double over or collapse as an example to the rest. And we all knew that bruises on your stomach don't show up when you're wearing a uniform. Again and again, with heavy blows he violated his orders not to touch the recruits. My face couldn't hold back showing the pain, but I didn't fall or utter a sound. He finally gave up, turned, and marched us back to the squad bay.

The blows had crushed every blood vessel on my stomach. First my wounds started to swell to the size of two fists. Then they discolored into a red-and-blue mound that shook like the mess hall's Jell-O. The blood blisters under my skin didn't stop growing until lights out.

I could have gone to medical. If I had, I was sure my assailant instructor would have been punished severely, but I could have been pulled out of the training sequence to help them build the case. Or I could just live with it and say nothing. Although it looked horrendous and it shook when I walked, ran, and did push-ups, it wasn't painful. I decided to keep my mouth shut, and I have for nearly sixty years until this writing. I noticed that it was slowly going down, absorbing back into the body. And thankfully, the occasion never arose when I had to reveal it. I did get the impression that Tchakirides knew and seemed on edge for a while, fearing I would turn them in. I hope he appreciated my silence.

I chose the path I did because I wanted to complete my training and proudly support the Corps. It was a cause bigger than I. Also, I couldn't bear the thought of explaining my failure to my dad, and I simply wanted to be a Marine.

I was awarded the American Spirit Medal, a battalion award of which I was immensely proud. And I was pleased that my dad, who'd retired as a brigadier general, USMC, was at my graduation from boot camp. I think it also pleased the officer corps to see a Marine son do well.

I felt better graduating from Marine Corps boot camp than college. After twelve weeks in the strict discipline of Parris Island, my platoon climbed a bus for the ride through Charleston, South Carolina, on the way to Jacksonville, North Carolina, and Camp Lejeune and the internal Camp Geiger, home of the Second Marine Expeditionary Force and Advanced Combat Training. Suddenly, without drill instructors monitoring every move, the newfound independence at this next level of training made us almost homesick for the tight, buttoned-up atmosphere of PI.

Days at Camp Geiger were spent learning everything from M60 machine guns to hand grenades, recoilless rifles, judo, and much, much more. One morning, we assembled as usual on the asphalt in front of the barracks, but our usual sergeants were not there to call us to attention for the short march to chow. We waited and waited until we realized there were no senior enlisted personnel anywhere in sight. It was like waiting at a traffic light that never changed to green. Finally, a three-striper showed up to say, "Listen up. The division pulled out last night. Right now, they're boarding transports at Morehead City with orders to stand by for a nice ride to Cuba. Invasion? Maybe. You'll be next in line after the division goes ashore."

This was definitely not training. We were several months from completing our courses.

"I don't know if you were watching President Kennedy on television last night, but he delivered an ultimatum to the Russians to remove their missiles from Cuba or else. Guess what? YOU are the *else*."

He added something to seal the deal: "After chow, we'll come back here, and you will fill out some forms. Your contact at home, your insurance beneficiary, and your blood type."

That was easy enough. I was O positive. And without a wife, I listed my parents, knowing my father would get a big kick out of it.

An intense anxiety washed over us all but quickly ended several days later when the naval blockade was lifted and the Marines returned to base. It was my first brush with history but hardly my last.

With the Cold War breathing easier after its most serious confrontation and my active duty completed, I was back in Kansas by the summer of 1963. I had taken a job at WIBW-TV, Topeka, where I would work part-time, first as an announcer and later as a weatherman, while attending Washburn University School of Law. Coming from small-time radio, I found that entering the world of television was an exhilarating sea change. Again, the pattern of cramming as much into my daily agenda as possible was part of my normal routine.

During my first weeks of law school, I made a startling new discovery: I actually enjoyed studying. It wasn't the average studying that I came to love. No, I actually hated the traditional method of reading cases and opinions late into the night, then sitting in class sweating bullets, dreading being called on by the legal minds of the great Washburn Law, William Harvey, James Ahrens, Robert Fowks, Ray Spring, William Robinson, and William Poland. Contracts, Torts, Administrative Law, Criminal Law—the usual suspects in every law school loomed in front of me like a muddy country road. And then there emerged the perfect blend of skills demanding my talents, moot court, a contest in arguing before an appellate court on an important issue currently before the law. It was goal-oriented research preparing for mock trials that became my obsession. Who knew my ego death on the KU debate team would pay off so quickly? Sure enough, debate proved valuable in transforming facts and judicial rulings into a legal argument, just as I had hoped it would.

To account for my short history at the bar, I'll quote from Dean James Concannon, who closed his tenure as dean of the law school by writing a 750-page history of the school: "The 1964 team, of Bill Kurtis '66, Stewart Entz '65 and John Prather '65 was Washburn's first to win the regional competition. Washburn defeated the University of Nebraska in the finals. The team received the top brief award and Kurtis won the American Trial Lawyers Association Award as top oralist." Imagine my thrill to hear the legendary jurist Harry Blackmun announce my name and compliment me on having the ability to hold attention by telling a good story.

Dean Concannon continued,

In New York, Washburn lost to the eventual winner of the competition, Ohio State University. Kurtis competed again in the fall of his senior year but the Washburn team was eliminated by the team from the University of Kentucky that won the regional finals.

Kurtis's practice was to go to the podium without a single note in hand. Faculty advisor Ray Spring overheard Nebraska's coach at the 1965 regionals telling his team, "Did you see what he just did—go up there without a note? I don't ever want to see you do that—unless your name is Bill Kurtis."

Amidst my own shock and surprise, I could only imagine what the smirking underclassmen from my KU debate team would think of me now.

Despite my growing reputation as a strong presence in the (mock) courtroom, I was still deeply insecure and unsure whether my academic credentials and practical talents were enough for me to really make it as a lawyer. Was it even worth trying? I mean, I was on track for a broadcast career with nearly seven years of experience under my belt and a secure television job that I loved. But I was still young, and with my baby face, I looked even younger than I was. Although I had the voice for radio, I knew my young looks would hold me back if I wanted to make a move to a bigger television market. On the other hand, I had already committed three years to becoming a lawyer. After my first taste of the courtroom, I began to wonder if maybe I should spend a few years practicing, just to try it out. So began an internal debate between broadcasting and law that was excruciating, and despite a job offer, I worried about making the right choice.

Although the decision about my future was never far from my mind, I had other things to pleasantly distract me. In my early days of law school, I married my high school sweetheart, Helen Scott Kurtis. She was a second grade teacher in Topeka. Our combined paychecks got me through law school. We had an apartment in the married housing units on campus. One bedroom, one living room with kitchen attached seemed like luxury.

I was in that living room on November 22, 1963, around 1:00 in the afternoon when my friend Ken Murrell pounded on our door. "Kennedy's been shot!" It's hard to relive the next four days of paralysis and mourning. All programming at WIBW was canceled as the national networks went into wall-to-wall coverage, documenting the assassination, President Johnson's swearing in on Air Force One, and the heartbreaking funeral procession that followed several days later. The unthinkable had happened, and America was shaken to its core. I was lucky to have "too much to do" to carry a heavy burden for long.

Another big distraction—this one joyous—came on December 22,

1965—our daughter, Mary Kristin Kurtis. And yes, the proximity to Christmas led us to the name.

Between law classes and parenting classes, I finally came to a decision about my future. With newfound worry about security for a family, I chose the safest path. I would be a lawyer. A two-man law firm in Wichita, John Frank and Pat Kelley, was looking for a young Washburn graduate and a potential courtroom lawyer. When they offered, I accepted.

Although the US involvement in Vietnam was escalating and my Marine Reserve rifle company was waiting to be called up, life seemed much calmer with a job in my pocket. Next stop, the bar.

The examination required to get a license to practice law in Kansas was akin to medieval torture. It was held in the largest chamber in the state capitol, the House of Representatives. We all took seats at the legislative desks and received the exam questions, which took hours to answer. Friends who had spent years studying and socializing were now fierce rivals, all set on edge with fear and determination. I watched to see who finished first and cursed them. Then I looked around at those still testing when I finished, strutting by with a feeling of superiority.

The stress didn't end there. Several days later, we all filed back into the hall. It was like visiting a battlefield, waiting for the casualty report. Would I be among the fallen? Or still standing and worthy of a future? It was one word, a simple *pass* or *fail*, sealed in an envelope. No "Thank you for your service" or "Sorry to keep you waiting" or "Better luck next time, bitch." And without private email, we had to receive the envelope in person by walking down the center aisle between all of our classmates. Some would open it immediately with instant smiles or frowns as they walked back up the aisle. Others left the building to join their wives and open the envelope together. One person went behind a tree on the lawn outside. Small rituals solemnized the determination of one's future.

Then came the sonorous voice over the loudspeaker: "BILL KURTIS."

I passed.

It was a tremendous relief, but the victory held less meaning because in the days leading up to the exam, the Topeka Tornado had completely changed the course of my life. I was going to be a broadcaster. One storm and those five words—"For God's sake, take cover"—had sealed my fate.

Several of the other members of the "tornado class" wondered if their careers would be shaped by the storm as well. We all wondered whether more of us had passed because the examiners had felt sorry for us after our law books had been found sixty miles away.

I tucked away my bar letter, wrote a letter of apology to John Frank and Pat Kelly to excuse myself from their generous offer to practice law with them, and started looking for a job in broadcasting.

With my future clearly in focus for the first time ever, the course of the past decade made perfect sense. It looked as close to true destiny as I think something can. The values of a loving mother and a committed military father; the lessons of rural immigrant grandparents and life in small-town Kansas; the devotion to teamwork, hard-won on Coach Emmot's field; the hardening maturation of the Marine Corps; the intellectual rigor of law school; performances in debate club and moot court. Not to mention a nearly unheard-of run of experience on the air. My first job at KIND, a Top 40 disc jockey at KTOP, classical music host at KANU, and weatherman at WIBW-TV. Everything fell magically into place. I felt it was what I was meant to do.

But it all seemed insignificant when compared with the videotape of my coverage of the tornado. That was what I sent to five television stations.

One responded quickly. WBBM-TV, the CBS station in Chicago. And that's where the story gets really good.

# FOUR

# Richard Speck

In many ways, during my first few months in Chicago, I felt like Dorothy, having been thrown about by a Kansas tornado and landed in the fantastical land of Oz. Everything about Chicago was still astonishing for a small-town Kansas boy. It meant my first time on an elevated train, first time to stare at an inland sea, first time to see a major league baseball game.

But those moments of magical fantasy were always quickly brought back down to a grim reality. My family and I arrived to a city gripped by fear. The bloody tragedy was the lead story on every newsstand. The picturesque suburban neighborhoods and iconic downtown avenues felt deserted. All of Chicago knew his name and spoke it in terrified whispers: Richard Speck. His lopsided, pockmarked face was plastered on every newspaper's front page.

On my first day at WBBM-TV, September 22, 1966, I had to get up to speed on what had already become a national story. I had only a basic knowledge of the mass murder that had taken place only several weeks before, on July 13. I had been preoccupied with the aftermath of the Topeka Tornado, passing the bar, applying for broadcasting jobs, and moving my young family several states away. But it didn't take long to catch up.

Richard Speck was a twenty-four-year-old ex-con from central Illinois. On the night of July 13, he'd been drinking and taking street drugs at the

Shipyard Inn, where he heard talk of an easy mark. There was a town house not far away where some student nurses were living together to save money. It was like a sorority dormitory. They were young and pretty and, to the blue-collar workers of the Shipyard Inn, exotic.

Making his way through the dark with a .22-caliber pistol and a hunting knife, Speck easily found the town house in a row of the Chicago-style living quarters. He pried open a rear screen and slipped inside.

As the nine students, ages nineteen to twenty-four, came home from work, Speck was waiting inside like a coiled snake. One by one, he tied them up with a bedsheet that he tore into strips, telling them he only wanted to burglarize the town house. But one student nurse spit in his face, and Speck broke into a drug- and booze-fueled rage. He stabbed and strangled three women to death on the spot. Then he took the remaining five into a separate room, where he tortured and killed them.

In the bloodbath and chaos, Speck overlooked one of the nurses, Corazon Amurao, who was hiding under a bed. After Speck left, she screamed for help on a window ledge until neighbors called police. She would become the primary witness and would send Speck on the road to conviction.

Even before the Speck murders, Americans were faced with a seemingly constant stream of unprecedented bad news. America's naive confidence had been shattered with the assassination of President Kennedy in 1964 and then the assassination of Malcolm X only a year later. The civil rights movement had been marching forward for years by this point, bringing with it social unrest, political upheaval, and violent chaos. Young people of all races were shaking things up with a vibrant youth culture that threatened the status quo. America's role in the Vietnam War was starting to spin up, and while the war had not reached its pinnacle of unpopularity, the draft, which had pulled 500,000 boys away from home since 1965, was already tugging at the seams of American society. Like many cities across the country, Chicago was a tinderbox, and Speck threw a match.

It was strange to think that if I had chosen to be lawyer only several months before, I would have been sitting at a small desk in Wichita, Kansas, working on mundane legal matters. But no, I'd decided to be a broadcaster, so here I was, assigned to work on one of the most significant crimes in the city's history and a criminal trial of national obsession.

Although I had just arrived at WBBM and had no TV experience, I was the only journalist with a law degree on the television station's reporting staff—and possibly the only one in the entire city. Thus, I was the natural selection to cover the trial.

If ever a trial seemed destined for a quick verdict, it was Speck's. Given the massive media blitz and the nature of the crime, I wouldn't have been surprised if the population had dragged him from the Cook County Jail and applied a little curbside justice. But even with my beginning status, I didn't buy that it was a slam dunk. My legal education gave me a different set of eyes. I could see things other reporters couldn't, things beneath the surface.

The issue of providing a fair trial and meeting the free-press demands had been argued for some time. But I didn't know that the Speck trial would become ground zero for the ultimate test between the law and the media. The palpable fear among the legal profession, from police to prosecutors, was that letting the media try the case could jeopardize Speck's *trial of the century.*

The first test was the case of *Sheppard v. Maxwell*, 1966. The Supreme Court had ruled that the trial was a horror in the courtroom. The Sam Sheppard trial became a landmark because of the press circus inside the courtroom. "The tidal wave of venomous press coverage" swamped the case and led to Dr. Sheppard being found guilty before the trial ever began. The *New York Times* called it a "roman circus." Excessive pretrial publicity had threatened Sam Sheppard's right to a fair trial. And that's an understatement.

The transcript of the *Sheppard* case was an indictment of the judicial system. The Supreme Court called the trial a "Roman Holiday." Reporters took every seat in the courtroom, and a long table was set up behind the counsel table to accommodate more. The reporters could have reached out and touched the jury. In an unheard-of violation of courtroom decorum, they were allowed to handle the exhibits! Today's practice of not allowing the media to interview, photograph, or even mention jurors grew out of ridiculous practices on occasions such as the Sheppard trial. Reporters could talk to jurors as they came and went from the courtroom. The local paper, the *Cleveland Press*, created a campaign of salacious stories against Sam Sheppard with no facts to support the claims. It was the worst case of trial by media one could imagine. If strict procedures had not been laid down at the Speck trial, the behavior of reporters could have been much the same.

Sam Sheppard was found guilty of murdering his pregnant wife and sentenced to life in prison. His son worked tirelessly to reverse the sentence and clear his father's name. In 1966, before the Speck trial started, the US Supreme Court determined that the "carnival atmosphere" surrounding Sheppard's first trial had made due process impossible; he was acquitted at a second trial.

How did this decision relate to Speck? For two days after the killings, the city shut down in fear. Four newspapers did their duty to spread every disgusting detail of the crime scene to a stunned public. Example: "When Chicago police entered the apartment there was so much blood on the floor they had to put boards down to avoid slipping." Police Superintendent O. W. Wilson stated at a news conference on July 16, "As far as I'm concerned, there is no question that he [Speck] is the murderer."

It was total coverage, absolute saturation with reporters competing for every bloody detail.

It posed a fearful challenge to prosecutors and the judge. Mark J. Phillips and Aryn Z. Phillips, in their review of the Speck case for the *Illinois Bar Journal* in November 2016, noted that the morning after the Wilson press conference, every Chicago paper, as yet unaware of Speck's capture in the early hours, carried banner headlines with Speck's name and photograph. The *Chicago Tribune* carried the front-page headline "Slaying Suspect—Man on Run."

National papers also picked up the sensational story. A front-page article in the *Washington Post* datelined Saturday, July 16, identified Speck as the killer of the eight nurses, fully reporting Wilson's press conference and giving a detailed description of Speck, including his photograph and tattoos. Even the *New York Times* that Sunday covered the press conference in its "Major Events of the Day," ranked in national importance after the Chicago race riots but before a labor strike against the nation's airlines.

Did the saturation coverage present the possibility that Speck could never get a jury that hadn't been corrupted by the media? I saw the vulnerability right away. Sometimes it takes fresh eyes and a newcomer's neutrality to provide a perspective that those closer to the story can't see. As in a debate, the "issue" to be argued in next year's moot court was indeed fair trial/free press. So the topic was hot in law schools, and I was sorry to miss it.

Then there was the issue of Speck's Miranda rights. In fact, there were no so-called Miranda rights when the Speck murders happened, as the Supreme Court had not yet handed them down on stone tablets. But no one was sure whether the Supremes would consider that an exception.

Ernesto Miranda went to trial for armed robbery, kidnapping, and rape. But in 1966, the US Supreme Court found that his Fifth and Sixth Amendment rights had been violated when police had failed to inform him that he had a right to silence and could refuse to answer questions or provide information to law enforcement officers that might be incriminating. The so-called Miranda rights are now the bedrock of every arrest we see on a television crime show: "You have the right to remain silent," etc.

I dug deeper into Speck's arrest. While police were still searching for him, Speck finally checked into a skid-row hotel, where he found a friend to drink with. He fell into bed to sleep off the drunken stupor, and his friend found him with cut marks on his wrist and arm, indicating an attempted suicide. He called police. They took Speck to Cook County Hospital, where a young doctor, LeRoy Smith, began the initial examination. When he scraped away the dried blood on the arm, he saw a tattoo that by then had been highly publicized across the country. It said, "Born to Raise Hell." And the police arrested Speck. But did they read him his rights? It never came up. The built-up hate rolled past the issue, probably not even knowing it was there. Speck had fallen into a void between a Supreme Court opinion and accepted Chicago justice.

It would take months for the city to calm down.

Ironically, the Cook County assistant state's attorney, prosecutor Bill Martin, was twenty-eight years old to my twenty-six. Both lawyers, I was looking in from the *outside* and Bill was facing a well-respected and clever public defender, Gerald Getty, *inside* the courtroom. Getty had never had a client visit Old Sparky, the Illinois electric chair. But Martin had an ace in his pocket: Corazon Amurao. She was the most desired remaining piece of the Speck puzzle. She held the absolute smoking-gun testimony as an eyewitness to Speck's rampage. But Bill Martin's team knew the entire press corps was after her to get an interview, so they kept her hidden for seven months prior to trial. They kept her first in a Chicago hotel and then in an apartment, where she got twenty-four-hour police protection.

Both sides would tiptoe through the judicial process so they wouldn't jeopardize the *"trial* of the century" for the *"crime* of the century." In response to the Miranda issue, the first precaution was that neither police nor lawyers would question Speck for three months prior to the trial. That's one way to handle Miranda rights: don't interrogate the defendant, and make sure he has a lawyer. Public defender Getty made Martin cautious.

I wondered whether the entire legal world had come to Chicago with me. Was Lady Justice taunting me by making my first case out of law school the biggest *random* mass murder in the twentieth century, as Martin put it?

As far as I could tell, I was the only lawyer among the Chicago press corps. That would change over the next fifty years, of course. But at the time, it gave me a distinct advantage. I could see ahead of the events and anticipate the legal maneuvering and arguments. I understood lawyer speak and was able to translate it into regular English that the average Chicagoan could understand. The television news business was far from hiring a specialist in the law, but a general assignment reporter who happened to be a lawyer was twice as valuable. I'd never thought when I was daydreaming in law school that a legal correspondent would ever be a real thing. But here I was, first job at a major television station, peering into the process of the trial of the century with knowledge no other reporter in the city had.

In the moment, however, the gravity of the situation was mostly lost on me. I was spending long, stressful days between courtrooms and newsrooms, figuring out how to translate hours upon hours of legal proceedings into a ninety-second report that was factual and understandable and trying to prove to the station and to myself that I could be a broadcaster. It was only well after the trial that I truly came to appreciate the significance of where I was and what I was doing. Perhaps the superhuman ego of any other lawyer-turned-broadcaster would have seen it, but I was just trying to keep my head above water in my first job out of school.

Still, my lawyerly instincts were running on all cylinders. As I was getting my head around the case and the trial, my first prediction was that the venue would have to be changed. I was quickly proven right. Upon Getty's request, in a pretrial motion, the judge granted a change of venue to make finding a jury that hadn't heard of the mass murder a little easier.

But where could the trial go? The entire nation was clued in to every whisper of the Speck case.

How about good old Peoria, 140 miles south of Chicago and big enough to handle the circus of media that would cover the trial? It would not be a long one.

Two years before a man walked on the moon, we were working without what we now take for granted—satellite communication. We didn't have videotape to use in the field; there was no electronic journalism. We were forced to use our ingenuity to speed up the competitive business. We weren't competing with the newspapers (they still ruled Chicago media), so we partnered with them. We shared a Peoria office with the *Chicago Sun-Times*. An idea floated through the media that a World War II fighter plane owned by a hobbyist could fly exposed film from Peoria to Chicago to beat the deadlines. That idea disappeared in the fertile minds of reporters used to pushing the limits of creative ways to beat the competition.

Covering the "law" in 1966 Chicago was like mid-nineteenth-century London, at least as described by Charles Dickens. One day, assignment editor John Lane sent me to the Cook County courthouse, the Gray Lady at Twenty-Sixth and California on Chicago's southwest side. When I got to the courtroom to try to arrange an interview with the famous author Nelson Algren, who was appearing on a charge of possessing marijuana, a crowd of fifty or sixty people was standing in front of the judge waiting for their case to be called. There was no order, no lines, no quiet except when the bailiff shouted like a human bullhorn, "Number 231, Marilyn Paulinski!" A woman standing in back stabbed the air with her arm, trying to get the attention of the judge. I don't know if she ever did.

I saw Algren leave the courtroom and caught him in the hall. He was not happy to see me and declined an interview. But the Man with the Golden Arm looked exactly like his photograph. Algren was a hero to reporters and authors for his books on the city, like *Chicago: City on the Make*, and would achieve a new level of interest with the news of his affair with Simone de Beauvoir, the wife of Jean-Paul Sartre, the French existentialist. It was a short ride from O'Hare to Algren's bed on the north side.

The judge had literally shut the courthouse down to press overage. I remember gathering with the other reporters on a sloping lawn outside the Peoria courthouse. It was where we received the restrictions that Judge Herbert Paschen issued to the media covering the trial. No cameras or electronic equipment would be allowed on the courthouse premises. Every person entering the courthouse would be searched. No artist's sketches were allowed. No telephone line would be allowed in the courthouse. No photographs of jurors were permitted. No publishing of their names or addresses. Witnesses, jurors, lawyers, staff, court personnel, and police were forbidden to make any statement in open court. The lawyers were forbidden to make their case to the press or by leaks. Only twenty-five press credentials were issued, leaving two hundred other requests denied. As if answering the Sheppard judge directly, Judge Paschen said no one except attorneys was permitted to handle exhibits. This was proof that Judge Paschen was listening when the Supreme Court spoke (in *Sheppard*). The Speck trial would be the first time *Sheppard* was tested. In one respect, it made our job easier. If we couldn't get information, we'd go to air with whatever we had, which was to report on the restrictions.

As expected, there was only one witness we were waiting for: Corazon Amurao. She was asked to point out the man who'd come to her bedroom door the night of July 13, 1966. Dramatically, she stepped from the witness box, and within a foot of Speck at the defense table, she pointed a finger at him and said, "This is the man."

Although it looked like the end, the trial was not over. Martin had more witnesses in case the jury chose not to believe Ms. Amurao and for the inevitable appeal process. And Getty still had his case for the defense. He presented an alibi from the owners of a café testifying that Speck had been there during the four-hour murder spree.

But on April 15, the jury began their deliberations in private while ordering lunch. Before the meals arrived, after only forty-nine minutes, word came that the jury had reached a verdict: guilty on all eight counts of homicide.

Despite Judge Paschen's restrictions, reporters bolted for the door and a few nearby phones outside the courthouse. Word spread quickly among those of us gathered outside. We set up our cameras and microphones and waited for Martin and Getty to make their statements and for the families to express their relief about the final judgment.

Everyone was relieved. The distance from Chicago made the coverage difficult for those of us who needed pictures. Even through my beginner's green eye shades, I thought the judge's new rules for covering trials were too strict. However, I thought they worked well enough considering it was the first time these rules had been applied since the *Sheppard* case.

We handed the film in four-hundred-foot exposed rolls, about eleven minutes, to couriers on motorcycles, and off they went to the great metropolis on the prairie an hour and a half away.

I would follow in my own car and get there in time for the 10:00 news. When the trial was still in session, the turnaround was tough. But that's journalism. I was the only reporter from WBBM-TV to cover the trial. There just weren't that many on staff. It was day to day but not more than a week. Once you start covering a trial, it's hard to pass along to someone else. You're both a conveyor of information and a file cabinet. That's why local stations find it expensive to assign one reporter to a full trial—unless it's red-hot important, of course.

In subsequent trials, I found that a looser application of restrictions worked well, allowing the lawyers to make brief statements after daily sessions to explain the legal procedures. It's an opportunity to educate the public about the legal process. The media appreciates it because it gives them something to report, and it benefits the law by using the platform to explain why various motions and objections were made. Throughout the next sixty years, I tried to explain legal jargon in layman's terms. This became one of my personal crusades.

In June 1966, Speck was sentenced to death. But while he was awaiting the electric chair, the US Supreme Court ruled that the death penalty was unconstitutional, forcing a resentencing for Speck. In November 1972, he was sentenced to serve between 400 and 1,200 years. He may have escaped the chair, but he would still spend the rest of his life in prison.

That 1972 sentencing had a certain finality. This is where the screen goes to black at the end of the movie and white text reads, "Speck died from a heart attack on December 5, 1991, one day before his fiftieth birthday." Roll credits. After that inescapable life sentence, and certainly after his death, no one expected anything else in the drama of Chicago's first infamous mass murderer. But the story of Richard Speck had an epilogue, one more horrendous chapter to shock us. And once again, I played a major role.

It was 1994, and I was well into the next chapter of my career—investigative documentarian and founder of Kurtis Productions. One of my producers, Glen Dacy, brought me a VHS tape that an attorney had given him to pass on to me. Ostensibly, it was some new revelation about Richard Speck. We were free to use it, but we couldn't reveal the attorney's name. To this day, some thirty years after receiving it, we have not revealed the source. News happens like that. Some sources are whistleblowers and want to right a wrong or change the world. Some turn to the media because the official channels of redress have become a dead end. Others have information that burns a hole in their psyche, so they have to liberate it. That's how cold cases are solved. Time loosens tongues, remember?

I took the tape into the screening room at Kurtis Productions and said, "Roll it." There in the twilight darkness loomed Richard Speck come back to life in a home video smuggled into prison. But how had they taped him? *Why* had they done it? Where were the guards? And how had the attorney got hold of it?

From the noise in the background of the video, we thought it was the kitchen. Speck sat on a bench with a companion. There was another inmate behind the camera who asked questions. The tape was an hour and a half, but in those first few minutes, we knew we had seen enough to send a shock wave through the Illinois penal community and extract the final confession to the eight murders that we had never heard.

The viewing was chilling, paralyzing. We couldn't take our eyes off the screen. We didn't really know how to describe it. We had heard of what goes on in prison, male-to-male sex, drugs available as easily as ordering through Federal Express, and cash flowing as if there were no walls. Here was proof in lurid, sickening detail that could not be ignored. Before listening closely to the sound half lost in the background noise, I wanted to confirm that what I was seeing was actually Speck. So I called Bill Martin, the prosecutor in the decades-old Speck case.

"You're not going to believe this, but I've received some video of Speck as you've never seen him, doing things I would guess none of us have seen before," I told him. "I need a drop-dead identification, and you're the best I could get. Also, it'll be good to see you again."

Who could turn down that invitation, especially the chief prosecutor of the man who'd killed eight student nurses? It was a process of buttoning up any loose ends, knowing critics and officials would be coming after us with their strongest criticism. The entire Illinois penal system was on the line for allowing the most hated man in Illinois, perhaps the country, to have the run of Stateville as if it were his playground.

Bill hadn't changed much in nearly thirty years, still fitting the legal scholar type, with curious eyes behind dark-framed glasses and a white crown of hair.

I greeted him, and we went straight to the screening room. I said, "I'll give you a few minutes to adjust to what you're seeing. It's a shock, I know that. Once you have seen enough and can firmly identify Speck, I'll stop it and we'll go again from the top because I'd like to confirm every act and statement he makes."

The video started, and as Speck took off his shirt, Bill gasped. Speck had what seemed to be full breasts that had been enhanced to appear female. I tried to convince myself that it was just the muscle loss and fat of an old man. But most people thought that he must have smuggled in breast-enhancing pills to become more womanlike to please other inmates in the penitentiary. It was anybody's guess. Speck disrobed until he was almost naked on the bench and casually carried out the instructions of the man operating the camera.

The question was heard from behind the camera: "How do you get along here?"

Speaking to the camera, Speck said, "If they only knew how much fun I was having in here, they would turn me loose."

He was playing to an audience of his fellow inmates, bragging about his sinister accomplishment. He took out a roll of one-hundred-dollar bills, which we could see in the video picture, and slowly unrolled it.

Why was the video made? After lengthy investigation, there's never been a good answer. The one I prefer is that it was pornographic jailhouse sex, which is available if you know which adult video stores to frequent. These jailhouse tapes are trafficked primarily inside the incarcerated network. Speck seemed to be doing it for the two other men in the room, perhaps in payment of a debt.

The tape rolled on, and Speck warmed to performing for the "boys." Noise from the kitchen grew loud and then quiet, not in sync with what we were seeing but adding a bizarre soundtrack from a place we had never been.

There was money and cocaine. Speck was slowly piling it into a small mountain of white powder. No, we didn't have any way to confirm that it was cocaine, but everything else was authentic; why not this?

During the trial, Speck never confessed and never gave an interview, with one apparent exception over the phone. He told Bill Martin that he had blacked out on drugs and could remember nothing about the killings. But after years in prison that were obviously not exactly cruel punishment, he felt confident enough in his safety to reply to a question from the camera operator about why he had killed the nurses.

Speck said, "It just wasn't their night." And laughed.

There was one more performance before the ordeal of the one-and-a-half-hour tape ended. Speck, now totally naked, leaned into the lap of his partner, Latimore, to provide oral sex.

The raw and authentic tape was a knife in the very heart of the Illinois penal system. It raised damning questions among law enforcement, politicians, and the people of the great state of Illinois. The day after this news piece aired on WBBM-TV, it seemed as if every serious news organization in the country, including *60 Minutes*, was calling to try to get the tape. In Los Angeles, the CBS station played the news piece several nights in a row. Ratings were out of sight. I also got in on the action with Kurtis Productions, offering my unique perspective in a one-hour documentary for my A&E series *Investigative Reports*.

The Speck tape was all over the airwaves for weeks. It was like looking at a terrible traffic accident and not being able to take your eyes off it. The pain reached down to Illinois's very soul.

Some viewers were shocked and offended. Did we have to show the sex and drug use? Wasn't it in bad taste?

My answer was, and still is, that's what we do. We show the entire truth. It's what the people deserve to know. And it can effect real change. It was pure, authentic truth carried by something that could not be denied—a visual record.

The Speck tape did create change. The day after WBBM broadcast it, a flurry of investigations were launched by the State House Judiciary-Criminal Law Committee, the Illinois attorney general, the Illinois Senate Judiciary Committee, and the US attorney's office.

Producer Mike Harvey accompanied me to Springfield, Illinois, to show the tape to the twenty-five members of the House Judiciary Committee. We arrived early in the hearing room to set up the monitors and playback unit. I wasn't looking at how many were attending in the visitor's section and was in for a surprise. When I did look around, it was filled with reporters, some even standing on chairs to get a better look. It was the first time our competitors had had a chance to get a recording of the tape, however short. More than a week had passed with video available only on CBS Chicago.

Committee Chairman Tom Johnson asked us to hit play. It lasted all of fifteen seconds before an audible gasp caused one female legislator to demand, "Please turn it off." The portion of the tape showed Speck leaning over into an oral sex position.

It didn't take long for them to see that everything they had heard about the tape was true.

The penal system had a couple other issues regarding losing control of the prisons. A gang leader was alleged to have set up a drug distribution system within the prison and was running his gang-controlled drug ring on the outside from inside the walls of Stateville. Another charge was that guards were having sex with inmates at a women's prison. Another Chicago street-gang leader had bragged about the freedom he and his top lieutenants enjoyed at Stateville. Federal agents charged that gang leader Larry Hoover had been able to build his gang into the largest in the state while incarcerated.

On the other hand, prison officials reasoned that giving inmates (gangs) freedom prevented possible riots.

State Representative Al Salvi said after seeing the tape, "I don't think any member of this committee is surprised by this. Some of these problems have been under our noses for years. And we need to do something about it."

Some say the Speck tape ignited the biggest change in the history of the Illinois penal system. Unable to deny the prison problems after seeing the Speck video, Representative Johnson's Judiciary Committee debated potential improvements for two years. They finally recommended creating one prison as a permanent lockdown facility, designating one gang-free facility, ordering new electronic equipment to check for contraband on anyone coming into the prison, and eliminating physical contact between inmates and visitors.

Once again, I was caught up in the whirlwind of history as it was playing out. But I wasn't just a bystander. I wasn't an objective reporter, calling balls and strikes. I was an active player. I saw how the line from the attorney's choice to send me the Speck tape to my choice to give it to WBBM and A&E cable network and everywhere else on the air led to real change happening. Decisions were made, problems were solved, and people's lives were changed, hopefully for the better. It was another reminder of the responsibility that journalists have, a reminder of why I got into the business in the first place.

# FIVE

# Chicago on Fire

The fact that my first assignment for WBBM-TV was the Richard Speck trial set the tone for my time in Chicago. In the immediate wake of Speck, everyone thought that the twentieth century had seen its biggest trial and the opportunities for a legal reporter at a local station were gone. The next few years would prove how wrong they were. Although I was already earning a name for myself as a legal specialist, I was still more often than not working the beat as a general assignment reporter. In 1968, before the next trial of the century, I was working the cultural tremors that were arising among the younger generation. It was clear that something was in the air.

I've come to believe that the foundational crack in the decade was the Kennedy assassination in 1963. It was a cruel splash of reality that America was not the impervious city on a hill we'd become accustomed to believing it was. The Warren Commission declared the assassination was the work of a single shooter, Lee Harvey Oswald, but the public found this hard to believe. One man? It gave license that it was permissible to reject authority. And so began the era of doubt. Vietnam would put a nail in that, followed by Watergate proving that even a president could lie to the American people.

My job as a reporter was to observe the changes creeping into view. It wasn't hard. People came marching down the streets carrying placards demanding equal rights for Black Americans, announcing the liberation of women, and condemning the Vietnam War. Anything that would shake the tree was fair game. When they weren't marching in the streets, the children of the sixties were practicing free love, smoking marijuana, and listening to new, subversive music featuring the authentic grassroots home-grown anthems of Bob Dylan and the bards of Woodstock. To me, it was a time when national stories jammed together without pause. It may have been exhausting to viewers at home, but to a rookie journalist, it was a welcome baptism by fire. I could tell this moment was important, but living in the middle of it, I couldn't yet tell how important it would become. I was still just trying to keep my head above water.

The Vietnam War needed manpower. President Lyndon Johnson decided to fight it by instituting a draft rather than calling up the reserves. With half the population under eighteen, young men were caught in limbo, facing an obligation to serve their country if they couldn't get a deferment and thereby postponing major life decisions. The risk of being shot at half a world away in a confusing immoral war provided a spark that set a whole generation on fire.

But antiwar protests weren't the only fire burning that year. Exactly one year to the day after the Speck trial started, April 4, 1968, Dr. Martin Luther King Jr. was standing on the balcony outside his second-story room in Memphis at the Lorraine Motel. He was there to march in support of a sanitation workers' strike and seemed to be relaxed as he surveyed the parking lot and beyond it a forested rise toward a brick building. He was waiting for others, including Rev. Jesse Jackson, to accompany him to dinner, but he didn't see James Earl Ray sighting in on him with a .30-06 Remington hunting rifle. A bullet severed King's spinal cord after traveling through his jaw. He was dead on arrival at a Memphis hospital.

I was in the newsroom when the bulletin came in. It was just after 6 p.m. I turned to Bob Harris, one of our producers and writers, and said we'd better get ready.

The network cut in with the bulletin, and we started to gather reaction on the street. Crowds pressed against plate-glass windows to watch the television sets inside. But it took the night for the heart-rending tragedy to sink into Black communities. It affected everyone, but especially the Black neighborhoods, whose hopes and constant prayers lifted King to sainthood.

On the first morning after King's assassination, news of dozens of chaotic protests poured in from every major city in the country. Looting, fires, beatings. Chicago was no different. The radio and television

stations in Chicago had a well-intentioned plan to avoid contributing to
the spread of unrest. They collectively agreed to withhold news of protests and riots for fear that covering them would only empower the protesters. But however well-intentioned, this approach turned out to be
deeply misguided.

It happened that my seventeen-year-old cousin, Greg Hecht, was visiting me. Sort of a right-place, right-time situation. I was getting ready
to head out with my film crew to cover the protests when he asked to go
along. He was considering a job in journalism himself, but I doubt he really knew what he was asking for that morning. He just wanted to go to
work with his cousin and see what working at a TV station was like. For
whatever reason, I invited him for a ride-along.

Charlie Boyer, Jim Yario, I, and my kid cousin hopped in the car with
plenty of gear and started driving west on Madison Street. Not long into
the drive, a car was stopped by a mob in front of us. They pulled the white
driver out of his car and into the street and kicked and beat him. I realized
that businesses were sending employees home early to avoid the coming
disturbance. But without knowing where the mobs were and what direction they were moving, innocent Chicagoans going home were driving
straight into the mayhem. The news media's failure to cover these riots
from the start, our failure to warn people of the danger on the streets,
however good the intention, was a major mistake I vowed never to make
again. We had abdicated our responsibility.

Jim Yario turned away from the biggest crowds in the intersections
and tried to stay ahead of the mob running from one burning building to
another, Madison Street stretched from the main thoroughfare at Mar-
shall Fields in the Loop all the way to the western city limits, about sev-
enty blocks. I'll never forget what I saw.

We watched the fires along Madison. While crowds beat innocent
commuters, I watched young men with torches running from row house
to row house, up the stoop stairs, lighting up the fronts of the houses.
Someone would pour gasoline onto a wooden door, and another would
touch it with a torch. They were hundred-year-old brick homes with
neighborhood businesses—whole communities woven together, now
being intentionally destroyed block by block. It was Chicago's history,
razed and replaced with a different kind of history.

We hung back, trying to remain unobserved by the packs of teens, but eventually we had to establish our own tactics. Jim maneuvered ahead full speed and then slowed down for filming. We stopped several times to warn people getting into their cars, "Hurry, the mob's just behind us. Better run." Adrenaline is a wonderful accelerant to fear, and there was plenty of it rushing through all of us.

We watched one typical attack on a business at Western and Madison. The mob was much more interested in looting than in attacking us, so we pulled over to see it start to finish. The storefront was secured by a folding metal barrier that could be pulled across the front at closing. It could be unfolded when the store was open and then shut at night. But the looters, grown men, dismantled it as easily as children smashing their toys. They pulled it down from the top far enough to climb over and through the broken front window. Then they went to the door and opened it from the inside. A burglar alarm was screaming, but it was just one more sound blasting away in the afternoon. It provided a dramatic soundtrack to the scene.

A steady stream of looters, from housewives to drifters to whole families, began carrying out television sets. One person even backed a car up to the door to fill it with electronic items—speakers, amplifiers, and TVs of all sizes. It didn't take long to empty the store.

The mood was electrifying as we witnessed crimes happening in front of us, otherwise law-abiding people joining their neighbors in getting "free stuff" without fear of being caught. Once or twice a squad car with four policemen inside drove by, and the crowd ran but quickly came back as if in a game at a festival. The police squad had more important matters, like protecting firemen farther down the street.

I saw it all start and grow until the fires had nothing to burn anymore. They left black, smoldering ruins filling the twenty blocks. The burned timbers stood in bizarre shapes where just an hour before a store had offered merchandise and welcomed customers. We watched children clinging to their mothers' skirts, wide-eyed on an adventure outside the house.

I think we probably heard it before we saw it, but that crowd got close suddenly. It seemed to close in all around us, and there was a crash—the sound of plate glass breaking—and then the volume of the voices went up, and the crowd was yelling at us. There was more crashing and glass breaking, and now it was a sea of bodies all around. Pinned in our lane, we were slowing and then stopped, with cars just a couple of feet in front of and behind us. Charlie was riding shotgun with the camera in his lap, mostly out of sight if you were outside the car unless you were really looking for it. He brought it up, aiming out the front and side windows, and captured a few seconds of footage. We could see storefronts with broken glass and people with rocks and bricks.

With the camera clacking, Charlie was getting great footage when someone in the crowd spotted him and realized that what was in that camera was evidence as much as anything else. A fragment of brick, or maybe cinder block, came smashing through the window and hit Charlie on the forehead and temple. Greg and I were in the back seat and saw his face as he turned away from the blow. He looked expressionless for a moment, and then a glint of surprise crossed his eyes as if he were wondering what had happened. He dropped the camera in his lap and slumped in the seat, out cold.

Another couple of rocks or bricks hit the car. The rear window behind me smashed. I had never seen safety glass crumple before and was momentarily amazed at how it formed into little square pellets instead of shards. The crowd got louder and quickly surrounded the car.

"Time to go," I told Jim, who was already trying to maneuver us out of the situation. Greg remembers me sounding very calm in that moment, but my heart was pounding out of my chest. In that moment, my mind was pulled in two directions. First, as a reporter, I was flooded with questions. How could this all have happened? Why would people destroy their own communities, burn down their own homes, loot their regular corner stores? And how would we ever put all of this chaos into a news package by deadline for the evening news? My other stream of consciousness was far more primal, more immediate: How the hell are we going to get out of this mess? We need to get Charlie help. Now.

Seventeen-year-old Greg Hecht remembered the view from the back seat. "Ever so slowly, Jim Yario eased forward and made contact with the bumper of the car in front of us. He gave it a little gas and pushed that car four or five feet. He backed up and did the same thing, giving the crowd time to get out of the way before he eased the car behind us back a few feet. Then he was able to break the wheel hard left and pull us into the next lane of traffic, mostly full of pedestrians. I remember that he moved slowly through them, back to the right, and at one point I think he actually had the two right wheels up on the sidewalk until we could reach an intersection, run a light, and break free.

Just as quickly as it had started, it was over. Charlie's forehead was bleeding. We found a place to pull off the street and then got to a phone. Within minutes, the newsroom had dispatched a motorcycle courier to pick up the film and run it through traffic to the lab for processing in time for the six o'clock news. Then we got Charlie to the ER at Rush Presbyterian Hospital.

Later, Greg told me that as he combed bits of glass out of his hair, he had never felt more sure that he wanted to be a journalist. When we knew Charlie would be all right and after the adrenaline left my body, I had the same feeling. This is what I'm supposed to be doing.

Driving past block after block of smoldering ruins, I couldn't help thinking, this is never coming back. The final numbers were smaller than the damage appeared. Nine people were killed, 300 were injured, and 2,000 were arrested. Whole shopping areas were wiped out, and more than 260 businesses were destroyed, including 116 along the twenty-block stretch that we traveled that day in our crew car. Another 72 were wiped out on Roosevelt Road. On Sixty-Third Street, an entertainment mecca for blues giants like Louis Armstrong and blues haunts where Muddy Waters and Junior Wells had nurtured a real American music culture, were gone. The only sound was the El train overhead, echoing off the plate-glass windows in the shops that were left standing. Some were mere shells of bricks left when the fire gutted them.

Chicago was rebuilt but was never the same. The city pushed out the communities that had destroyed it, failing multiple generations of Chicagoans. Close-knit neighborhoods were replaced with corporate offices. Underground blues joints and mom-and-pop diners never returned, replaced by the United Center and James Beard Award–winning restaurants. And after that TV storefront we watched being looted was long gone, a supermarket took its place. In some strange twist of fate, I was invited to the grand opening of that new addition on the corner of Western and Madison. When I pulled up in the exact parking place where our camera crew had stopped in 1968, I felt a deep pull of nostalgia. I mourned what was lost as I looked at what had risen from the ashes.

I had seen firsthand what can happen if unaware, innocent people stumble into danger and what our responsibility as broadcasters should be if we are in a position to warn them. We're the ones with the microphone. We're the ones who must issue the alarm. Whether it's an oncoming tornado or angry mobs waiting to beat commuters leaving work, our words can save people. To choose not to broadcast the truth is to abdicate the basic tenet of our profession.

It was April 1968. I had felt the heat of homes on fire and watched angry mobs pull drivers from their cars because we had failed to warn them of the danger. I was only two years into my chosen career and thought, *What events can possibly be bigger than a city on fire?*

I was in for a surprise.

SIX

# Four Days in August

In 1968, it seemed like the news never stopped. For an ambitious, energetic, up-and-coming newsman, nothing could have been more exhilarating. For a small-town kid with a young family and a strong moral conscience, nothing could have been more exhausting. It was memorable, to say the least.

The nation had barely processed the assassination of Dr. King when, on June 5, the unthinkable happened again. Senator Robert F. Kennedy was killed in Los Angeles. News was becoming more and more national, and the Chicago air was thick with social unrest, political anxiety, midwestern heat, and the smell of the stockyards near the International Amphitheatre, where the Democratic National Convention was to be held.

The coming convention brought with it streams of young people appearing on the streets and in the parks. They wore tie-dyed T-shirts, colorful long hair, and sandals. The emerging "counterculture" had reached the Windy City in full force.

June was suddenly July and then, just as quickly, August. The city was negotiating with the gathering numbers of self-declared "Yippies," now full-fledged "antiwar demonstrators" who were seeking a permit to sleep in Lincoln Park. It had become their unofficial campground anyway.

Most of us regarded them as more *interesting* than truly a matter of concern. Anyone who passed by Lincoln Park had their senses assaulted by aromas of incense, herbal tea, and marijuana; scenes of Technicolor communes and dance circles; and mystical music from acoustic guitars and Indian sitars. The counterculture haven was like something out of an exotic dream, not a violent nightmare.

But Mayor Richard J. Daley took them quite seriously, appearing as a gruff-looking grandfather afraid these creatures would soil his city, lace the water supply with LSD, and nominate a pig for president.

Despite the theatrics (one act in the demonstrators' literal makeshift theater was a skit in which they referred to themselves as "Groucho Marxists"), there were also foreshadowings of more serious intentions. When I arrived in Lincoln Park to put together a report for the evening broadcast, there were lessons underway on how they might use karate to defend themselves from attacks by the Chicago police. Some were jumping up and down in conga-line fashion shouting, "Death to the pigs."

On August 24, two days before the Democratic National Convention began, the city informed the Yippies that they would not receive a permit to be in the park after the 11:00 p.m. curfew. This caught my attention, and I began to believe that this free-love occupation could in fact become something more serious.

The three national networks, CBS, NBC, and ABC, rolled into town and promptly took over the airwaves. I was anchoring the 10:00 p.m. news on WBBM-TV that summer and was pleased to give my slot to my heroes: Walter Cronkite, Eric Sevareid, and the roster of network correspondents. National coverage also meant a little vacation time for the local talent. I could have chosen to take the time off, but I decided to pursue what I loved more than anything—more work—especially when it involved being a witness to history. I headed back to the streets, but now as citizen Bill Kurtis rather than "Bill Kurtis, CBS, Chicago."


The first confrontation came on Sunday, August 25, in Lincoln Park. The Yippies had begun their "Festival of Life" with about two thousand people listening to a rock band, MC5.

By Mayor Daley's order, the police would clear out anyone in the park after the curfew. His reasoning was to break up the encampment and avoid the threatened march to the International Amphitheatre forty blocks south the day before the arrival of the convention delegates.

I could see the long line of CPD officers stretching on a rise above the common green where the Yippies were camping. Their silhouettes, backlit by streetlamps, had the look of Native American warriors on a ridgeline before they came riding down on settlers in a John Ford movie.

At 11:00 p.m., a bullhorn announced the city's intentions and warned that anyone still in the park would be arrested.

Then, step by step, the entire police line, probably two hundred yards long, started moving in a silent skirmish line toward the crowd in the park. Slowly and relentlessly they came, clubs in hand, silently walking down the rise. It was the first contact between protesters and Chicago police. There was no outburst in the darkened campground. The music stopped.

There were calls of "Pigs!" and "Fascists!," but there was no clash that night. The ominous presence of the police seemed to have its effect. The crowd dispersed.

I moved to the intersection of North and LaSalle, the southwest point of the park, among cars that were jammed in traffic from running demonstrators and clouds of tear gas pushing the slow walkers out of the park. Cars were trying to get through the traffic jam. Members of Students for a Democratic Society were near me. Months later, during the trial that prosecuted participants in these four days in August, I would realize that I had walked alongside defendant and courtroom celebrity Tom Hayden. As the protests reached the edge of the trees, I think I heard Hayden yell around the departing protesters, "Let the revolution start now!"

It hardly felt like a revolution where I was. Lincoln Park on that Sunday night was not the site of either a police riot or violence against protesters, save for a few encounters.

The media produced a different story. I saw a cop chase a reporter down an alleyway and pop his head with a baton, sending blood down his face. I had to relive the moment when it was published later in *Time* magazine. In addition to cops, the media provided easy targets for the antagonistic Yippies. Some went after cameras when the photographers turned their way. I realized that some members of the police had taken off their name badges to avoid being identified, both in the moment and after the fact. Amidst it all, I was glad that I wasn't there on assignment. I was just a mild-mannered Chicagoan along for the ride. The more law-abiding protesters knew there were orders not to attack any members of the news media and tried to pull their men off, but they were hard to control. The lack of discipline and training was evident. And it was only Sunday night.

I was more startled than angry. The cops were not provoked, but it was clear that they had a plan—to get the media. But why? In my mind, we the press corps had not yet been critical of the Yippies or the Chicago police. The police aggression seemed to be gratuitous, taking advantage of the situation. The only answer must have come from the squad rooms where they had received orders regarding what to expect. I thought that must have been where the attitude had developed that "outsiders" had come to their town to raise hell, and the cops were going to fight back. It would be at the level of a street fight. That was where the leadership fell short and failed to instill the professionalism to hold their lines tight, respect the right to protest, and keep the peace. The rank-and-file police planned to get their "licks" in.

To be there, night after night, was instructive. It was as if there were two cops in one. The cop beneath the police uniform was in control, baton at the ready around the waist, blue helmet on, waiting and watching, careful to keep his line. But the cop on the outside was not in control; he was driven by emotion and fear. He heard the chants and saw the missiles lofted toward him, the bottles and rocks, and felt the urge to charge.


Things were heating up by Tuesday night, the halfway mark of the Democratic National Convention. Dan Rather and Mike Wallace were shaken by security guards as they tried to interview delegates in the crowd. Outside, the protests moved to the Coliseum south of the Loop for a performance by Peter, Paul and Mary as the planners staged an "Unbirthday Party for LBJ." The city continued to deny permits for sleeping in the parks, marching in parades, and gatherings through Monday and Tuesday. Reports of sporadic dustups filtered in. I felt as though every march in the city was meeting with overaggressive security. The feeling that the cops were not their friends was rising among protesters. The young people, already experiencing their adrenaline rush, accepted the challenge.

Farther north at Division and Wells, there was another demonstration. CBS News cameraman Del Hall was covering it and reported that two Chicago policemen were successfully handling some two hundred protesters who were carrying signs and shouting loudly: "The cops had even kept them on the sidewalk instead of the street. That was a big step because without permits for a parade, a group in the street would stop traffic, making the group liable for arrest [violating city ordinance] or physical altercation. But around the corner came a bunch of cops who were bent on going physical." The first contact was Del Hall, with a camera on his shoulder. A cop, without ordering him to clear away, hit him with the butt end of his baton. The blow hit Del right above the eye, where boxers most often start bleeding from facial blows. Del was the same. The blood was running down his face. His CBS News correspondent, John Laurence, grabbed the camera and saved it. Del needed medical care, so he was taken to Northwestern Medical Center for stitches.

Del said, "As far as I knew there were only three policemen chasing this crowd back and I didn't even see the police. I'm not expert on preventing riots, but one of the problems was that the crowds got too large before the police tried to disperse them. If you'd just kept the crowd from reaching that stage, but by the time they did go in it was too late. I have a theory about television news that no matter what you say, it's only what you see that you remember. That's from my point of view because I'm a cameraman. I think the combination of seeing and hearing that night had a big effect. The world was watching. It was a television event that happened where live cameras were."

When the city finally granted a license to gather and present speeches in Grant Park on Wednesday afternoon, the stage was set for the biggest confrontation yet. With CBS News still on the WBBM airwaves, I was still free of my duties as a correspondent and anchor. Obviously, I made my way to Grant Park.

Crowd estimates varied, but it was reported that about fifteen thousand protesters had assembled. Black Panther Bobby Seale from Oakland, California, spoke from a bandshell stage, and it appeared to be a peaceful gathering until a young protester climbed a flagpole and pulled down the American flag. I was just arriving when I saw police already in the crowd, having knocked over wooden benches to get to the protesters, dispersing them within minutes but not without injuries. One of the organizers, Rennie Davis, was beaten bloody. The police were not waiting for a buildup of violations. The American flag was the red line, and it had been crossed. I thought at the time that their action had come too soon, as they had waited with a hair trigger for the slightest excuse.

The crowd scattered. Would they go south toward the Amphitheatre or east toward the Loop, about three blocks away, and the front line of buildings on Michigan Avenue?

The core of the protesters knew they had no permit to march, but they could walk on the sidewalks. I was with them, hearing shouts of "Let's go to the Hilton."

The Balbo bridge over the South Shore railroad line that ran parallel to Michigan Avenue was barricaded by a National Guard unit. Concertina wire was strung across it, and the soldiers had their rifles at the ready, sealing off the street. The next access across the tracks was farther north on the south side of the Art Institute, Jackson Boulevard. The flow was picking up, and there was a relaxed feel as we boldly crossed onto Michigan Avenue. It was like two rivers joining with tourists and delegates also on the street. I joined the flow on the sidewalk toward the Hilton Hotel, where a number of delegates were staying the night.

Would-be candidate Senator Eugene McCarthy was ensconced there along with his young supporters. Looking down from their rooms, they watched the growing numbers of demonstrators against the Vietnam War.

Like coffee pouring into a cup, the crowd filled the intersection to the brim, which stopped traffic and allowed the protesters to lay claim to the area inside the four compass points of the corners. The crowd was now big enough to start an impromptu rally right there. Speakers gave it the appearance of an ad hoc gathering. Or had it been planned this way all along?

A year later, a national trial would hinge on this very moment. But right now, all we could do as reporters was observe and describe what we were seeing. We had limited perspective, little protection, and no foresight. We were in the eye of the storm.

Confusion and chaos whipped around us from every direction. I walked through the hotel and smelled the stink bombs that had been dropped inside. I looked at the plate-glass window that shattered when police pushed people against it. Delegates wandered stone-faced, some looking for a cocktail. The conventioneers were waiting to ride to the Amphitheatre for the convention speeches.

There was anticipation in the air, a foreshadowing of something bigger about to happen. Those who could see it set their eyes on the intersection full of young people. It was a theatrical climax to many marches and confrontations so far, as if two rival football teams were meeting for a final contest.

There was no live television coverage, a strange anomaly for a political convention. Mayor Daley had restricted the large television trucks from parking on the street. But the networks did the next best thing: they set up studio-sized cameras on the overhanging hotel entrances and recorded the activity below on two-inch videotape machines, the largest at the time. It was at least five years before the miniaturization of electronic news gathering would be introduced.

Time got away from me in the volcanic milieu. I could feel the lava rising beneath my feet. It wasn't hard to predict. I knew the thousands of demonstrators didn't have a permit to be in the intersection. They wanted to keep marching south on Michigan Avenue, but they had no permit for that either.

A line of police stretched across Michigan Avenue at the corner of Balbo. They stood stoically with their batons ready. Their helmets began to glow in the streetlight as the sunlight withdrew. Their blue shirts seemed strangely unprotected without the bulletproof vests that would come years later, adding to the likelihood that the police would be prone to move into the crowd and clear it if bottles were thrown.

I wasn't on assignment, but my journalistic instincts were flaring. I may not have had a camera crew, but I still wanted to get the perfect shot. So I looked for a vantage point. A car was illegally parked under the traffic light at the corner—it couldn't have come any closer to the action if I had parked it myself. So, in the spirit of the moment, I climbed on top of it. Several others followed—a still cameraman for *Time*, the owner of the car, and a few more. We were all crowded on top when the roof depressed in one big dent. The owner, whom I knew from the streets, looked at me with a half smile and a shrug. He said, looking at the dent, "What the hell, it's history."

It was a remarkable position. The police line extended from straight under me next to the driver's side across the street, shoulder to shoulder to the far curb. The cops were facing north toward the crowd. Commander James Rochford was in charge, walking the line, talking to the demonstrators.

The trees were full of late-summer foliage. Some protesters were hanging there; others had climbed up streetlamps. The crowd was sitting as they had been for an hour and a half, during which time the dark sky had crept up on us. The intersection was now fully lit by streetlamps.

There was one incident that a lot of reporting missed, but since I had such a good view, I saw it clearly. Hosea Williams of the Southern Christian Leadership Council leaned down from the bench seat of a wagon pulled by two mules, leading the Poor People's March to the International Amphitheatre. They *did* have a permit, and Commander Rochford waved them through.

In the chaos at the time, I had a bad feeling. The crowd behind the wagon was pushing hard as it slid through the police line. The crowd thought they were being permitted to march through too. But the police line closed after the wagon squeezed through. That upset the demonstrators.

There was pushing and shoving against the line, and from my vantage point looking down from the car top at the point of pressure—protesters against cops—it appeared that the demonstrators were trying to force themselves through the line, to break it. If the police line had broken— and it could have with ten thousand people pushing against the single line—the demonstrators would have had a clear path to the Amphitheatre, or there would have been a bloodier confrontation farther down Michigan Avenue when the police reinforcements put up another line.

What happened next has been seared into the history of Chicago. It was a tremor felt and heard round the world.

It was interpreted as a split between law and order and anarchy, and it polarized the nation in a debate over half a century about whether it helped or hurt the protest against the Vietnam War.

When the pushing was on the edge of a breakthrough, Rochford, feeling under siege, gave the order to "clear the intersection."

Television may not have carried it live, but the mounted cameras in the hotel had a full view. They videotaped the phalanx of police charging the crowd, swinging batons, calling for squadrols, and fighting with their fists. For fifteen minutes, in muted color, the blue helmets waded into people, their batons held over their heads for more leverage. Some officers were hit. Later reports told of bags of feces thrown at the cops. Rocks and bottles were thrown, their liquid flashing like crystals as they were lofted in the otherworldly light of the bluish sodium-vapor lamps, until the police squadrols were full and the intersection was clear.

I was riveted on the line in front of me, watching the mules go through and the protesters try to follow. I decided *that* was ground zero, starting with a push by demonstrators and reaction by police. But months later, I learned a valuable lesson in *perspective*. Truth depends on your physical point of view. But different positions had different light, different angles and views. It was easy to lose track of the bigger picture, to forget that my narrow view, however critical, was a small part of a much larger event.

A friend of mine, Sam Iker of *Time* magazine, told me three months later that he was watching from the second floor of the Hilton, looking down on the intersection from a north window near the corner. He saw what I couldn't see. He said a platoon of Chicago police reinforcements estimated at two hundred, looking ready for business, came marching aggressively up Balbo toward the intersection. The crowd gathered in the street recoiled from the police reinforcements. That movement pushed the entire protest throng into the police line on Michigan. What appeared to be protesters attempting to break through Rochford's line caused him to give the order to clear.

One might argue that it made no difference because the result was the same. But the appearance became the reality—the appearance of what appeared to be an unprovoked attack by Chicago police excessively assaulting unarmed kids.

For the antiwar movement, it was perfect. What appeared to be a spontaneous political rally was stormed by police and eventually broadcast to the nation raw. Even Walter Cronkite was shocked as he watched the tape roll in its unedited form at his booth at the convention. He saw it for the first time along with the nation and expressed his rising emotion at the chaos, jumping to the conclusion the police were out of control.

It was not apparent that even Mayor Daley knew that thirty seconds on television of his police force wading into protesters swinging their clubs would create an indelible wound on the city's reputation that would last for years. Tolerance was lost in the battle, lost to adrenaline that translated shouts of "pigs" into insults that must be answered.

Reflecting on the event, I still find it hard to say it was *planned*. But protest organizers certainly seized the moment and took advantage of it. Regardless of what was premeditated and what was improvised, they provoked the police into violence, revealed Mayor Daley's control over free speech, crashed the convention, and gave a national platform to the anti–Vietnam War movement.

It was a time of reckoning for many journalists, of choosing between traditional straight-down-the-middle reporting or becoming an advocate for one side or the other. In the moment, I was relieved not to have been on the clock and had to make that decision. It was so hard to record what was happening at all that I can't imagine having the time to think about allegiance. That had certainly been my experience in trying to capture the riots only several months before. And this wouldn't be my last social upheaval either, for better or for worse. It was my job to capture police abuse and instigating protesters all the same, and I did my best to do that.

Through it all, I've tried to remain committed to the truth that is in front of me on the ground, in the moment. That's all any reporter really can do. Standing on top of a car at Michigan and Balbo taught me that. We're all limited by our perspective. Just be there, be first, record the scene, and be as accurate as you can. Easier said than done.

# SEVEN

# Tokyo Rose

It was fall, only a fog's breath away from Chicago's dramatic seasonal change. I was coming off a reporter's high from covering ground zero of the summer's protests, so I started looking around for scraps of stories. Mass murders, race riots, and national antiwar protests don't just fall into your lap. Well, not usually. I was combing through loose ends at the WBBM offices when I came across a story that caught my attention: Tokyo Rose, the infamous Pacific siren of World War II. It was a long shot, but my journalistic Spidey senses were tingling, so I had to chase it down.

Like most people, I knew the *myth* rather than the *reality*—that the enchanting voice of Tokyo Rose had broadcast Japanese propaganda by two-way radio across the Pacific to US troops with the intention of weakening the morale of the Allied forces. None of the broadcasts reached the United States, but the image had been cultivated in movies and radio productions. The sailors and Marines aboard ships did listen to an American-sounding voice featuring a disc jockey named Orphan Ann who spun popular records interspersed with Americanized "patter," and the GIs gave her a name, Tokyo Rose, like Kilroy or Axis Sally.

I found out that Tokyo Rose lived in Chicago and worked at her father's grocery store and mercantile business on Clark Street. I didn't know that this lead was mostly a joke, bait laid for newbie reporters. The senior editors got a laugh because they knew Tokyo Rose hadn't given an interview since she had returned from Japan for her trial in 1949. I didn't find out that the lead was a hazing ritual until after the first interview with Tokyo Rose—*my* interview—was already on the air.

So off I went toward Lincoln Park, the same street Al Capone's boys had used on their way to shoot up the gang of Bugs Moran in a garage at Dickens and Clark in 1929, more familiar as the Saint Valentine's Day Massacre.

The store was Chicago chic, two large windows fronting a long, narrow building with several floors above. On the north side, paint was peeling down to the first or second coat, like modern art if you looked at it the right way. It was standing alone next to a vacant lot and was scheduled to be torn down. Inside, yellowed lighting from single bulbs hung from twenty-foot ceilings.

It was a Japanese grocery all right, with shelves filled with rice products in cans and cloth bags along one wall and many, many labels in Japanese. I loved it. Like a movie set from the forties that smelled of a foreign country, having aged over many years. But those years were dialing down. The neighborhood would soon be the victim of a changing city pushing little quaint stores like Toguri's farther north. Soon the grocery would look like the vacant lot next door.

The current attention-getter in the room was actually a four-foot-long tuna, just arrived from the West Coast. A white-aproned Japanese man was drawing a knife across the thick silver fish at widths of one and a half inches to make patties. The slices were deep cherry red and glistening fresh.

A short line had formed after I entered the store, people who knew this was the place to get authentic Japanese products. They were part of an all-Asian clientele.

A small Asian woman stood behind the counter working an abacus. Her hands moved like lightning before adroitly placing the goods in unmarked paper bags.

I asked to see Mrs. D'Aquino, and she looked up as if wondering how I knew her name, so she must be the one, I thought. After the glance, she turned back to her customers, not hiding but appearing to hope that I'd go away, like so many rookies before me.

She was small with quick movements, as if she knew exactly what she was doing. Her almond eyes were bright and alert. She avoided eye contact, but I had a feeling she had already sized me up. Dark hair was mixing with gray and was tied behind her head, out of her face. A dark mole on her upper lip appeared to be a natural beauty mark decorating a face that was still attractive if you handicapped for age.

She finally looked at me and said, "Who are you?"

I said, "Bill Kurtis. I'm a reporter at Channel 2."

"Ah, I thought I'd seen you before. Television, right?" I was stunned as she spoke. Not a trace of a Japanese accent. She spoke like a native Chicagoan. "I don't talk to the press."

I needed a quick pivot as I leaned toward the door. "Yes, I understand that. I just came in to say hello. I like soy sauce."

That brought a smile, a flash of a woman much younger than sixty, almost coquettish, but that could have been my wishful thinking.

Near the door, I turned back and said, "But I see you're busy."

"Yes, I am. But don't you want your soy sauce?" she said, testing me and knowing I was testing her.

"I'll come back for it," I said, walking out the door with a smile.

So it began, a friendship with Iva Toguri D'Aquino that lasted fifty-four years.

I'd drop in once a month to say hello and cultivate a friendship that eventually grew to mutual admiration and, most important, trust. In between visits, I did my research, looking for every newspaper clipping and radio report that I could find. Finally, I had enough to realize that her side of the story had never received the full explanation it deserved. I thought, *This is one hell of a story, and I'm going to tell it.*

I got the feeling that she wanted her story out but had been double-crossed by the press so often that she had sworn never to trust a journalist again. Until me. I knew that if I were to get her side of the story, she needed to trust me. Where so many reporters before me had come in fast and brash and made the hard sell, I tried a different approach.

After several months of building our acquaintance into friendship, I asked if she'd give me an interview for a documentary on Channel 2, CBS, in Chicago. She was torn between entering the cycle of publicity that had persecuted her in the first place and whether to put her trust in me, a true friend. It would be the first interview since her return to the US for trial. I let her know that I would make sure that *her* story told *her* way would make it on the air. I wanted the truth, not the distorted, villainous mythology that had been swirling since the end of the war. Looking down at the worn wood slats on the floor, she nodded yes.

I didn't want to alert anyone about the story. Just the announcement of such an interview would attract the attention that could blow the story before I even had it. I also knew that any preview would drive speculation and only fan the flames of misinformation. I wanted to keep Iva safe and let her tell her story. Iva's only request was that she be allowed to wear sunglasses, one last shield from the history behind her.

I asked for a crew to meet me on Saturday in Lincoln Park so Iva and I could walk down the tree-lined promenade. As we got into position, I realized this was exactly where the Yippies had been cleared out at the beginning of the Democratic National Convention just a few months earlier. When we got to the park, it was cold and rainy. Our 16-mm news camera didn't have much latitude in low-light conditions. We could "push" the film in the lab to get another stop of exposure, but I didn't want to take any chances with such a historic interview. Another problem was that we didn't have wireless microphones. Yes, it was that far back.

I had chosen an outside location because of our need for secrecy, and the challenges were a little unusual. Such are the woes of a filmmaker, especially working with a news crew instead of a well-equipped documentary crew.

How to adapt? I pulled the crew car onto the walking path down the lane. The cold and rain kept people out of the park. The cameraman, Charlie Boyer, sat in the trunk with his legs dangling over the bumper. Iva and I walked together behind the moving car with our mics connected to the sound man, Pete Stanish, by cables. I said we should shoot close enough that they wouldn't see the exhaust fumes in the shot. Iva and I were both wearing raincoats. The rain became a light mist that frankly was a blessing that we could never have planned. It created a mysterious ambience on a darkened, lonely path that looked like the Orson Welles movie *The Third Man*, shot in Belgrade. I felt better years later when a history professor at an East Coast university reviewed it as a brilliant directorial choice to set the history-making first interview with Tokyo Rose/ Iva Toguri in the United States in something that looked like a Humphrey Bogart movie. I told Iva that I'd refer to her as Iva D'Aquino, her married name, to further protect her.

All I wanted was a few minutes to have Iva Toguri D'Aquino tell her story. Fortunately, all the trouble was worth it. The Library of Congress put it in the archives and preserved it for history.

She started at the beginning with her trip to Tokyo before the attack on Pearl Harbor.

"I had gone over there to visit a sick aunt, my mother's only living sister. My mother couldn't go because she was ill herself. She asked me to go to see how her sister was but take her something she needed. They were very short in material things because Japan had been at war with China for so long. So this is what I did, went over there to visit the aunt."

I described her as a woman caught between two countries at war. "This is the story of a woman who maintained American citizenship while broadcasting for the Japanese, who denied the title Tokyo Rose and denies ever broadcasting propaganda but who was convicted of treason."

Even in her midsixties, Iva had an appealing voice. It was immediately clear how it would have been attractive to US servicemen who hadn't seen a girlfriend, wife, or frankly any woman for months in the Pacific theater. It sounded very "American," which of course she was—100 percent.

Iva Toguri D'Aquino was born in California on the Fourth of July, 1916. Her father was a citizen of British Columbia, and her mother was of Japanese descent. Medical research was her main interest, and she graduated from UCLA with a degree in zoology. It was in July 1941 that, according to Japanese custom, she became the family representative at the expected death of an aunt.

It was like fighting the tide of history as events swept relentlessly toward total severance between the US and Japan. Neither country wanted to bend to help the other or its citizens. For those unlucky few caught on the wrong side of the equation, the odds of getting out of Japan were slim.

Iva explained as we walked that she had sought passage back home, but when she applied to the US State Department for a passport, her request was denied. The State Department sent word that her citizenship had not been proven. Although she had been born in the States and was a full citizen, the racial element set against the politics of the tension between the US and Japan worked against Iva. Whether on purpose or by accident, it was an obvious mistake since her later trial for treason was based on her citizenship—but it was fateful.

It came one month before the Japanese attacked Pearl Harbor. She was trapped by red tape and politics. The Japanese, however, considered her a citizen of the United States, and she was immediately placed under the surveillance of an internal security force, Kempei Tai.

And so began the unluckiest set of life events I'd ever heard. Even her family was fearful.

Her aunt feared retaliation for harboring a US citizen, and Iva was turned out on the street to hunt for new quarters and a job. She took small ones until the fall of 1943, when there was an opening for a typist at Radio Tokyo. She would listen to shortwave broadcasts from US radio and then transcribe them for staff typists to translate into Japanese.

It was uncomfortable in the rain, but I soon forgot the chill when she described the turmoil inside Radio Tokyo. There was pressure to use the powerful broadcasts to demoralize the US troops. I asked, "What was the pivot that turned you from typist to broadcaster?"

She continued, "The war started. There was very little work that I could do because I did not know the Japanese language, and all I knew was typing and English. So I got a job as a typist at Radio Tokyo. And after I'd been there for some time, the head of the department asked me, not asked me, he said we have an order from the, I guess at that time it would be general army headquarters, I guess, saying that you are to participate in a broadcast with the Allied prisoners of war who are being, not used, but they are running a program here at Radio Tokyo. You have been ordered to broadcast with the Allied prisoners of war. And this is how it started. I had never seen a mic before, but the head of the department said that the Allied prisoners of war had selected me and wanted me to work with them to put on this particular program."

I asked her, "You were an enemy at the time?"

"That's right."

"What were some of the scripts that you read?"

I was looking for the content that she had been accused of broadcasting. Anything containing treasonous comments that gave aid and comfort to the enemy.

"Well, the scripts were like introductions to music and giving some information on the content of the music. And ask the listeners to join in a singsong in a sort of a get-together type of script. You see, the Allied prisoners of war had written the script, and of course they were pros at it, and they were able to prepare the scripts in such a way so that they were entertaining and humorous without any of this so-called material which is intuitive to this particular broadcast. A very free, easygoing, fun type of program."

Her segment was part of the Zero Hour broadcasts. She participated in 340 of them as hostess of a fifteen-minute segment under the name Orphan Ann. The value of those segments as propaganda is questionable. If across the Pacific the aim was a decline in Allied morale, it was an utter failure. Most GIs laughed at the programs. Many enjoyed them. Some said they could use them to detect the weather conditions over Tokyo, useful if you were going to bomb it. Later, Japanese authorities said that from their headquarters, the object of the Zero Hour was to cause Allied troops to become homesick and disgusted with the war. One said the purpose was entertainment only. Some prisoners of war said they saw it as an opportunity to dilute the Japanese propaganda effort. They confirmed that they had asked Iva to join their team. They believed they could trust her.

She was perfect for the job. In her twenties, Iva not only sounded like a red-blooded American fresh out of college, she was just that. Her sound was cute and appealing to the GIs, as the male listeners could easily project a picture of a girl back home. I could tell from her voice that it was upbeat and enthusiastic, which of course is what the POWs wanted. She was one of the "team."

"Oh, I got along very well with the prisoners of war. It's a very strange feeling to see that the Allied prisoners of war who are forced to broadcast, they welcomed the chance to talk to someone from the United States, although there was one from the Philippines and one from Australia. They all liked to talk about the States and the progress of the war, and some of the news I was able to get because through an agency where my later husband was working, I was able to get Allied news, and I was able to take the news over to the prisoners of war."

I asked her if she did more than slip information to them.

"Not much, but I was able to supplement their diet with whatever I was able to get them, with whatever was available in vitamin pills and food of which they ate seeds, skin, and all because of the danger of pellagra. And they were short of blankets and things, and they used to take them under their coats into the prisoners-of-war camp. Many times the prisoners were having malaria attacks and they needed blankets, so they used to take them in for me."

A point missed during early reports about the so-called oriental siren was the number of women on the air. There were some twenty women broadcasting for Radio Tokyo. Their scripts were more aggressive than Orphan Ann's. In fact, one strategy was that the Japanese were using Iva's very American-sounding delivery to attract an audience that was followed by the more propagandistic content of the other women and their programs. The POWs testified later at her trial for treason that they had deliberately kept propaganda out of their scripts to maintain an American integrity.

In my research, I found a film made by Allied correspondents in 1945 when they entered Tokyo. The recording was a re-creation of the Orphan Ann show produced for the reporters who demanded to hear "Tokyo Rose." This report never made an effort to distinguish between the women, treating the entire campaign as if it had come from a single person. This became the dominant story, so when the war ended, no one in Japan or among the Allied forces really knew who fit that name. The myth had begun, and the symbol of Tokyo Rose had surpassed any single person. When the military police entered the offices of Radio Tokyo looking for Tokyo Rose, the staff was confused.

Iva was not holding anything back. She'd been waiting for twenty years to tell her story to someone she trusted. I explored every possible question.

So why did Iva Toguri wind up as the voice they identified as Tokyo Rose?

It was easy for American citizens to become Japanese citizens during the war and occupation. All they had to do was sign a document choosing to make the switch. They thus avoided any prosecution for treason by giving aid and comfort to the "enemy." It was a common choice in the last days of the war.

But Iva refused to make the switch. She became the only American among the broadcasters to not give up her US citizenship. Consequently, she was the only one eligible for prosecution. The radio staff made sure the authorities looking for Tokyo Rose focused on Iva.

"Well, one of the fellows in charge who incidentally was born and raised in the US, his wife had substituted [as a broadcaster] on this Zero Hour. When the army or CIC [Counter Intelligence Corps] went to Radio Tokyo to search for someone to be associated with this image, he more or less directed them over to me to get them off his back."

Japan was a defeated nation. Food was scarce. The occupation government ruled. It was total confusion. And caught in that confusion was a twenty-nine-year-old woman from Los Angeles, California, who had married and was now waiting to go home. But she would go home the hard way.

"I was put in jail for over a year in Japan."

"Under charges of treason there?"

"No specific charges. I was just dragged off and put in jail and left there. Everyone forgot about me. I couldn't get any legal help, no counsel of any kind, and at the same time I was questioned all the time, daily, by all branches of the United States government and the army."

"Were you released at all from jail?"

"Yes, after completion of over a year, they released me under orders from General MacArthur's headquarters, and I understood that General Willoughby's orders said that there was no evidence to connect me with this case, so they released me."

Specifically, that government release order said that the Department of Justice no longer desired that Iva Toguri D'Aquino be retained in custody, October 6, 1946. Upon that release, she applied for a passport to the United States. Some say it was a radio broadcast in 1948 by Walter Winchell prompted by a Gold Star mother (who learned that "Tokyo Rose" had applied for a passport) that brought pressure upon the Department of Justice to reopen the case. Others felt it was the work of two journalists, Harry Brundage and Clark Lee. They allegedly had interviewed Tokyo Rose and obtained information that they turned over to the Department of Justice, although none of the prisoners of war who had produced the programs had been prosecuted. One had even been promoted. In 1948, after a year in jail, Iva was arrested again and this time charged with eight counts of treason. She was tried in San Francisco.

"Well, it took over thirteen weeks. There was just a multitude of witnesses that appeared who I had never seen before, I'd never heard of before, and yet they professed to have known me and testified that they saw the broadcast, heard the broadcast, which was impossible because the Allied prisoners of war were under guard and they couldn't have got into the studio, but they all testified that they heard me say these things and they saw me perform. Many of the witnesses were brought over here. . . . It was after the war, and the people who were asked to come were willing to come because they were given so much per diem, three meals a day and a trip to the United States. A lot of people just jumped at it. Didn't make any difference what sort of witness they would make."

The indictment charged that her activities had been intended to destroy the confidence of the members of the Armed Forces of the United States and their Allies in the war effort to undermine and lower Allied military morale and to impair the capacity of the United States to wage war against its enemies.

The government presented forty-six witnesses, the defense forty-four, nineteen by deposition. The prosecution argued that Iva had worked to create nostalgia and war-weariness among members of the Armed Forces to discourage them.

The defense tried to show that she'd been part of a team working to water down the Japanese effort and that she had broadcast under duress. A jury of six men and six women came back once during deliberations, unable to reach agreement. The judge urged them to try again. After five days, they brought in a verdict: innocent on seven counts, guilty on one, that on a day during October 1944, she did speak into a microphone concerning the loss of ships.

Iva didn't have a chance. In the United States, the postwar hatred for Japan was still so strong that dropping two atom bombs on the island nation hadn't fazed anyone.

I bought the transcripts of the trial and saw clearly that the prosecution had used the hate in their case. They brought into court a stack of large wax discs that had allegedly been recorded at listening posts throughout the Pacific. They kept them in clear view of the jury throughout the trial. But they didn't play any of them because they didn't have Iva reading the treasonous words that convicted her. Thus, the prosecution still made it look as if they had the recordings without ever actually playing the discs.

The two witnesses who were brought from Japan, Kenkichi Oki and George Mitsushio, to provide the necessary testimony that would meet the Constitution's treason requirements—two witnesses to the act of treason are required—recanted their testimony several decades later.

Nineteen of the prosecution witnesses were transported from war-torn Japan, where food was scarce and jobs hard to come by. They were paid ten dollars a day for their testimony and were given new clothes. The trip of a lifetime to the United States allowed them to see relatives and get some relief from the poverty conditions in Tokyo.

Still, the jury found Iva innocent of seven of eight counts and guilty on one.

I asked Iva, "And you went to jail. For how many years?"

"About six years. Time off for good behavior," she added with a sly smile.

For the record, I asked, "At any time did you feel that you were collaborating with the enemy? Or that your acts were treasonous?"

"No, I never felt that. I guess it was mainly because at the onset, the Allied prisoners of war placed the whole program in front of me; they wanted me to become a member of *their* team, they wanted to put on *their* type of program so that they could send these messages home . . . because it was the only way they could send these messages home to the other parents to let them know their [sons and daughters] were living and well."

"And that is not collaborating in your . . ."

"Well, I felt that I was working with them to help them do what they tried to do in an enemy country for their own purpose."

"You were and you are now and you remained at that time an American citizen, didn't you?"

"Yes, I did, and it was pretty rough at times because it was an easy procedure to become a citizen of Japan. All you had to do was sign in a word, and that would have prevented all of this. If I had any feeling that it was going to hit me like it did, I just would have gone in and become a citizen of Japan and not be liable."

Chicago in 1969 was a long way from a broadcast studio in Japan, the war, a trial, and prison. With time off for good behavior, Iva D'Aquino came to Chicago in 1956. There was a small Japanese American community, and she worked in a shop in what was left of her father's mercantile store on Clark Street. Here, she could seek anonymity among friends. Her father was here. Her mother had died during the war in a relocation camp for Japanese Americans, Nisei, in Gila River, Arizona. The work and family became her life. They'd had their own problems during the war, and the family had known nothing of what had happened to their daughter. Iva said she felt it may have been hardest on them.

"We're all rather stoic, and I think this is characteristic of the thing that has bound us together, and they are very loyal, and I'm very proud of that. I really don't hold any bitterness. I don't think it's very healthy, number one, and I think you gain nothing from being bitter."

A lack of bitterness does not mean lack of feeling. Twenty years after, she could relive it like some Monday-morning quarterback.

"Actually, looking back when you analyze something like this, if I had any fear of guilt after my initial release from the army—the army was in control then—since I had been married to a Portuguese national, I could have been free from any charges by becoming a Portuguese citizen, and in fact the Portuguese consul offered me free transportation to any position in Portugal. But I said no, I'm not running away from anything. And I kept my citizenship. I believe that a leopard just doesn't change its spots."

So for Iva D'Aquino, despite the years, it was hard to forget. But harder still to resist speculation about a slightly different set of circumstances. Would she be convicted today?

"I don't know anything about law, but reading so many decisions handed down by the Supreme Court, it seems there's points of law that protect the individual. I don't know whether it's been clarified or relaxed, I don't know the correct terminology, but I assumed that anyone tried for a capital crime has the right to legal counsel, which I never did have until I came back to San Francisco. I think it's a span of three or four years after the cessation of war in 1945 . . . it was about four years subsequent to that that the trial actually began. I have reason to believe there were a lot of opinions formed during that time. But you have to sell newspapers, and you have to sell magazines."

After six years at the West Virginia Federal Reformatory for Women, Iva returned to Chicago to work in her father's store. She left her husband in Tokyo and saw him only once to protect him. He arrived during the trial and was vilified. Such was the wave of hatred of anyone Japanese.

Iva D'Aquino will be remembered because the story of Tokyo Rose will not be forgotten. It is a memory of a generation caught in a world war. It is one of those comfortable pieces of history pigeonholed in its proper place. The case is closed for everyone except Iva Toguri D'Aquino. The truth lies somewhere in the nagging dissimilarity between a legendary oriental siren and the bookkeeper in Chicago two wars later.

Iva was pleased with her story after it aired. When I was working on cutting together the final interview that all of Chicago saw, I kept my promise. I let her tell her own story in her own way.

If you're lucky enough to be first with a story and tell it well, your work will become a keystone in a wall upon which truth will grow. In 1976, I got a call from Lowell Bergman, producer for *60 Minutes*. Could I help get him an interview with Iva? I told her this was one she should do. They would do right by her, just as I had. I told Iva that I thought a *60 Minutes* interview could rewrite history. I was right.

In addition to *60 Minutes*, Ron Yates, the Far East correspondent for the *Chicago Tribune*, revisited the story of Tokyo Rose on the other side of the Pacific. He interviewed two key witnesses who had testified at Iva's trial that they had seen and heard Iva broadcast, "Orphans of the Pacific, how will you get home now that your ships are sunk?" It was the key testimony against Iva since treason requires two witnesses to the treasonous act. Yates interviewed Kenkichi Oki and George Mitsushio, who admitted that Iva had done nothing wrong and their testimony had been coerced.

The case was made. On President Gerald Ford's last day in office, he issued a presidential pardon for Iva Toguri D'Aquino. The World War II Veterans Committee in Washington, DC, honored Iva Toguri with the Edward J. Herlihy Citizenship Award. After Iva's story was printed in their newsletter, committee president James Roberts said the reaction moved them to award her a medal. He said, "Not one veteran said they were demoralized in any way by the broadcasts. She remained loyal to the US when many others may have turned on it or given up." Attending the ceremony were the three principals she most associated with helping her clear her name: Wayne Collins Jr., son of her devoted primary lawyer; Ron Yates, who procured the two interviews recanting the treasonous testimony; and me, the twenty-eight-year-old reporter/lawyer from Kansas who earned her trust to begin to tell her story the right way.

Until her death in 2006 at the age of ninety, Iva and I remained close friends. Iva was a wonderful auntie to my two kids, Mary Kristin and Scott. Though I sought her out that day on Clark Street, chasing down a story, it became more than that almost immediately. Some reporters might say that we should always be objective observers, completely separated from our subject. My experience with Iva proved that wrong. Had we not built a trusting friendship first, Iva never would have shared her story, and I might not have given it the care it deserved. Her friendship and her story deeply impacted my life, and being able to help her tell the truth was a great honor. It was a highlight of my career to have known her.

EIGHT

# The Trial of the Chicago Seven

I had been at 'BBM for three years but had already covered enough high-profile stories to give any journalist a lifetime of bragging rights. While I was now measuring my time between major stories in months rather than weeks, I was still caught in the whirlwind of the 1960s. And I was loving the ride. In the fall of 1969, I was assigned to cover what would become one of the most highly publicized trials of the twentieth century. Ironically, one of the only other trials to be eclipsed by this one in notoriety—Richard Speck—had been my first assignment. The combination of law and journalism that I thought was impossible had dropped into my lap. Once again, I would learn that the Washburn years had given me a special set of eyes in the courtroom, a remarkable advantage.

While years later, I would look back on those days in the courtroom as one of the most thrilling experiences of my career, a dream for any lawyer/reporter, at the time, I was mostly oblivious of the profound historical gravity of the moment. I still saw myself as a young reporter in his first job, trying to give our viewers hard facts and good stories, trying to impress the producers, and just trying not to get canned. So, as in most of my career, when I covered the trial of the Chicago Seven, I wasn't covering history; I was just reporting the news.

It was September 24, 1969, thirteen months beyond the anniversary of those infamous four days in August when ten thousand antiwar protesters had come to Chicago to disrupt the Democratic National Convention and denounce their nation's warmongering in Vietnam. Now, those protesters faced a legal reckoning. Thirteen months before, I had just been

Bill, a Chicagoan with no visible press credentials and no story to write, pulled along in the riptide of youthful defiance. Now I was Bill Kurtis, WBBM-Chicago, reporting on the trial of the century.

From the outside, the Mies van der Rohe glass-and-steel building looked like all of his designs—impenetrable and sterile, devoid of emotion, which was as it was supposed to be. The air crackled with anticipation of what was to come, like the moments before a great athletic contest.

Inside, the US Federal Court of the Northern District of Illinois faced a red-hot issue: Had protesters come to Chicago to exercise their constitutional rights to speak and protest? Or had they conspired to cross state lines with intent to incite a riot?

I spent five months sitting in the federal courtroom, a high-ceilinged room that would become the theater of the absurd. TV news had yet to dominate the media landscape. To further remind us that print was still king, cameras were not allowed in the courtroom. But artists were. Howard Brodie, for CBS News, was the reigning royalty among courtroom sketch artists. So I gathered plenty of pens and paper, took my seat next to Brodie, and got ready to work.

The drama of the trial was clear from the first moment in the courtroom. Everyone in front of the bar looked like they were straight out of central casting. The key figure in any trial is the judge. He sets the tone for the trial and enforces the word "fair." It's best to picture Judge Julius Hoffman as Napoleon, short in stature and short in temper and never slow to assert his authority as absolute.

One of Hoffman's primary targets was William Kunstler, the flamboyant, agonizing civil rights lawyer who was thwarted at every turn. Kunstler brought New York City culture to the midwestern courtroom. He called an array of celebrities who made some headlines but looked like they had been called from a liberal New York City cocktail party. During the trial, Kunstler's legal reputation was protected by the bizarre actions of Judge Hoffman, who dominated the media attention, leaving the impression of Kunstler as a sympathetic figure struggling for justice within a system controlled so tightly by Judge Hoffman that the statue of Lady Justice seemed to expel tears like some religious painting.

Co-defense attorney Leonard Weinglass, a more cerebral lawyer, provided the real defense. He quietly labored over his notes while the defendants, seated together, acted like the class bell would soon ring, allowing them to change rooms.

The prosecutor, US Attorney Thomas Aquinas Foran, was the best lawyer in the courtroom. His reputation had been made by prosecuting organized crime members. His score was 150 successful convictions. He was a torpedo bomber pilot in the service and a tough Irish trial lawyer who rarely had an objection overruled.

Assistant Prosecutor Richard Schultz joined Foran both in his firm and in the courtroom. He was listed as chief prosecutor but followed the direction of his boss, US Attorney Foran. Clean-cut and a good lawyer, he was ready for the fight.

As I stood at the back of the courtroom, the center aisle seemed like a path to Saint Peter sitting above the latest candidate awaiting judgment. The public sat in the front half of the room until the seating reached the bar, a short fence that holds little importance other than to separate the rabble from the "learned ones" who will dispense and receive justice. In the case of the eight defendants gathered around a large wooden table on the right side of the courtroom (on the judge's left), it was like an arrow pointing to the *accused!*

I thought the grouping of the defendants together around one table, with their attorneys sitting at one end, had the effect of creating a classic conspiracy pose. In fact, most of them had not come to Chicago in a group and knew of each other only by media attention or public appearances. But in the definition of a conspiracy, none of the members had to know each other. These defendants had been chosen for their leadership, public notoriety, and past roles in organizing protests. The prosecution also relied on the testimony of undercover police who had infiltrated various strategy meetings prior to the convention. These were the names that surfaced most often.

Putting all the defendants together had the appearance of a cast of a musical comedy, without the music.

Abbie Hoffman was the most colorful of the pack, with his curly black hair billowing around his face and neck and a habit of being quick on the trigger with a comment. He was well-known as an activist and as cofounder of the Youth International Party, or Yippies.

Jerry Rubin was a cofounder of the Yippies with Hoffman. He was an actor who could also do outlandish things, once coming into court in judge's robes. Rubin campaigned to elect a pig for president. It was street theater, and he and Abbie Hoffman were the leading actors.

Rennie Davis was the buttoned-down version of the activists, the strategist and front man when wearing a suit was needed. He later started a venture capital company and advised Fortune 500 companies, leading to some descriptions of him as the businessman activist. He cut his hair, put on Madison Avenue clothes, and slid into the business world more easily than the other seven defendants.

I always thought Tom Hayden was the smart one. He knew what he was doing. His life was dedicated to protest. He was a founder of Students for a Democratic Society (SDS) and wrote the manifesto called the Port Huron Statement that was adopted by many college students in the movement to stop the war. Gradually, he chose a political career and was elected to the California legislature as an assemblyman and state senator for ten years. He told me after a panel on the protests, "Bill, we did cross state lines to start a riot!"

David Dellinger was balding and fifty-four, giving him the image of "the old man" among the young activists. His record of jail terms for protest actions like refusing to serve in the army was so long that it's hard to categorize. He was quiet but sincere and was always the one steadfast believer whom his colleagues rallied around. If protesting were a profession, Dellinger would have been a card-carrier.

John Froines was one of two defendants who seemed out of place sitting at the defendants' table. A PhD from Yale, he rarely spoke out during the trial. He was surprised by his arrest but surmised that undercover police thought he was responsible for the "stink bomb" at the Hilton Hotel, cloth soaked in butyric acid. He later had a remarkable career studying environmental contaminants and worker safety. Judge Hoffman treated him with respect.

Lee Weiner earned his PhD in sociology but continued his work as a fundraiser for members of Congress and nonprofits. He and John Froines would be acquitted of the charges.

Final defendant Bobby Seale got the party started early.

When I heard Kunstler read from a written statement in his opening arguments, "We intend to make this trial a schoolhouse for the nation on the war in Vietnam," I came to attention in my hard, uncomfortable seat.

I thought, *He knows better.* A trial is usually narrowly designed to reach truthful facts that the jury can use for a conclusion to the indictment question: did these defendants cross state lines to start a riot? To make it anything more and somehow sneak in propaganda against the war would not only be hard but also draw a big bull's-eye on Kunstler's back.

The trial began with a mistake.

A conspiracy indictment threw all the defendants together around a rectangular wooden defense table. In fact, no one of them knew all of the others. But in a conspiracy, they don't have to.

Hoffman and Rubin had cooked up the Yippie name and avatar to attract media attention by organizing concerts, political demonstrations, and a Festival of Life to be held in Lincoln Park. Rennie Davis and Tom Hayden had their own constituency of protesters against the war in Vietnam from Tom's SDS days. David Dellinger was a legitimate conscientious objector, which made him the most sincere antiwar protester. John Froines and Lee Weiner had been included for tech support.

An eighth was included in the indictment because he was a founder of the Black Panther Party and represented the target of the government's long arm into the Black community. Bobby Seale had been scheduled to give a speech in Lincoln Park on Sunday night, substituting for his fellow Panther Eldridge Cleaver. He'd been in Chicago for less than forty-eight hours.

I watched the first day as Jerry Rubin set the standard of conduct by blowing a kiss to the jury when they were brought in. As would become the norm, both the judge and the prosecution vigorously objected.

No one realized it, but that small act and reaction would telegraph the entire trial to come.

Judge Hoffman definitely had a chip on his shoulder. In the spirit of small men, he spent his life convincing others that he was just as big as anyone. He sat perched behind his commanding altar of justice, his bald head alert as an eagle scanning a lake for a fish. God help the soul who artlessly disrespected the US district judge of the Northern District or his court. From the beginning of the trial, the judge's Napoleon complex was easy to distinguish—diminutive men who overcompensate for their lack of height by excessive aggressiveness. It was clear but not talked about.

As the trial began, I was still the straitlaced young lawyer sitting in a federal courtroom filled with enormous respect for the setting, especially the judge. This was the World Series. I took my place in line outside the courtroom behind other reporters and artists, right where I would be for the next five months. Protests raging outside the building, the knowledge that crowds were growing on college campuses around the country waiting for the nightly newscast. They were keeping score, prosecution or defense, while we reporters were mostly occupied with the outlandish.

There was one not-so-little matter that the judge had to get out of the way before the "teams took the field."

Bobby Seale was an outsider to his fellow defendants. He didn't know them and didn't want to know them. What he really didn't want was to be forced to accept William Kunstler as his lawyer. Seale originally had retained Charles Garry, a well-known civil rights lawyer in Oakland, California, but Garry needed gall-bladder surgery, and when the trial started, he couldn't travel. Kunstler said he would represent Seale for the sake of a pretrial motion only, but Hoffman insisted that Kunstler's signature be extended for the entire trial. It was another clue to the judge's obstinate nature that he wanted to take advantage of weakness in his enemy.

That description will please most trial observers, but it is a little harsh considering what the judge faced. He faced the threat of failing to handle disruptive defendants and beyond that losing control of his courtroom. For the judge, the entire judicial system was at stake, and he was not about to let the hooligans around the defense table win.

Arrayed before him were eight of America's most outspoken contrarians, dedicated to turning the court into a "schoolhouse" for the nation on the Vietnam War.

From the beginning, it had the feel of a street fight among rival gangs, and Judge Hoffman acted like he was fighting eight opponents at once. The courtroom was the ring. Rules of evidence were used as uppercuts or below-the-belt jabs. The prosecution was ahead in points from the beginning, but the defense attorneys rallied again and again, with each witness finally succumbing to the combination of blows from the judge and the government.

Maybe the image of a cantankerous bantamweight fighting above his class was the best definition after all. I could almost hear an echo from the high ceiling: "Let's get ready to rumble."

Black Panther defendant Bobby Seale drew the first round before the trial even got started.

Seale's strategy was that every time his name was mentioned, he would stand and insist loudly that his constitutional rights were in play if he didn't get his choice of lawyer, Charles Garry of Oakland, California.

It eventually brought the trial to a standstill when Seale refused to be quiet and instead, in addition to demanding loudly that Charles Garry be his attorney, said he would remain quiet if he could be his own attorney and cross-examine witnesses. Suddenly the puppet was manipulating the puppeteer, or trying to.

I realized that the trial could not go on without a resolution. Seale was not only the elephant in the room, he was a herd of elephants that on a stampede's trigger could overrun the system of justice. Additionally, a contingent of Seale's Black Panther "brothers" sat in the audience as long as Seale was there. It added spice to the face-off, knowing the Panthers would carry out orders.

I knew it was Hoffman's first real test to remain in control, and I also knew he did not want to back down and show weakness. I was observing the most rebellious defendant I could imagine, especially having come from the cloistered confines of Kansas justice.

After court, I found my way to the law library of Northwestern University School of Law, located just two blocks from the television station. Dark wood paneling led me to the stacks of law books, or rather the smell that I loved. Their largest classroom, which served as an auditorium, was patterned on the House of Commons in England's Parliament. A shaded courtyard set among stone walls reminds one of the spirit of English common law and suggests that law is the proper course to a destination, not the ruler.

The legal battlements were in danger of being breached.

I found my answer, later confirmed in a hall conversation with Prosecutor Tom Foran, that the judge had very few options. He could sever Seale from the case and lose face by admitting his original mistake. He could remove him from the courtroom and risk being overruled for denying Seale his constitutional right to confront his accuser, or he could force Seale to be quiet and not disrupt the trial proceedings against him. The quandary was *how* he would do the latter.

I put my research to work and discovered an opinion that seemed on point. It was from the Seventh Circuit Court of Appeals, from just a few floors up, dealing with a case a few months prior to the conspiracy trial.

Some defendants had thrown chairs in the courtroom, jumped into the jury box, and physically shaken the jurors. The judge had been allowed to bind and gag them to force-feed them their right to due process. I asked Foran about whether this earlier case was an answer to how Hoffman would handle Seale and said, "Don't answer but I'll take your silence as a yes." It was a good way to avoid the gag order without violating the judge's order. The solution was something no one believe could happen or wanted.

The trial moved rapidly into the fog of waiting for a solution. It was the judge's call. Meanwhile, the pressure built. Members of the Black Panther Party didn't have to say a thing, just sit there, their black clothes and faces injecting a new element into the audience of predominantly white people in a trial that had barely started. Intimidation. I could see that the judge didn't know what to do with the Panthers. They were not noisy and did not attempt to stop the proceedings. But Seale was continuing to talk, even while the jury was coming in. He said the Panthers would not take orders from "racist judges," but he would tell them himself.

As I looked around the room, there were now eleven marshals, serious and exceptionally big, standing around the courtroom. For my own safety, I checked the exits in back and the side door to a hall that led to chambers and access to holding rooms and cells.

The other defendants took the opportunity to join the fray. Jerry Rubin brought a birthday cake for Seale into the courtroom. When marshals took it away, Rennie Davis said aloud, "They arrested the cake." It could have been an Aaron Sorkin play, with lines and action coming from off camera to contribute to the disturbance.

David Dellinger spoke up: "I think you should know that we support Bobby Seale in this." The trial decorum had broken open. It appeared that Judge Hoffman had lost control.

In the afternoon, while the jury was still filing into their seats, Seale was forcing himself into center stage with a monologue demanding action from Hoffman. The judge could not let it go on.

The jury was dismissed to go home for the day while Seale tried to be his own attorney. Still in control, he said, "You think Black people don't have minds, good minds. We got big minds, good minds. Did you lose yours in that Superman syndrome comic-book stories?"

Hoffman tried one more time in the hope Seale might quiet down if the trial started. He allowed the prosecution to present a witness, an undercover agent who had been present at Seale's speech in Grant Park. Seale shouted to be allowed to cross-examine him. The judge said, "You have a lot of contemptuous conduct against you."

Seale rebutted, "I admonish *you* you are in contempt of people's constitutional rights."

Imagine the drama for all of us sitting there, not believing what we were seeing and frankly challenged by trying to capture it all for ninety seconds of television reporting or a column in the *New York Times*. It was a spitball fight in a classroom at a boys' school, a confrontation between bully and challenger on the school grounds. There was so much action, we reporters had to divide the scene among us: "You take the judge, I'll watch the defendants," etc.

At any second, we expected the air to fill with objects thrown by the spectators or defendants. It felt like you could *see* the electricity.

More than any other time in the trial, I was on alert for the possibility of defending myself, most likely against the burly marshals wading into the spectators to get at the Black Panthers or the defendants throwing things.

I can't remember how much disruption occurred in front of the jury. The judge had them come in and then dismissed them when Seale erupted. They had to have seen some of the craziness going on. It was as if Hoffman were setting up his contempt citations, embellishing them, luring Seale to sink himself and justify Hoffman's inevitable contempt rulings.

The judge laughed nervously and then admonished everyone not to laugh, including anyone who had seen him laughing.

It must have been exhausting for the seventy-four-year-old jurist. Finally, after sending the jury out for the day, he told Seale that in order to assure his right to due process, it was the judge's duty to have him bound and gagged to force him to be present at his own trial. Hoffman could have added, "The system is at risk!"

Seale answered, "Gagged? I'm already being railroaded."

The bailiff asked everyone to rise as the judge left the courtroom.

Seale refused.

So did the other defendants.

The next day, the number of marshals standing by the walls around the courtroom had increased to twenty.

Seale told the Panthers that since their party had been founded on self-defense they could defend themselves if the marshals attacked them, but they should not start anything. Otherwise, he instructed them to be quiet and to leave if asked to do so.

Assistant Prosecutor Schultz reported to the judge that Seale had told the spectators about an "attack by them," implying that Seale had told his cohorts to attack the court.

Seale blew. "You're lying. Dirty liar! I told them to defend themselves. You are a rotten fascist pig, fascist liar, that's what you are."

There was laughter, and the judge said if there was more laughter, "I will clear the court." He then said, "Let the record show that the tone of Mr. Seale's voice was one of shrieking and pounding on the table and shouting,"

Schultz apologized, saying he'd been lost in the furor of the judge's indignation.

But Seale was more than warmed up. Since Hoffman had warned him the day before, he might have figured that this was his last chance to speak freely. He pointed to the portraits of the founding fathers on the wall, saying, "What can happen to me more than what George Washington and Benjamin Franklin did to their slaves?"

As Dellinger tried to intervene between the marshals and Seale, the judge motioned to Seale and said, "Take that defendant into the room in there and deal with him as he should be dealt with in this circumstance."

End of Act One.

We sat and waited. Binding and gagging. What would it look like? I had made sure I was near the front of the line waiting to enter that morning so my seat would be in the front row. Seale would be less than six feet from me, across the bar at the defense table. I knew that we would see history in the making: either a victory showing how a judge could successfully handle a disruptive defendant or the attempt going down in flames. Then the question would become how does the trial go on? The judge would have to do what he should have done weeks earlier: sever Bobby Seale from the other defendants or declare a mistrial. That would be a blow to the ego of the small judge. The last thing he wanted to do was give the defendants anything to celebrate.

The jury was not seated when the marshals carried Seale back into the courtroom and placed him at the front of the defense table. A white handkerchief was wrapped around his mouth and tied at the back of his head, Yes, just as outlaws would gag a captive. His wrists were hand-cuffed to the sides of a metal chair, and his ankles were tied to the legs.

The courtroom was frozen. The normally verbal defendants were paralyzed. I could feel my pulse literally begin to race. I was short of breath, afraid to move.

It was a scene not to be believed—in the United States of America, a spectacle that harkened back to the days of the Wild West. I couldn't even describe it as a re-creation of a cowboy-movie scene because even the movies hadn't touched it. This was original. This was real.

But there was a flaw in Hoffman's attempt to follow precedent. His order to gag Seale was based on a contempt citation: that Seale was obstructing the judicial process. The goal of a contempt citation is to impose the penalty close to the time of the offense to reduce the disruption, which lets the offender know what can happen if he doesn't cease. The limit of the contempt penalty is usually six months. But Hoffman held all his contempt citations until the end of the trial and then added them all up for a total penalty much longer than six months. For Seale, even though he was no longer even present at the end of the trial, the judge imposed a combined penalty of four years. In the three days of the Seale incident, Judge Hoffman would impose about one-third of all the contempt citations in the five-month trial.

It's good to remember the adage "Don't poke the bear."

The sound of the metal handcuffs against the metal chair was just as disruptive as Seale shouting from his seat—not that the scene needed a metallic soundtrack. No one in the courtroom could take their eyes off the man sitting before them with a gag in his mouth. Talk about disruptive. There was an urge to run and help him, to rip off the gag. As if we were witnessing a car wreck but unable to stop it.

Seale was mumbling, trying to shout from behind the gag, added to the clanking as he pulled against the chair. At one point, he swung his head toward the spectators in the front row, looking for his wife. I remember that his eyes were straining, laced with the red blood vessels of someone who couldn't fully breathe, struggling for release.

Kunstler was beside himself, giving a play-by-play for the court reporter.

Finally, the judge told the marshals to take Seale out and deal with the matter.

We sat looking at each other. I wondered if my seatmates were as shocked as I was. There was no rush for the exit. The courtroom was locked down. Of course, we didn't know what would happen next and didn't want to miss it. We didn't want out; we wanted to keep our seats. The incident left us dumbfounded, paralyzed. How would we describe what had just happened?

Once we did get out, the binding and gagging exploded in the media across the national newscasts. Without cameras, all eyes were on the artists. Howard Brodie could have been more popular than Picasso. His style of many strokes evoking movement captured a Black man affixed to a chair, forcing him to face his own justice. It was a case of an image that needed no words, that spoke of four hundred years in a single glance and like a shriek in the darkness said, *We haven't come very far, have we?*

Marshals brought Seale back in with the gag reinforced and the handcuffs adjusted to prevent him from making the metallic noise.

I thought the judge was out of his mind to allow the jury to come back, but he did. Seale was sitting there when the jury realized what was before them. A few of them looked away. One woman teared up. The others were solemn, both quizzical and alarmed.

On this first day of the gagging, it was as if a bomb had gone off in the trial. The act had accelerated the notion that what was happening inside Judge Hoffman's courtroom was a reflection of what had happened a year earlier in the streets. And it finally had the full attention of the nation. This alone bumped up the importance of the trial to Code Red and reached through the newsrooms to grab assignment editors by the collar. Viewers were polarized. Students on campus waited for the news reports. They staged their own demonstrations. They knew the names of the players. It was as if someone was writing a script for reporters that needed no embellishment.

If there is one image that fifty years later comes to me at the mention of the conspiracy trial, it is from the second day of the Seale incident.

Two large bailiffs (marshals) entered the courtroom from a side door, carrying Seale, seated now in a *wooden* chair. His arms were tied to the chair arms (no metal this time), and his hands were almost completely wrapped to prevent communication with his fingers. His head was covered tightly with white cloth and cotton held in place by medical elastic tape over the hair, behind the head, and across the mouth and nose, leaving two holes for his nostrils. He could see out, but the eyeholes were little bigger than slits.

Seale was trying to talk, but it was impossible to understand him. Kunstler leaned over him to hear better. And then Seale slumped forward in full collapse, straining against the restraints, his head bobbing down.

Kunstler yelled, "He can't breathe. Pull the tape off."

Rubin and Hoffman shouted, "Help him. He can't breathe."

Marshals ran to Seale and began unwrapping the swaddling over his face. They were working hard, but the covering was thick, and it took some time to unwind the tape. I was concentrating on the scene in front of me, so I can't remember the judge's reaction. I believe he sat without saying a word as the marshals struggled against time. The entire courtroom felt the tension, and we held our breath, hoping the marshals would make it before a human disaster occurred. When enough tape had been removed to assure that Seale could breathe, they carried him out.

We sat like inanimate objects. Judge Hoffman's remarks from the day before seemed very appropriate for knowing his state of mind and how he was absorbing the verbal blows from Seale: "There comes a time when a federal district judge is called a pig in open court before a hundred people, publicized throughout the country . . . to be called a fascist racist."

I'm not saying he was happy to see Bobby Seale smothering while bound in a seated position. But those words caught the essence of his feelings. He was hurt so deeply by Seale's actions and words that as a narcissist, he had to strike back and make it hurt.

Hoffman called for a two-day break. There was only one question looming: where do we go from here?

When the trial came to life again, Prosecutor Schultz started, "If the court please, Seale was trying to build error into the record. . . . None of us like to see the defendant gagged. It is an abhorrent sight."

The judge said, "I implored him, I beseeched him, I urged him."

Seale spoke to the judge about his blood circulation being cut off by the bandage around his head. Richard Schultz reported him saying, "Even if the words fascist and racist come into it, I am trying—don't you see—to persuade you to concede my right to defend myself." The statement was unusual because it sounded so reasonable.

Kunstler moved for a mistrial.

Foran said, "No man has a right to disrupt the trial."

The trial was obviously in tatters. Emotions ran from anger to deep disappointment at what had happened. Everyone concerned was in distress.

Seale was talking, as before, wanting to defend himself, when Hoffman told two marshals to "have that man sit down."

But it didn't shut Seale up.

Hoffman called a recess until after lunch, and when he came back, he methodically read sixteen times in the record when Seale had interrupted the court and spoken disrespectfully and therefore would be held in contempt and sentenced to three months for each citation. In total, the amount of punishment for contempt was four years beyond what had been thought to be the limit of such a punishment.

Then Judge Hoffman lit the dynamite he had been holding back in a matter-of-fact manner: "There will be an order for a mistrial." He fixed a date for a new trial in April 1970.

Bobby Seale was severed from the other defendants and would make only one appearance later in January.

The reporters bolted from the newsroom in a "devil be damned" mission to break the news to editors and producers; in some cases, they would break live into broadcasts.

The next day in the courtroom as the trial of the other defendants continued, it was as if someone had opened the ceiling to let the sun shine in with fresh air. For the defense, it was all smiles.

And so the trial began from the point where it should have started in mid-September. Ahead of us, months of witnesses would take the walk to the witness stand, be sworn in, and add their substance to the growing pages of testimony. The prosecution would present more than one hundred witnesses, and the defense would follow. The prosecution was methodical, trying to "build a house starting with the foundation, brick by brick."

Trials don't provide a Perry Mason moment every day. It's often slow and tedious work. First, Foran had to get the defendants to Illinois. Then there was the testimony of the airline clerk at the counter who had checked David Dellinger in. Police officers who had seen the defendants at the demonstrations did their duty on the witness stand. Which one? Which location? Who else was there? What did they say?

The defense challenged each sighting. After all, it's easy to mistake one demonstrator for another in the chaos. But the most damaging witnesses were undercover police officers and occasional students who had attended planning sessions and SDS strategy sessions. In other words, they had been inside the core group. And for the trial, they told their stories. It would take a few months to "build the house" and another few to attempt to tear it down.

If the climactic moments of chaos had offered me any illusions of historical grandeur, the slog of daily courtroom reporting was sure to snuff it out. For most of those seemingly endless weeks of coverage, it felt as if I was just working my day job like any other American. It was just that when I walked to work, I walked through a parade of radical demonstrators into a federal courthouse and got into the elevator with national celebrities. Yes, I often rode up to the courtroom with Tom Hayden, Rennie Davis, or David Dellinger. Whenever I got into the elevator with them, ice seemed to form on the walls as they stared me down, trying to convey their disapproval at my reporting. I didn't mind their venom. I was just flattered that they knew who I was.

Still, my focus was mostly on the job. What happened today? Was there enough to even report on? And how do I translate legalese into plain English and condense it into a sixty-second report before deadline?

In October, a tip pulled me out of the courtroom and back into the streets. The story of the days of rage that followed—a sort of epilogue to the original protests of 1968—needs telling, especially since I was there.

A tip came in that a relatively new protest group called the Weather Underground was planning a reprise of the first Lincoln Park dustup a year earlier. They had missed the big show at Balbo and Michigan and were anxious to breathe new life into the antiwar movement. "New life" meant raising the tension and headlines by bringing violence to the party. This approach was controversial within the group. Many felt that injecting violence into the cause was beyond their commitment, as if saying, "Hey, we won the battle. Why fight it over again?"

They had hoped fifty thousand protesters would show up, but only a few hundred made the date despite active promotion. One poster said, "Bring the War home. Chicago. Oct. 8–11."

The conspiracy trial was underway, and the defendants had enough problems without reminding everyone that it wasn't over. One sarcastic comment was "Why don't they just say sure, the defendants wanted to start a riot, just like these jokers. Were they sorry they missed the first one?" There was even agreement among the Seven not to show up or take part.

I arrived after dark to find a ragtag group huddled around a small fire in the park. No police were in sight. They were gun-shy from having borne the brunt of so much criticism raised by Dan Walker's "police riot" report. They had adopted the strategy of avoiding provocation. But they were there. Along streets, down blocks of the Gold Coast, an upscale community of high-priced homes. Unseen.

The fire looked inviting as a barrier to the chilly October night. I moved closer to steal some warmth. Right off, I knew the group was a step up from the Festival of Life protesters. Lots of leather shone in the campfire light. I thought, *The perfect battle dress for a rumble.* These costumes were topped by motorcycle helmets. Shadows from dancing flames created a cinematic quality to the bearded faces and long hair. The voices were more murmurs than rousing attempts to increase adrenaline. I could see that this was no fraternity sing-along, especially when my gaze dropped to fists around baseball bats taped for a better grip. This was planned.

I had one cameraman with me. I didn't expect to get much footage in the darkness of Lincoln Park and the side streets. But then, that was the idea of this kind of protest: to stay concealed where possible. There was no overt attempt to create a parade of placards and cute signs. It was Weathermen versus police.

We were part of the crowd, and no one seemed to pay much attention to us.

Then, I heard some kind of signal, maybe a loudspeaker, that was the beginning of a running, shouting melee pouring into the narrow confines of the near north side neighborhood. The entire body of ruffians poured out of the park, leaving the fire as they ran across the street.

I felt like I was being carried in a whitewater stream, unable to get out. By now, I'd changed from "protesters" to "rioters" in describing the violent action.

There was a large restaurant window overlooking the street. A couple was sitting at a table near it. I saw someone in front of me in the crowd throw a brick at the window, and I froze for a moment, thinking of the injuries and damage. Should I do something to stop it? Too late. I didn't see the result as the rioters pushed me farther down the street. I never found out what happened to the couple.

The sounds of car windows being battered was strong, like drums keeping rhythm on a march. The rioters were bashing hoods, car tops, headlights. We came upon a line of storefronts, and I watched two young men work their way down the strip of shops, smashing large sidewalk-to-roof windows. CBS News cameraman Del Hall got some iconic footage of a lifetime just by holding his position and watching the rioters smash their way down the strip of stores. That instinct to let it happen within a single frame of 16-mm film was truly professional. The thirty-second sequence became a repeated emblem of the entire night.

Where were they heading? Many of the town houses had been built a hundred years earlier and were made of granite carved by old world tradesmen. The three- and four-story single-family homes looked warm and cozy with their jack-o'-lantern orange glow lighting the inside.

I came upon a large mansion built so durably that it looked like someone many years ago had prepared for just this threat, rioting mobs in the street. In fact, this was Chicago's history as immigrants poured into the city looking for a better life and jobs. Eastern Europeans, Irish, and Germans all arrived when Chicago had mostly wooden shanties, and this single strip of homes had been built for the ages. They'd seen a lot and were still standing. The Weathermen may not have realized it, but they were small players in history, repeating emotions that had been expressed before, using violence to express dissatisfaction.

We came around a corner and saw that Chicago police had set up a barrier across the street. It turned the rioters east on Elm Street, and they flooded onto the inner Lake Shore Drive. I was still near the head of the snake, tired from the running and high tension, but it seemed like the leaders were trying to get to Michigan Avenue, only a block away, to gain access to the apartment of Judge Julius Hoffman next to the Drake Hotel across Michigan Avenue. I held my breath because there was no police barricade in sight, nothing to stop the rioters from reaching their destination. The cops had been caught by surprise.

And then, before they reached the busy intersection, I was privy to the most remarkable piece of police work I'd ever seen.

By now, I estimated the marauding rioters numbered about three hundred. Suddenly, at the point where Elm Street reaches the inner Lake Shore Drive, an unmarked police car drove directly into the swarm, stuttering on the brakes as if on ice.

When it slowed, bodies ricocheted off the fenders and bumpers, cutting off the spearhead of about twenty Weathermen.

It was a Trojan horse. Six police officers jumped out of the car and into the street, armed with batons and with guns drawn. The doors were left open.

I knew the sergeant in charge from the Eighteenth Police Precinct. I'd ridden with his men before and regarded them as a tactical unit often used for the "big stuff." In the words of the street, they proceeded with one humongous ass-kicking.

It was a scene of flying batons and falling rioters. From both sides of the car, the police rolled out to face an overwhelming foe. It was the Spartan battle of Thermopylae. Before I knew it, the twenty on the south side of the police car were on the ground and the 250 on the north side were running hard up the inner drive.

I witnessed two singular incidents that I will never forget. One of the officers had a young man on the ground ready for handcuffs. The cop saw me and said to his captive, "Please stay quiet, sir; you're under arrest." I almost laughed. I figured he wanted to impress me with the training and instructions the police had received after the 1968 convention.

I say almost laughed because I was expecting the normal verbal command: "Be quiet or I'll bust your fucking skull wide open. Give me your hands!"

I also saw the same cop fire his weapon into the crowd. I heard the gunfire and saw the crowd wheel away from him. I looked but could find no one wounded and figured it was a blank round used for crowd control.


The October protests ended quickly, and the eyes of the nation shifted back into the courtroom. And while the prosecution witnesses were paraded daily, each dropping facts like Easter eggs on a green lawn, the defense followed with a Broadway production. It was filled with celebrities, well-known liberal supporters of Kunstler. They provided the entertainment for which the trial is known. A few stand out in my mind as especially memorable.

I think a New York lawyer is more impressed and more comfortable with those from his own culture, which I would describe as urban East Coast or hardcore New York City. After months of trying to adapt to midwestern Chicagoans, he may think he knows them and risk underestimating their sensitivity to things that are "different" and not as tolerated as in the world from which he came.

A parade started of a series of witnesses who seemed designed to impress the media more than the jury. Names like Pete Seeger, Judy Collins, Phil Ochs, and Country Joe led off the defense witnesses along with Allen Ginsberg, the poet from Greenwich Village who was a friend of Jack Kerouac and William S. Burroughs of the beat generation. To young people and, frankly, older folks of the beat generation age, Ginsberg was an icon, a founder of that counterculture that was against militarism, materialism, and sexual repression. It was the latter that Prosecutor Tom Foran chose to discredit.

Ginsberg was the perfect person to describe the Festival of Life in Lincoln Park. I had seen him perform there, sitting on a raised platform to address the crowd of young people much as a yoga instructor would, with legs folded one on top of the other, trying to raise everyone's consciousness to delight in the world around them.

Some leaves had been turning color, which had provided a natural proscenium arch above Ginsberg. And then, he'd led the crowd in his famous humming of the word "ommmmm." The theory was that if enough people *ommmmm*ed, they could change the world and stop the war. He started to do it from the witness chair until the judge cut him off.

I thought he actually was being successful in calming the room after the hurricane that had passed through. It was a gentle, peace-loving approach that reached into the jury box. There was nothing to object to, even as he described the Festival of Life as a benign gathering of young people just wanting to protest the war peacefully.

That is, until Tom Foran stood up to cross-examine the defense witness. It's the job of the defense attorney to draw a distinction between testimony that is given without examination on direct and what the prosecution extracts by cross-examination that brings it closer to reality. The jury must decide which is the truth.

Foran wanted to break the spell of the exotic cultural leader. I'm fortunate to have had the opportunity to witness one of the classic examples of destroying a witness with cross-examination, something that I found my colleagues downplayed or missed completely.

He handed Ginsberg a copy of his book with his poem "The Night Apple." When Foran asked about the religious significance of the poem, Ginsberg said it was about a wet dream. He laid out its "religious significance" by describing how dreams can connect with reality. Foran played him as carefully as if slowly pulling in a walleye in Lake Michigan, letting the fish believe he is free until the moment when the fisherman pulls the line tight to set the "hook."

Foran asked Ginsberg to read from his poems.

"You also wrote a book of poems called *Reality Sandwiches*, didn't you?"

Ginsberg answered with pride, "Yes."

The reading extended to Ginsberg's poem "Love Poem on Theme by Whitman," which dealt with homosexual and bisexual love. Foran asked him to explain the poem to the jury. Ginsberg started with an explanation that is difficult to follow even in print but included several phrases that shocked the court. To lift them from their context, they were "sandwiches of human flesh, which include dirty assholes, because those are universal images that come in everybody's dreams."

I whipped my view to the jury box, and sure enough, the facial expressions were like walking into the first cold blast when leaving a building. In seconds, all the positive vibrations created by Allen Ginsberg were gone, at least in my mind and observation. I could even see Kunstler bow under the weight of losing the positive momentum he'd built.

Ginsberg was continuing with a description of yoga, and within the monologue were phrases that underscored the shock of the previous comments. One dealt with yoga meditation and examining thoughts in dreams like "sleeping with one's mother or sleeping with one's father or becoming an angel or flying." After the phrase "sandwiches of human flesh which include dirty assholes," I didn't concentrate on the rest of Ginsberg's testimony. And I was sure that many on the jury had written him off as a radical homosexual who was using filthy language to promote gibberish. I felt it was as serious a blow to the defense case as Abbie's long hair and contemptuous manner.

In the final vote toward a verdict after months of testimony and upheaval, I expected a majority of the jurors to make their decision based on whether they liked the defendants. And aside from the intellectual content of the testimony, it's my opinion that Tom Foran blasted a major hole in the defense case.

By mid-December, the defense team had been blocked, it seemed, at every turn. Almost every objection was denied. The judge admonished the defendants constantly while at the same time granting the "good boys," the prosecution, a pass and therefore a subtle endorsement. They were the "good lawyers," and Kunstler and Weinglass were treated as inferior—outsiders who were from "out of town." You know, from New York.

It was in keeping with Hoffman's reputation as a prosecution judge. But was it a fair administration of justice? The answer was clearly no. Foran and Schultz were even sheepish at receiving so many trial decisions, like when the Bears football team scores so many points that it's embarrassing. A poor analogy, since it hasn't happened in my lifetime and I'm sure never will, but you get the idea.

It may be unfair to judge Judge Hoffman totally in one dimension, as a little toughie. But a deeper shadow hung over his bench. Could American justice survive the assault of the disruptive defendants before him? Would the rules of evidence produce the truth? If defendants don't obey the rules, how do you make them? The judge was driven by the fear that they would win, and in my estimation, that fear made him bear down harder.

With the talk of contempt incidents, I thought I could also detect a weariness in Kunstler and Weinglass, a feeling that they had given up all hope of winning the case. Of course, they would finish the trial as best they could, but there was depression in their faces.

Then came one of the highlights of the trial, the day Chicago Mayor Richard J. Daley was called as a witness by the defense. I was there early to get a seat in the first row. The courtroom filled quickly, with friends and family in the back rows and plenty of prosecution "helpers" in the far-side benches.

Daley entered in good spirits, dressed in a mayoral dark suit, ready to take his medicine or whatever was coming his way.

Among the celebrities called by Kunstler, Daley was perhaps the crowning "get." He was both celebrity and substantive witness. He had been the symbol of the trial in that the defendants had pointed to his actions as the violator of their constitutional rights with his restrictive orders, specifically as a dictatorial politician preventing their right to assemble outside the convention to prevent Hubert Humphrey from being nominated for president.

Instead of police versus demonstrators protesting the war at Balbo and Michigan, it was now Mayor Daley versus the defendants who embodied the ten thousand demonstrators.

The jury was not yet in the courtroom, and if my memory serves me right, the judge had also not yet entered. Daley walked straight up the aisle, went through the railing, and was directed to the witness chair. Strangely, unlike anyone else appearing as a witness in the trial, he climbed right into the chair situated slightly below the judge. He was not sworn in as he sat waiting for Judge Hoffman to come in.

The *other* Hoffman, Abbie, was not one to miss an opportunity. He squared off with the mayor, *Gunsmoke* style, with his hands at his sides where the six-guns would hang. He said to Daley, "OK, Mayor, why don't you and I settle this right here? To hell with this law stuff." Daley loved it and laughed heartily, as did spectators still filling up the court.

Kunstler mistakenly believed that Daley would be judged a *hostile* witness. He had good precedent. It's hard to think of someone who would have been more hostile to the defendants than Mayor Daley.

Under *direct* examination, the defense counsel could not ask leading questions of their own witness, but under *cross-examination*, Kunstler would have had greater latitude and been free to pose leading queries. But Judge Hoffman denied Kunstler's request to have Daley declared a hostile witness, saying, "He has answered in the manner of a gentleman." Furthermore, he said that nothing in the mayor's behavior justified calling him a hostile witness.

Here's a good lesson for law students. What will you do when you come to court prepared only to ask leading questions of a witness when the witness has not been declared hostile? The answer is that you must be prepared to adapt quickly.

It threw Kunstler into a tizzy. I saw his legal pad. It had eighty-three leading questions written out and carefully listed. I remember thinking at the time, *Is he going to ask them anyway?* There's a rule of thumb that I first saw in the movie *Anatomy of a Murder* with Jimmy Stewart, who did go ahead and ask leading questions even against the judge's sustaining objection after objection to each question. The jury still heard the questions (without answers) and got the idea. You can't erase a thought from inside one's brain.

Kunstler decided to become Jimmy Stewart. He asked all eighty-three leading questions accompanied by roughly eighty-three objections from the prosecution, which were all sustained. There was actually a rhythm to it in court. Kunstler fell into the trap.

At the end of the trial, Judge Hoffman found Kunstler in contempt for those eighty-three leading questions.

There was at least one question that caused a stir. Kunstler asked, "Did you say to Senator Abraham Ribicoff, 'Fuck you, you Jew sonofabitch'?"

You can imagine Foran jumping into the air with an objection. Kunstler said, "But there was a lip-reader there. There's clear video of Daley sitting with the Illinois delegation when Ribicoff was giving a speech at the convention criticizing the city for its 'gestapo' tactics. Daley held his hands to his mouth megaphone style and let 'er rip."

The mayor left out the back entrance past chambers, to the chagrin of the defendants. They had hoped to embarrass him, but a Chicago newspaper summed it up: "Mayor Emerges Unscathed."

It's dangerous when a lawyer calls a witness without preinterviews to know exactly what the witness is going to say. Take Norman Mailer, for instance. He said that Jerry Rubin had said that the presence of 100,000 young people would cause the establishment to commit all the violence in Chicago. At first it seemed, well, there goes the case if Norman Mailer said Rubin was talking about plans to provoke violence in Chicago. And then he repeated the comment on cross-examination. But Mailer was so witty, enjoyed himself so much, and provided so much laughter that it was hard to gauge how the celebrity had scored.

One other memorable moment in the trial came when the contempt citations were handed out. Four years total for the seven defendants. No one escaped. But each was given the opportunity to express himself to the court. These were people who embraced crowds and delivered orations pressing their cases. It was a series of exit speeches for the conspiracy "drama."

All of them made political speeches except Tom Hayden, who, in addition to some not-so-kind words about the trial, Judge Hoffman, and the prosecution, said something so personal and touching that it stopped the recitations: "I don't want to go to jail because I'd like to have a child."

Tom was full of surprises. Years later—more than forty, to be exact—he leaned over to me during a panel we were both on and said with a smile, "Of course, we did come to Chicago to start a riot."

Did the prosecution team of Tom Foran and Richard Schultz prove that the defendants had crossed state lines to incite a riot? Yes and no. The jury found that five of them, Hayden, Hoffman, Rubin, Dellinger, and Davis, were indeed *guilty* of crossing state lines with intent to riot. And they were convicted. Froines and Weiner were *acquitted* of all charges.

But on February 18, 1970, all seven defendants were acquitted of the *conspiracy* charges. Each was fined $5,000. They also received prison sentences for 170 contempt citations. And then in 1972, all charges were *dropped* by the Seventh Circuit Court of Appeals.

The appeals court blamed Judge Hoffman for an aggressive application of rules of court that resulted in an unfair trial. A following report, the Walker Report, concluded that the violence at the convention had been caused by the Chicago police.

One witness for the defense, Richard Goodwin, an aide and speech-writer to John F. Kennedy and Lyndon Johnson, said of Julius Hoffman's trial that the judge had used rules of evidence like clubs and kept such tight control on all parties that he squeezed out justice.

The Chicago Seven conspiracy trial entered the annals of legal history as one of the most disruptive trials ever. I would add, one of the most dramatic trials. Over time, it shifted from the news of the day to one of the great moments in American history. It captured the national imagination and became the topic of books, television series, and motion pictures. For me, it led to a new job: network correspondent for CBS News in Los Angeles. It also pointed me toward my third trial of the century.

Bill and his Grandad Bert on the Horton Farm in southeast Kansas. To Bill, Grandad was hard work personified, and always looked old.

Suited up and ready to play quarterback for the Independence Community College Pirates.

In the KANU studio, the highlight of Bill's time at the University of Kansas. A place of academic refinement and classical music, this was where Bill honed his iconic broadcasting voice.

Sergeant Bill Kurtis of the US Marine Corps, standing aboard a training ship.

Even when celebrating his graduation from Washburn University School of Law, Bill was still uncertain which path he would take: lawyer or broadcaster?

"For God's sake, take cover." Bill standing in front of the weather wall during the Topeka Tornado. This was the moment that solidified the trajectory of his life toward broadcasting.

Bill preparing his notes before a broadcast in the original WBBM-TV studio in the late 1960s. This was before Wussler and Sauter rebuilt the WBBM newsroom and moved the news desk from a sound stage into the working newsroom.

A still from the first televised interview with Iva Toguri D'Aquino, better known as Tokyo Rose. Cameraman Charles Boyer had to sit backwards in the open trunk of the crew car to get this shot of Bill and Iva walking through the rain in Lincoln Park in Chicago.

Bill, a cameraman, and an audio engineer, in 1967 on assignment covering bears at the Brookfield Zoo for WBBM-TV. The team is geared up with top-of-the-line mobile broadcasting equipment.

DEPARTMENT OF THE

# SHERIFF

## COUNTY OF LOS ANGELES

# 1970
# PRESS PASS

WILLIAM KURTIS

CBS NEWS

This is to certify that the above-named person whose photograph appears hereon, is a duly accredited representative of the press.

*Peter J. Pitchess*

**SHERIFF**

Bill's official press pass from the Los Angeles County Sheriff's Department, issued during the coverage of the Charles Manson trial.

Bill's words and Howard Brodie's sketches were the only way CBS viewers could experience the drama of the Manson trial. Brodie's skill at capturing the very soul of his subjects is part of what made the coverage of the trial must-see television.

Judge Charles Older, here watching Manson take the stand, was committed to see a fair trial was given and justice was served. Easier said than done, in the face of everything the unorthodox, chaotic Manson Family threw at the wall.

Linda Kasabian, the prosecution's key witness, on the stand. Her innocent, flower-child beauty and her grisly account of their murderous night at Sharon Tate's house captured the hearts and imaginations of Americans everywhere.

Brodie's rendition of the infamous moment when Manson vaulted over the defense table to attack the judge, only to be tackled by the bailiff.

Reporting live from the floor of the 1972 Republican National Convention in Miami Beach, Bill is wearing a state-of-the-art headset and antenna, which made mobile reporting possible. Only four years earlier, at the iconic 1968 Democratic National Convention, CBS reporters were tethered to the studio above the convention hall.

## IT'S NOT PRETTY. BUT IT'S REAL.

In an age when Chicago news shows have theme songs and expensive settings for their broadcasts, Channel 2 has returned to the simple life.

We're doing our news from our newsroom.

Frankly, we were starting to gag on the plastic and tinsel that has surrounded television news for the last couple of years, including our own.

The result of our change, is that TV2 News is a lot more real and a lot more interesting.

Certainly, our co-anchormen Bill Kurtis and Walter Jacobson are not going to put you to sleep. Both are bright, young, dynamic newsmen.

And everywhere around them, things are happening.

Reporters are returning with stories.

Film crews are going out.

...pes are teletyping.
...ole newsroom is busy
with ...y. And all of it's real.

If you get a chance tonight, take a look at a news broadcast without the plastic or tinsel.

You just might think it's beautiful.

## TV2 NEWS
With Bill Kurtis & Walter Jacobson
6 & 10 pm. CBS©2

Bob Wussler and Van Gordon Sauter stripped WBBM-TV Chicago of its previous sterile presentation and made television news real, serious journalism. With Bill Kurtis and Walter Jacobson as the frontmen, the maverick spirit of the revolutionary newsroom is on full display in this advertisement.

Two of the most talented, ambitious, and competitive journalists Wussler and Sauter could find, Kurtis and Jacobson worked behind the anchor desk together for nine years and changed the nature of local television news.

Bill in the WBBM-TV studio, preparing for the next broadcast at his typewriter.

Bill established a reputation by using his previous experience as a correspondent to cover international news for WBBM-TV's local Chicago audience. This included traveling to South Vietnam in 1975 to cover the last days of the war.

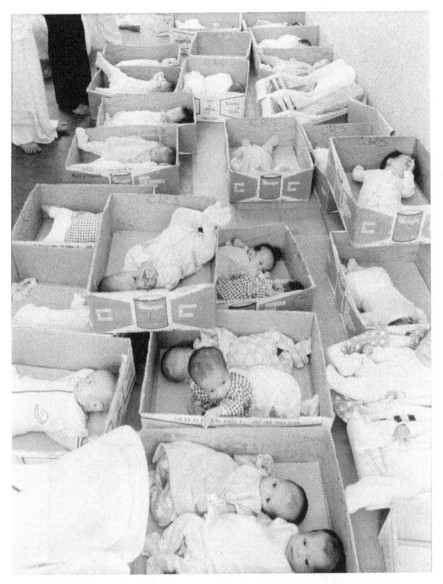

The last orphan lift to leave Vietnam before the end of the war. Cared for by Catholic Relief Services, these babies lay in makeshift cribs near the Tan Son Nhut airport before boarding their flight for the United States. Photo by author.

A still from Bill's coverage of the Pokot raid against the Turkanas. His news team was flying in to cover a doctor's work in northern Kenya when a radio transmission redirected their plane to the site of the massacre.

After the Agent Orange reporting broke, Bill was invited to Hanoi to get the other side of the story. In what used to be an area covered in mangrove trees along the Mekong River Delta, now decimated by Agent Orange, Bill prepares for his report.

Bill surrounded by children in the streets of Ho Chi Minh City, who became the unexpected focus of his second trip to the country.

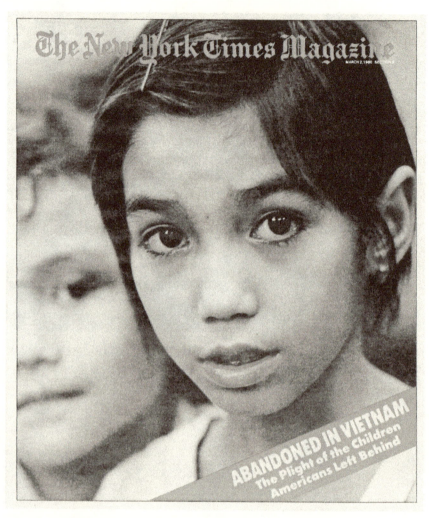

The New York Times Magazine

MARCH 2, 1980  SECTION 6

ABANDONED IN VIETNAM
The Plight of the Children
Americans Left Behind

The cover of the March 2, 1980, edition of *The New York Times Magazine* featuring Bill's article, "Abandoned in Vietnam." After submitting an unsolicited article on spec, Bill never expected his writing to make it to print.

In 1982, Bill got behind this desk as a network anchor, fulfilling the dream of every television journalist.

Diane Sawyer and Bill Kurtis, cohosts of *CBS Morning News.*

Muhammad Ali relaxing with Bill on a couch in between shots for his feature in CBS's *The American Parade*. Ali's familiar, easy-going charisma captured on film helped his fans process the public announcement of his Parkinson's diagnosis.

Bill Kurtis and his wife, Donna LaPietra, in the early days of Kurtis Productions. Donna is the vice president and CEO of Kurtis Productions, a longtime producer.

Bill (*center*) and Harvard professor Dr. Richard Wilson (*left*) approach one of the most infamous sites of the Cold War. The documentary team for PBS NOVA were the first American television journalists to return to the Chernobyl Nuclear Power Plant, less than two years after the disaster.

Dr. Richard Wilson and Bill note an alarming rise in radioactivity while touring Chernobyl.

Bill Kurtis and Peter Sagal, laughing at the week's news during a live taping of *Wait Wait . . . Don't Tell Me!*

# NINE

# Charles Manson

After the Chicago Seven verdicts were handed down, I had a brief moment to catch my breath. It felt like I had been spinning nonstop since I had first set foot in Chicago four years before. Richard Speck, the second Great Chicago Fire, the Democratic National Convention, Tokyo Rose, the Chicago Seven trial. My unique experiences and skill set I had brought with me from Kansas had been caught up in a perfect storm of good timing and a bit of sheer luck. It began to dawn on me that Chicago was experiencing year after year of historical significance, and I was there for it all. I was living every newsman's dream. *How could it get any better?* I wondered. But I should have known, journalism is a carousel—you get on and you get off, but it never stops. And I wasn't getting off. The best was yet to come.

In the late winter of 1970, John Lane, the CBS News Midwest bureau chief, called me in. He had been talking with the network bosses in New York, and they had offered me a job as a reporter with the West Coast Bureau. I was ready to go.

Arriving in California after a late spring in Chicago was like walking in the aromatic air after a thunderstorm has passed. It was everything I expected. Palm trees lined the boulevards. Everyone in short-sleeved shirts. It was *el paraíso* to a Chicago transplant.

As I got ready to move my small family across the country, I realized it was not so different than the transient life of a military family—a life I had experienced only a few decades before. Looking like a vaudeville troupe carrying trunks and suitcases were my wife, Helen, daughter,

Mary Kristin, and I. Chasing a dream, we followed the bright lights and headed toward an even bigger city. As for many correspondents at the time, it was Helen who set up the base camp, finding a suitable place to live and checking the nearest school, playground, dance studio, hospital, and shopping mall. It was the heavy lifting that allowed the ambitious white-collared correspondent to work the job that required a hair-trigger reaction to the news of the day. I held my breath with every headline, waiting for the call to come in from New York: "Stop what you're doing, get your ass there, and COVER IT!" If I had told Helen I'd be gone two hundred days out of the year covering eleven western states, I'm sure she would have told me to get an apartment in LA and taken Mary Kristin to establish a permanent base in our hometown of Independence, Kansas.

As much as I focused on chasing newsworthy stories, I did feel obligated to contribute as much to the family outreach education as I could. When home on weekends, I set course to visit every one of the theme parks and natural environments in the greater Los Angeles area. I know it sounds self-serving, which it was, but it was also fascinating. From Disneyland, the original, to Yosemite, Sequoia and Kings Canyon, Joshua Tree, Death Valley, the Channel Islands, Santa Catalina, and La Jolla. In 1970, California was crowded with twenty million people. By 2020, that number would double. I'd say the Kurtises hit the orange groves of sunny Southern California at just the right time.

We chose Pacific Palisades to live, a very nice community at the end of Sunset Boulevard. We had a comfortable apartment above a two-car garage, overlooking the Pacific if you squinted through the trees. Hollywood actors were scattered throughout the neighborhood, and to my surprise, Carroll O'Connor, star of *All in the Family*, was our next-door neighbor in a surprisingly modest bungalow.

Six months after our arrival, my son, Scott, was born. We were suburban quiet, miles away from any hippie culture with an orange tree in the backyard—how perfect.

Helen was a small-town girl used to the same streets and neighbors who watched the kids on the block growing from the first arrival home from the hospital to that nervous first attempt to ride a bicycle to noisy high schoolers going to the prom, then going away to college with occasional return visits to the folks until starting their own families. That comes pretty close to the life cycle of America encapsulated in one block.

It was stable and predictable. With two children, Helen's new neighbor-hood was confined to the two-bedroom apartment and its tree-filtered view of the ocean.

The CBS West Coast Bureau offices were in the lower level of CBS Television City, an enormous building housing five soundstages, which could have that many shows running simultaneously. When I arrived, giant billboard posters decorated the outside walls with the names of Glen Campbell, Cher, *All in the Family*, *The Carol Burnett Show*, and the Smothers Brothers. It was a CBS world of the Tiffany Network.

Out the back door, where trucks were delivering the workings of show business, was the famous Farmers Market, an open-air thirties- and forties-style group of stalls that hadn't changed since the time when Hol-lywood stars like Clark Gable had meandered the aisles. I took to it like a Kansan to the wide-open prairie. I visited again forty years after that initial walk-through, and not only had the stalls not changed, but neither had the menus: Italian mostaccioli; Greek saganaki; American hamburg-ers; juice bars; ice-cream counters; Japanese sushi, tempura, and sake; and Middle Eastern marinated feta.

It was pre–shopping malls, and it caught the spirit of California when orange groves and oil wells stretched from Santa Monica's beaches to the La Brea Tar Pits, where pools of crude oil and tar had trapped prehistoric animals that roamed the desert before it was filled with *Homo sapiens* seeking sun, fun, and retirement living.

Inside the basement bureau, John Harris was the bureau chief who communicated with New York, offered what was happening in twelve western states, and then send his correspondents, Bill Stout and Terry Drinkwater, to cover those events. The LA bureau worked three hours behind the network in New York. The early mornings and extremely tight deadlines must have been karmic punishment for our summer weather.

In August, less than six months after I got to LA, was one story loomed at the top of the daily log that was something of a dilemma for the seasoned correspondents. The trial of Charles Manson was about to begin. It was a high-profile crime—a shocking murder that had frightened the citizens of Beverly Hills and Bel-Air—but taking the assignment meant locking in to a potentially long trial and extended days in the courtroom, most of which would probably be mind-numbingly boring. Neither of the two senior correspondents, Drinkwater and Stout, wanted to get caught up in yet another long, tedious courtroom assignment. Terry had covered Robert F. Kennedy's assassination in the Ambassador Hotel, and Bill had done his time with court coverage in the trial of Sirhan Sirhan, who had been convicted of the murder of Bobby Kennedy.

No one was expecting more than another mundane courtroom drama. For that reason, they would rather have the assignment go to the new guy. Once again, my background helped. I had a law degree and had made my name in the news business on Richard Speck and the Chicago Seven. Who better to slog along with the murderous Charles Manson and his family of hippies and drifters for as long as it would take?


The trial was in the Hall of Justice, an old eight-story gray building in downtown Los Angeles filled with courtrooms. The television show *Dragnet* liked to shoot the exterior as a police headquarters.

That's one thing about LA—since the movie industry is there, every corner looks familiar, having been filmed for forty years of filmmaking. The streets had become the archives of our cultural lives.

If it sounds like I was dazzled to be in La-La Land, you're right. As Chicago had its own magic, I was beginning a new experience in exactly the same mood, which could best be described as "doing what I loved in a remarkable new setting." That positive attitude turned everything into an adventure and every encounter into an extraordinary experience. That is a one-way ticket to success because the flow of energy creates its own *luck*. Praise those who find it, and pity those who don't. They'll keep looking all their lives.

Philosopher and chief editor of Britannica's Great Books of the Western World Mortimer Adler injected the word *luck* into a conversation we had about success. He was arguing that no matter what we do, it takes *luck* to really succeed. I followed him to the Aspen Institute for a more extensive explanation, and after some thought, he explained it as part of a serendipitous life's journey. He finally conceded that *luck* can trigger success, but only after preparation, as in "cultivating the field to grow the best crop" and recognizing the best time to harvest.

In my case, that particular time was August 1970 at age thirty. With my law degree, with four years of on-the-job news experience, and having within the last eight months witnessed the most disruptive trial in American jurisprudence, I was poised to receive Adler's "luck."

Being chosen to report on the Manson trial for the number-one television news organization in America was indeed the *luck* in Adler's equation.

At the time, none of us knew we would be participating in what would become America's horror story and the end of the wide-open era of sex, drugs, and a culture turned upside down—the sixties.

Chief prosecutor Vincent Bugliosi was not as confident as the rest of the country that a guilty verdict would be easy to obtain. Four defendants were charged with murder: Charles Manson, Susan Atkins, Patricia Krenwinkel, and Leslie Van Houten. Tex Watson, who was the primary killer, would be tried separately.

Bugliosi's problem was that Manson had not been present when his four followers had entered the house of Sharon Tate and killed her and four friends who were "babysitting" the actress during her last month of pregnancy. Her husband, Hollywood director Roman Polanski, was out of the country. Bugliosi had to prove that Manson had controlled the defendants so completely that when he had directed them to kill everyone in the house, they had been carrying out his orders as if he were with them. The legal theory is called "vicarious responsibility," a secondary liability that arises under the common-law doctrine of agency, the responsibility of any third party who had the "right, ability, or duty to control" the activities of a violator.

To do that, Bugliosi had to re-create the bizarre world of the Manson family, crazier than anyone had ever heard before, and explain how Manson had controlled the defendants and why he had sent them to kill.

Put yourself in the position of the chief prosecutor—you've got to establish Charlie's cult, how the use of sex and drugs had taken over their minds and turned them into zombies capable of murder. That was no small task. It was no slam dunk.

Even a free-love youth revolution has to be careful about who comes to its party. On the streets of the hippie mecca, the Haight-Ashbury neighborhood of San Francisco, the milieu of faces, psychedelic colors, sounds of guitars and bongo drums, human smells of days without showers saturated with clouds of marijuana smoke, and swollen red eyes from harder drugs was teetering on the apex of an era known as the sixties.

To a river of runaway kids just off Highway 101, it was heaven, the land of the lost boys and the girls looking for them, a place where they made their own rules, did what they wanted, and never thought of tomorrow. Each was running away from something and looking for an intangible essence. Maybe it was truth. Maybe it was love. Maybe it was Daddy. But they thought they'd know it when they saw it or smelled it or heard it.

If they were unfortunate, they would hear Charles Manson. He was sitting on the sidewalk, cloaked in a white robe and strumming a guitar over legs folded yoga style. His voice was pleasant in the folk style of the day, with interesting lyrics of his own. His face was appealing too. His head was half covered, which gave him the look of a religious ascetic, even Jesus. A slight beard helped. And of course the hairstyle of the day, stringy and shoulder length.

It was just a step or two to join him in a sitting position and another short distance to an old school bus and later a Volkswagen van. These were mostly young girls—in their twenties—looking for that . . . something. At the van were other young girls who hugged them as long-lost companions and who seemed to know what they were thinking. They'd been running too until they'd found Charlie. Charlie? Yes, Charles Manson, they would say, "the most remarkable man you'll ever meet. He has the answer."

Like an itinerant wise man, he was on an idyllic journey similar to that of the runaways, trying to find a home to make a family, a family they'd never had or were running away from—or so he said.

Would they like to join them? "We'll be like a band of lost souls together."

Charles Manson was thirty-three, older than his followers and therefore more experienced and "wiser" in their eyes. He became the father figure they were looking for.

When he revealed his background, it was taken by the runaways not as frightening but as transparent and truthful. He seemed to be showing what people were afraid to do—reveal themselves, sharing his reality as they should share theirs. On paper, Charlie's reality *was* frightening: no obvious parents, no mentors to keep him on the right track, years in juvenile detention facilities, and no safety net to save him. So he had reared himself.

His teachers were felons. His school was the street. His hippie appearance as a peaceful teacher/folk singer fit the times perfectly but went deeper. He was an evil shell of resentment that would erupt someday to "get even with the world" for stealing his youth, his soul. He had been abused and in turn abused others all his life. The ultimate abuse would become his life.

When there were more followers than would fit in the van, he needed a home. The runaways' highway down the coast of California led to a rustic old movie ranch at the far side of the San Fernando Valley in Chatsworth. Secluded within huge boulders where Gene Autry and Roy Rogers had churned out their career B movies, it was like a setting for another movie, this one to be called *The Manson Family*. It had everything any kid would want. A boardwalk along a string of Western storefronts used as a movie background set. A barn, fences, and a dirt road leading into the rocks and wagons and buggies. Charlie moved the "family" into one of the larger buildings, where they set up housekeeping.

The ranch was owned by a man named George Spahn, who was bedridden most of the time and easily persuaded to take on a lovely bunch of young people as "guests." They would care for him, fix meals and keep him company, and even occasionally service him with sex.

It was something of a work in progress. In other words, there was no plan at the beginning. Things just happened.

There were a few rules—made by Charlie. The girls had to have sex whenever a male wanted it. Charlie allowed some men to enter for a while and provide protection in exchange. Motorcycle gangs would come by, attracted by the drugs and sex.

Over about a year, the Family grew in more ways than one. In the evening, they'd gather for a meal. There was no television, so they would sing hymns and popular songs for entertainment. Patricia Krenwinkel was the "mother superior" of the household, cleaning during the day and supervising the meal at night. When an attractive young hippie walked into a supermarket, there would always be a young man or woman willing to supply his brothers and sisters of the movement with the throwaway food from the day's commerce. Foraging raids supplied the meals.

With sex available on demand, there were soon babies, all part of the

Family. Although physically small at five foot two, Charlie was clearly the alpha male. When a new recruit wanted to join, he would have a "talk" and then sex with them. His approach was much like that of a street pimp using mind games to control his prostitutes. He had been arrested many times for crossing state lines with women for purposes of prostitution. He told them what they wanted to hear, that they were looking for their father. His final revelation was that they should think of their father when they had sex with him because "every woman fantasizes having sex with their father." "We must destroy your ego," he said. His goal, of course, was to become their father, what they were looking for.

There were drug orgies with the Family gathering on mattresses under the picturesque rocks. The drugs were not from a pharmacy or even a dealer. They were foraged from drug stores or traded for sex. From mushrooms to cocaine and heroin, never clearly identified, it was a smorgasbord of hallucinogens du jour. LSD was a key to what was to come.

Whether or not he knew what he was doing, Charles Manson was creating a cult. There was one source of information—him. No radio or television to check the accuracy of his views. Charlie could tell the Family anything he wanted, and they would accept it without questioning. Lynette "Squeaky" Fromme told the group that she was walking with Charlie in the garden and saw a dead bird on the ground. He picked it up and blew on it to give it life, and it flew away. The Family speculated among themselves that Charlie, the perfect man, was actually Jesus Christ. There was the name, Man-son, son of man.

Creating a cult is not as hard as it sounds. Charlie gave his followers what they wanted: security, a feeling of belonging to a close, intimate group that fit the definition of "family" perfectly. The women were seeking that, including a father. They quickly accepted his invitation and obeyed him to the letter. I heard them say, in court and outside, "Why don't they let us tell the truth? That we were happy. We were family and loved each other. Charlie was our father."

During one family session after dinner, Charlie was studying the Beatles' *White Album*—first a cut called "Revolution 1" and then trying to decipher the lyrics that he claimed were meant for him in the song "Helter Skelter." His mind was influenced by drugs, just as the others were, and he fashioned a theory of what was happening in 1968 when the cities were burning. He thought if he could create something terrible and make it look like the Black population was responsible, whites would rise up to stop a revolution. Then the whites and Blacks would kill each other, leaving a void to fill. The Family, having moved to Death Valley to avoid the apocalypse, would come out of their hidden lair to rule the world.

Manson told the Family that they might have to show Black people how to start Helter Skelter. He became paranoid and started to defend the Spahn ranch with night patrols.

On August 8, Manson told Linda Kasabian, Patricia Krenwinkel, Susan Atkins, Leslie Van Houten, and Tex Watson to go to "that house where Melcher used to live and totally destroy everyone in it as gruesome as you can." "Melcher" was Terry Melcher, a record producer and son of Doris Day who had turned Charlie down for a record deal.

But what would the terrible act be?

I'm not sure when it dawned on Manson that he had created the perfect murder machine. And whether he got the idea that family members would commit the murders and he didn't even have to be there, allowing him to declare his innocence and never be convicted. For the rest of his life, he would maintain his innocence because he was never at the murder scene. The perfect murder? It might have been except for one man. The prosecutor, Vincent Bugliosi.

Once again, my legal education and journalistic experience helped. Three years at Washburn had given me a knowledge of the obscure corners of legal proceedings and courtroom maneuvers that was unmatched among the LA press corps. Better yet, I was fresh off the trial of the Chicago Seven and the only reporter with experience covering a consequential gag order. When reporters would swarm Vince in the halls after the day's session, he would have to explain the gag order imposed by Judge Charles Older and excuse himself. So I let the other reporters ask away, and when they drifted off to meet their deadlines, I'd ask for a few more minutes. In the course of explaining what the legal procedures would be, without divulging any substance, Bugliosi would outline his strategy for me. As the trial progressed, I'd get to see some exhibits, like photos of the murder house and bodies. The descriptions that reached the public seemed more horrific than the black-and-white photos shot by the police. A rope hung from the beams of the California frame house. Scribbling on the wall made by a towel dipped in blood declared, "Death to pigs."

The prosecution strategy was similar to preparing a news story: get the jury's attention so they'll want to hear the rest of the mystery and put it together in their heads. Then, carefully present evidence from witnesses to fill in the holes as was promised in the opening argument. The problem with long trials is that it's almost impossible for the jury to remember each witness and how they fit into the case. That's why having twelve people in the jury room for deliberations is so valuable—someone among the twelve has usually heard and remembered a witness and can fill in gaps in memory.

What is almost never analyzed after a trial is what effect sequestration has on the jury. In Manson's case, 225 days was a long time to be "held hostage" at the Ambassador Hotel in LA. That was the record until the O. J. Simpson jury beat it with 265 days. The dynamics of spending that long with twelve strangers is akin to cruel and unusual punishment.

Charles Manson thought he was so smart that he could trick the jury into believing his theory of "I wasn't there. Therefore, I'm not guilty." Or he believed that he could play the women (defendants) so that they would disrupt the trial with antics. Both plans backfired. When Charlie came to court with an X carved in his forehead, and the women then followed with the same sign, it was clear that he controlled them. If he could do that, then he must have had enough control over them to send them on a killing mission.

On July 24, 1970, I submitted my first report to the *CBS Evening News* on the first day of the trial. It was before the Manson story "blew up" to become America's most gripping murder mystery. I tried to set the scene of a courtroom inside which little monsters were gathering.

In a typical report, I said, "The trial began nearly one year after the murders. The three female defendants grinned at a packed gallery. Charles Manson had, in his words, 'X-ed' himself out of society by scratching a symbolic sign on his forehead."

I had Howard Brodie's artwork to turn my words into accurate images. Prosecutor Bugliosi used his opening statement to describe the complex and bizarre story of Charlie's perfect murder scenario: "The evidence will show that Manson had the infinite humility to call himself Jesus Christ. He was a killer who masqueraded as a hippie, and he so dominated these defendants that they did his bidding. They, not he, committed the seven Tate/LaBianca murders, but he is equally guilty as a member of a conspiracy to commit murder."

The jury listened attentively as Bugliosi detailed Manson's fanatical obsession with "Helter Skelter," a concept he got from the Beatles' *White Album*. Manson was quiet as Bugliosi continued. Those in the press corps and visitor galley could be heard only by an occasional cough, otherwise afraid they would miss something important in this first account of the prosecution's case. The combination of "mystery story" and historical relevance elevated the significance for everyone.

"The evidence will show that Manson intended to start the Black/white revolution by making it look like Black people had murdered the Tate/LaBianca victims."

Bugliosi tried to make his complex strategy clear: "You have to realize these murders were bizarre, and they're not going to have a garden-variety motive. Linda Kasabian's testimony will clearly show that on this particular night, no one in the metropolis was safe because they were looking for their victims totally at random."

The idea of an opening statement is not to try the case but to outline the story for the verdict, to make it interesting and hold the jury's interest. It didn't take much to accomplish that in the Manson trial.

Defense attorney Paul Fitzgerald, a young court-appointed attorney for Leslie Van Houten, did what he could to lessen the blow: "We took particular exception to the very vituperative comments made by Mr. Bugliosi. We thought that his opening statement was slanderous, defamatory. We thought it did very little in elucidating any evidence that the prosecution might present. We thought the opening statement degenerated into some form of name-calling."

Bugliosi was able to present testimony from Sharon Tate's father. It was a major moment in the courtroom, and I had thirty seconds on the air to talk about it: " Evidence came today from several witnesses—Sharon Tate's father—to establish that she had lived in the murder house. Other witnesses began a meticulous re-creation of what happened that night. There will be many witnesses from both sides as what the prosecutor described as a long hot summer. Bill Kurtis, CBS News, Los Angeles."

The long, hot summer had begun. Ahead of us was not only the Los Angeles heat but the fall and winter seasons too. The courtroom would be home away from home for a cadre of a dozen reporters servicing the three major networks, local television stations, the *Los Angeles Times*, and the UPI and AP wire services carrying the story around the world.

We knew it was important, but we didn't realize how the airwaves and wires were heating up to service overwhelming demand. It was an early form of audiobooks, Raymond Chandler novels, Capote's *In Cold Blood*, and Jack the Ripper murder mysteries. The insatiable interest in crime stories, especially the bloodiest, most gruesome cases, was yet another element that fueled the notoriety of the Manson case. Manson had it all: Hollywood stars, weird hippie killers, and the hard-to-believe set of facts—America's new horror story.

My routine in "filing" a story was complicated. Because California did not yet allow cameras in the courtroom, we turned to artists. I had worked with Howard Brodie at the conspiracy trial in Chicago, and I knew I was working with the very best among courtroom artists. He'd covered World War II, the My Lai massacre, the trial of Bruno Hauptmann for the kidnapping of the Lindbergh baby, and countless events in between. One famous drawing that had made it to the front page of the *New York Daily News* was the execution of a man in the electric chair.

Howard brought his colored pencils and large sheets of thick drawing paper into a front-row seat that happened to be quite close to Manson. Over the course of the trial, Manson would take great interest in Howard and even exchange sketches with him. Howard is the most humanly sensitive man I have known, and he was touched by Charlie's overtures. Some would say Howard was "drawn in" to the Manson orbit. Others would say Howard was so focused on discovering the essence of a killer or the beauty of Linda Kasabian that his concentration led to being enamored with the Family. It was an interesting glimpse into Howard's immersion in his craft, with concentration so complete to find the "soul" of a subject that he blocked out all around it. As for Charlie's part, I viewed his interest much like the action of a cobra hypnotizing its prey.

It's one thing to obtain images of key actions within the courtroom. It's another to actually send them to the Cronkite-anchored evening news in New York—in the world of the 1970s.

At the noon recess, I would tuck the large paper drawings under my arm and ride down the elevator from the eighth floor to the parking lot where my tiny Austin-Healey Sprite sports car stood. The car was California fun but hardly a commuter's dream. In fact, it was something of a nightmare.

I covered the art and hit the Santa Monica freeway due west to Television City. In traffic, I was always looking up at larger cars jockeying for a few extra feet of advantage, and I felt like a flea at a dog's kennel waiting to be barked off the road. The tiny Sprite was the closest to suicide I ever got.

It may sound primitive in the era of advanced technology forty-two years later, especially compared with the press corps of three thousand that covered O. J. Simpson's trial, but the dozen of us did what we had to do. In one sense, it was the best of television production instead of being crushed by instant satellite speed.

I would take the artwork to the bureau in Television City, and then it would go to one of the soundstages upstairs that happened to be shooting. We needed access to live studio cameras. For news coverage, there were as yet no electronic cameras being used by news crews on the street. We were still shooting 16-mm film.

I was assigned the studio where *The Carol Burnett Show* was taping—Studio 33. That means there was a live studio audience of about five hundred. They had come to see a television show with Tim Conway and Harvey Korman playing with Carol that just happened to be the highest rated in the country. So when the floor director walked to center stage and said in true entertainment style, "OK, kids, take five!" it meant that everyone onstage except the cameramen vanished. There was a brief apology to the audience and an explanation that the "news guys need to use the studio for about fifteen minutes." The audience didn't budge and kept their eyes on what we were doing onstage.

There was no other way to get Howard's images on videotape than to send them via coaxial cable to New York. We put them in front of a studio camera and directed the cameramen to zoom in or out, pan left or right and dissolve from Charlie's face to Linda Kasabian's, zoom into the X on his forehead and then to the women standing with their own swastikas scratched into their flesh, and so on for weeks of reports.

The art cards were placed on three easels, and the director took over. Let's face it; they were rather simple moves from one easel to the next. It was the setting that was disconcerting.

Onstage interrupting *The Carol Burnett Show* in front of a live audience in Television City had to be one of the more interesting chapters in the history of television news. Should I say we "went Hollywood"? I maintain that the production moves requisitioned by Bureau Chief John Harris on Howard's art helped make the Manson story a global event. The Brodie artwork and the smooth moves and close-ups added a touch of moviemaking that made Kasabian look like a beautiful Botticelli Madonna figure and quite innocent and Charles Manson look like a sinister madman. Add to that Kasabian's tale of drugs, sex, and murder and you had a blockbuster.

On one occasion, while our director was positioning the cards, I climbed to the upper seats and a small room off to the side of the control room. It was the announce booth where I would read my script as the cameras caressed the drawings. I was usually so rushed that I had no time to appreciate the moment, but on this day, when I entered the announce booth, I found a cigarette tracing a thin line of smoke toward the ceiling. When I looked at the script lying on the small table under the microphone, it had the name of George Fenneman, the greatest announcer of the day. I was as thrilled as a kid getting an autograph from Mickey Mantle.

In her first appearance, the prosecution's key witness, Linda Kasabian, became America's macabre sweetheart. The horror-filled Manson story was not the kind of fare the *CBS Evening News* was used to, but if Walter Cronkite's producers had planned to drop the Manson story from the evening lineup after the opening-day testimony, there was a quick change of heart. The testimony was so compelling that viewers demanded every word. The Manson trial was red-hot for news consumption everywhere.

Linda Kasabian was everyone's perfect flower child of the sixties. She entered the courtroom like Angela Lansbury coming on the Broadway set of *Sweeney Todd* dressed in a flowing white dress tied at the waist. The only thing missing was a bouquet of daisies cradled in her arms. Actually, a meadow of embroidered flowers swept in a border under an open neck. Another column of a Dutch design ran down the front of the dress. Her hair fell straight to each side, divided in the middle and tied but not braided.

She was only twenty-one and very attractive, with wide-set eyes and cheeks slightly hollowed to catch a shadow when the light fell directly on her face. And when she looked down and to the side, she was as beautiful as any movie star. On cross-examination, she described herself as "a little girl in a forest," exactly the *look* she presented on the stand. And it all just "happened." You would think some entertainment agent was crafting a public relations campaign for his client who turned out to be a natural "star."

Bugliosi should have been a Broadway producer. His star witness was everything he had planned and could have asked for. He later told me, "She was the best witness I have ever seen."

With the opening argument laying out the strategy, Bugliosi began to prove his case with his strongest ace in the hole, Linda Kasabian.

When I reread my reports for the Cronkite show, I think it is no wonder the story overwhelmed any other headline.

I said, "Linda Kasabian today had regained her composure after testifying that she had seen three persons stabbed and shot at Sharon Tate's house. She told of stopping at the front yard of a home to wash off the blood. She said that Patricia Krenwinkel had hurt her hand from stabbing so much. After the killing and at a conversation at the ranch, she said that Tex Watson said he told the people in the house that 'I'm the Devil here to do the Devil's business.' He told Charlie there was a lot of panic. It was really bloody. Bodies laying all over the place, but all are dead. Manson asked them if they had any remorse, but they all said no. Continuing then, she said Manson told them, 'We're going out again tonight.' Last night was too messy, and he was going to show us how to do it. The LaBianca murders occurred later that night, even more brutal than the Tate slaying."

In a later report, I concentrated on the women: "The three female defendants, their hair in braids, wore dark clothing today. They and Manson stared for long periods at Linda Kasabian. Their lawyer talked about their attempts to reach her. But there is no communication between the former Family members. One of the girls mouthed to Linda softly, 'You're killing us.' She replied, 'You've killed yourselves.' And today, when Charles Manson said, 'You're lying,' she spoke into the microphone and said, 'You know it's the truth, Charlie.' Bill Kurtis, CBS News, Los Angeles."

I think the trial was effectively over at the end of Linda Kasabian's testimony. She was that strong Even when defense attorney Paul Fitzgerald asked if she had ever used the drug LSD, she repeated Bugliosi's direct examination: "Yes, fifty times." He was trying to show that she was mentally ill from the drug use, but Kasabian was so lucid, alert, and articulate that it went nowhere.

Direct and cross-examination went on for eighteen days before Linda Kasabian left the stand.

The judge, Charles Older, faced the issue of disruptive defendants when the female defendants cut swastikas in their foreheads and stood to recite poetry. But he pressed on to prove that justice could prevail even against the greatest challenge.

He should have asked me. I was the only one in the courtroom who had been an eyewitness to the other "most disruptive trial." And I knew exactly what should be done.

I had seen how a judge could handle defendants who tried to force their own mistrial. Looking back only a few months, the US Supreme Court had provided some help to Julius Hoffman in Chicago after the Bobby Seale gagging disaster. Their answer was simply to give defendants the choice of either behaving themselves in the courtroom or being removed to an adjacent room to listen to the proceedings on a speaker. That happened to Manson and the female defendants.

One day, the three defendants stood silently and refused to sit down. The jury couldn't take their eyes off them, and neither could I. Another day, they started singing. Same effect. Finally the judge removed them to the jury room next to the courtroom. Each day, they were brought into the main courtroom and were asked if they wanted to remain quietly. When they said no, they were removed. Same with Charlie.

Frankly, I thought it worked well. The judge quickly established that he was in charge and would not allow a defendant to disrupt their own trial, establishing that a defendant can forfeit his or her right to face his or her accuser. The constitutional right is not absolute.

Charlie thought he had one thing working for him—his appearance. But he couldn't have been more mistaken. It as a look that had appealed to his young harem—hair dropping below his neck and curling forward at the chin, creating a frame with a full mustache and beard set perfectly above his prison dungarees. It focused attention on his face, specifically the eyes, dark and sunken. The effect was hypnotic, as if inviting you to explore deeper, a journey into the soul—yours and his. Howard Brodie would draw large close-ups of him, and I'd dissolve one upon the other, suggesting that within the deep sockets were pools of evil without ever having to state it. Manson was so short at five foot two that how he survived inside the joint is a wonder. The answer is by illusion.

Contrary to public perception, every day in the Manson trial was not filled with fireworks. It was the work of justice, slow and deliberate and often boring. But outside the Hall of Justice on the street, the carnival continued. Members of the Family sat on the curb outside their van, talking with anyone who stopped. They were twenty-year-olds, sometimes holding a baby or playing music from the van radio, re-creating the feel of a folk concert of the sixties. One day, I asked what they were making. Squeaky Fromme said it was a magic vest for Charlie. I said, "Can you talk to Charlie while he's in jail?" They said, "Oh, yes, he sends us messages and tells us what to do."

I actually believed there was some crazy communication network of inmates that may have sent them messages. Maybe I was getting too close to the Family and too inclined to believe the fairy tale. Manson was in a holding cell in the basement of the Hall of Justice. His only contacts were with prison attendants and a few visits from Family members and deputies. To believe in my "network of communication," you would also have to believe the deputies were bribed—certainly not impossible but improbable. The dungeon-like cell was a location I didn't know during all those months of trial.

During the same conversation with the six Family members on the curb, I noticed a .45-caliber pistol on the front seat. I asked if the police had seen it, and they said, "Yes, it's not loaded." At which point, I wished them a good day and went back to trial.

Then there was the day when one of them said, "Hi, Bill." It meant either that they had watched television when Walter Cronkite had introduced me as Bill Kurtis or that Charlie had sent them a message to harass and scare the news media. I've felt two serious chills in my fifty years of journalism: one was when Sam Giancana's in-law suggested that I "cool it," and the other was when a tiny member of the Manson Family addressed me by my first name.

We called Los Angeles La-La Land after Ulysses's odyssey when he was warned about the sea monsters Scylla and Charybdis. The thought came to me as I looked up at the palm trees, felt a soft ocean breeze glide down the sidewalk, and reflected on how reality mixed with fantasy here in La-La Land without being able to tell the difference. There was Disneyland, dedicated to a fantastical re-creation of reality. And there was reality with the patina of make-believe on every corner. The main industry here was bringing dreams to life.

That same night, I was sitting with Helen, Mary Kristin, and Scott in our living room on Sunset Boulevard when there was a knock on the door. I opened it to find a young woman about eighteen years old on the porch with mascara and tears running down her face and hair matted from the rain. She cried, "Would you help me? Please call the police. I want to go home."

My first thought was that she was a runaway or, God forbid, a Manson Family member. I didn't let her in but said, "Of course I'll call the police."

As I went for the phone, I told Helen to take Scott and Mary Kristin into the bedroom. But when I came back, the girl was gone and in her place was a strapping young man, taller than I, also wet, and looking for the young woman.

I explained, "Yes, she was here a moment ago. Asked me to call the police, and I did."

He said, "I'd like to find her. She's tripping out on marijuana and needs help."

I felt like saying *I* needed help.

We stood there looking at each other. He was trying to get a look inside in case I had let the woman in and was protecting her or perhaps wondering whether he could come in himself. I was not going to allow that. Finally he turned and half leaped down the porch stairs and was gone before I could say anything.

Now I waited for the police. Los Angeles County is the largest county in America, and it requires both a police department and a quasi-military sheriff's department. I guess I didn't have the urgent sound to my voice. It took the sheriff's department officers twenty minutes to arrive. By that time, I explained, the young people were gone. I had no idea who they were or what they were doing so far from a shopping center where they might be expected to gather.

Was it the Manson Family? Or just a random brush with drugged-up hippies? Coincidence? I tucked it away as the latter, although it had never happened before. In fact, we had never seen runaways or druggies this far toward the end of Sunset Boulevard—Pacific Palisades.

Charles Manson was trying to cause a mistrial, and the Family members and codefendants were playing their part. But when they had run out of antics like carving swastikas in their foreheads, Charlie was able to act on opportunities.

The sequestered jury was transferred each day from the Hall of Justice to the Ambassador Hotel across town. The sheriff's deputies had covered the insides of the bus windows with white shoe polish. One juror, apparently hungry for some connection with the outside world, rubbed a hole in the shoe polish so he could see the street. It happened that it was the day the *Los Angeles Times* ran a headline in big, bold type: "Manson Guilty, Nixon Declares." The juror saw it on a newsstand on the way to the hotel. If that wasn't enough, Susan Atkins's lawyer, Daye Shinn, brought the newspaper into the courtroom and laid it on the defense counsel's table like putting cheese in front of a mouse. Manson grabbed the paper and held it up to the jury, which strangely had been seated this day before the judge came in. That was all it took to shut down the trial for the rest of the day.

Judge Holder was committed to pressing on with the trial, but he had to respond to the defense motion for a mistrial. Irving Kanarek, Manson's lawyer, said the jury was in danger of being biased by the president's statement. The judge brought each juror into the jury box and asked them under oath if seeing the headline would make it impossible to render a fair verdict. One juror said, "I think if the president declared that, it was pretty stupid of him." Another put a cap on the matter with the statement "I didn't vote for Nixon in the first place."

On another occasion, Charlie leaped onto the defense table and lunged toward the judge. Howard Brodie captured the move of Charlie in flight being tackled by a bailiff. By this time, deep into the trial, Judge Older took it as a routine matter, sitting and just staring Charlie down while he was placed back behind his table. The Family had lost the value of shock and surprise. It was just another day in the Manson court.

When the defense took over, Manson wanted to testify, and did. He told the same story he always did: "I wasn't there, and to be honest with you, I don't recall ever saying, 'Get a knife and a change of clothes and go do what Tex says.'"

The three female defendants also wanted to testify to say they took full responsibility for the killings and that Manson had nothing to do with them. Bugliosi saw Manson's hand in this. The defense attorneys did too and refused to let his clients take the stand.

Near the end of the trial, at a time when the attorneys were working on their final arguments, Leslie Van Houten's attorney, Ronald Hughes, turned up missing. It was his first trial, as he had passed the bar only a few months before. He first represented Charles Manson but then was replaced by Irving Kanarek. Hughes moved over to Leslie Van Houten, remaining a fixture at the defense table throughout the trial.

He had decided to bring along transcripts of the trial to study while on a camping trip to Sespe Hot Springs, north of Ojai, California. It was a well-known hippie destination, although it required a rather strenuous hike. While Hughes was there with two neighbors, a massive rainstorm rolled in. It scared off the neighbors, but Hughes decided to stay, perhaps with the vision of relaxing in the steaming springs while reading the transcripts of the Manson trial.

The court convened as usual on Monday, November 30, without Hughes. A search for him was launched, and when no trace was found, the judge decided to move ahead. It delayed the trial for two weeks while the judge found and appointed a new attorney for Van Houten.

They were so close to making it to the finish line that it was as if everyone, except Charlie, was holding their breath, fearing some dramatic incident that would throw the trial into more chaos.

When a week had been lost to finding another attorney, the story emerged of what the Ventura County sheriff thought happened in Sespe Hot Springs.

The rainstorm had caused flash floods that cascaded down streambeds that were ordinarily desert-dry. Hughes's body wasn't found until the following March, ironically on the very day that the four defendants received death sentences. The sheriff speculated that Hughes had been caught in the flash floods and carried down the stream until his body wedged in the rocks. It was found by two fishermen, decomposed beyond recognition and with one arm torn off. He was identified by a dentist.

The ghoulish similarity with a killing gang like the Manson Family raised the possibility among those of us at the trial that Charlie had made one last attempt to blow up his trial. Even Bugliosi said later when he published his book, *Helter Skelter*, that he harbored suspicions that Hughes had been murdered. Family member Sandra Good allegedly said that Hughes's death was the first of the family's retaliation murders. No evidence has been found of foul play in Hughes's death, which officially remains unsolved.

On January 25, 1971, all four defendants were found guilty on each of the twenty-seven separate counts against them.

Before the verdict was read, all the reporters were instructed to stay in their seats until the judge released us. I can't remember if we actually waited to be formally dismissed, but we almost immediately lunged for the doors in typical journalist style when we heard the news. We had been allowed to install telephones on a shelf just outside the courtroom doors. The world wanted to know the verdict as soon as it came down. They couldn't wait for me to make it to the *Carol Burnett* soundstage or even to a camera outside the courthouse. A phone booth—that was the cutting edge of instant news.

I reached mine before the others. As I picked up the receiver, I heard the sound of a CBS News bulletin starting to play from New York. They were waiting. I made the announcement, "This is Bill Kurtis in Los Angeles. Charles Manson and three defendants have been found guilty of murder on all counts." Be first, and be accurate. The thought that I was being heard all over the world has stayed with me all these years.

On April 19, 1971, the defendants were sentenced to death. The following year, the Supreme Court of California struck down the death penalty and automatically commuted the death penalties to life imprisonment. When I heard the news, I was hit with a strange déjà vu. Hearkening back to my time in Chicago in the wake of the Speck trial, I realized this was the second time one of my subjects had slipped past the controversial death penalty.

When the verdict was delivered, I felt as though a war was over. The single story that had consumed every working moment of months of my life had come to an end. This wasn't my first rodeo, and I knew there is always another story waiting just around the corner. But the end of the Manson trial felt different somehow. A new decade had begun. The sixties were now in the past. As time marched forward, today's news became old news and old news became history. Youthful revolution, racial strife, antiwar protests, free love. Could it be that everything that had defined my whirlwind of a career up to this point was really coming to an end? If so, what would come next?

TEN

# Earthquake

Reporting a breaking story tests a journalist in ways that other stories just can't. And not the kind of breaking news like reporting the Manson verdict. We all knew it was coming that day—the phones outside the courtroom were set up, the networks were ready, and the world was watching. It's the truly unexpected stories, those acts of God that no one could ever see coming, that are the real test. It's a race against time. The gathering of facts. Finding the truth amidst the chaos. Writing, editing, and memorizing for the spoken presentation on the fly. The technology of 1971 certainly held us back, but the basics have always been the same. Be first. Be accurate. Be good.

It was shortly after 6 a.m., February 9, 1971, in Pacific Palisades. Helen, Mary Kristin, and Scott, the newest addition to our little family, were still sleeping. I had gone to bed the night before planning to head back to the courthouse to continue my coverage of Manson's sentencing, where the prosecution was arguing for the death penalty. I was awakened by what I thought was a subway running beneath us. Then I remembered there was no subway in Los Angeles.

I got out of bed and checked through the house. All the hanging lamps were swinging, but there was no damage beyond that. It was an earthquake all right—6.5 on the intensity scale. The Palisades were on the edge of the zone, but I could tell it was likely worse elsewhere.

I called John Harris at the West Coast Bureau. He was already waking up everyone who had somehow slept through the earthquake. "I've got a crew coming for you," he told me. "You'll be heading into the Valley to find whatever you can." He meant the San Fernando Valley, which stretched from LA proper across an equally populous area filled with generally cheaper houses and apartment buildings.

We drove north through housing developments, shopping malls, and office complexes with minimal damage until we hit Sylmar on the far edge. Along the way were the unmistakable fingerprints of an earthquake. Houses without walls. Families wrapped in blankets on the front lawn. No one wanted to chance going back inside. In small shopping centers, broken water lines spurted into the air like geysers in Yellowstone and broken gas lines were on fire. It was just a matter of time before the entire center would burn to the ground. The fire departments were already overwhelmed, and the morning chill had yet to lift. People just stood and watched the fires burn.

We reached the foot of the hills denoting the Simi Valley and Sylmar. There was a sign at the bottom of the hill for the West Los Angeles Veterans Hospital with an arrow pointing up the hill.

We had yet to roll a foot of film, so I told cameraman Larry Travis to backpedal to the nearest destruction for some basic damage shots while I walked to the top of the hill to see if the Veterans Hospital had been hit.

I jumped out of the car and started half jogging up the hill, remarking on the view across the entire Valley, home to millions, shining in the sun with columns of gas fires painting traces of the earthquake that had just shaken people awake.

As I crested the hill, the sight took my breath away. The third floor of one of the hospital buildings had pancaked all the way down to the ground. I realized that men who had survived World War I and World War II had just lost their lives to an unexpected, unavoidable act of nature.

Chain saws were already filling the air with that familiar whine, chewing into the roof to reach anyone still alive. Those living and dead were being laid nearby under white sheets on the emerald-green lawn. That's a memory that will never fade. White sheets, rich green grass, a destroyed building with rescue crews climbing over it, set against a campus of other buildings. If you blocked out the destruction and bodies, it would have been a tourist poster for sunny California, land of orange groves and palm trees.

I recorded my impressions for CBS Radio, but with all the phone lines down (and satellite broadcasting still years away), I had no way to get it to the station.

I ran down the hill to our drop-off point to tell the crew what was at the top of the hill. We drove up to let Larry out with his sound man. He would win an Emmy for his footage. I looked around and was astonished to realize that we were the only news crew on the scene—almost by accident.

The network was gobbling up any coverage it could, and I had the real story. But where to hook up with a telephone line? Poles were toppled into the streets as far as I could see, so I headed back down the hill with the car and kept going until I reached the end of the main damaged area.

It was still farm country in transition to some housing development. There were dirt roads and small houses alongside plowed bean fields. I pulled into one small house where the door was ajar. I knocked, and a young woman holding a baby opened the screen door. I said, "I'm sorry to interrupt, but I'm a reporter for CBS News Radio Network, and I need to use your phone. Is it working? The Veterans Hospital has been damaged, and . . ." She nodded, and I pushed past her toward the kitchen.

"That's where the phone is," she said, pointing to the wall above the kitchen table. She went back to feeding the baby. I could tell it was a one-year-old.

I called New York. They were desperate to hear from someone on the scene rather than getting impressions of what it was like to be in an earthquake.

I twisted the plastic off the speaker end, placed alligator clips to the posts, and rolled my tape recorder. I could hardly hear it myself, but I knew it was making it through. Fifteen minutes of chain saws whirring, some excited rescue workers in tears, and a little on-scene narration to fill in the picture of how the bulk of the Veterans Hospital had disappeared from a campus where 2,800 veterans lived and from which 1,460 would soon be evacuated. There were fifty-eight deaths in the Sylmar earthquake. Forty-nine of them were at the Veterans Hospital.

In one of those moments that capture a Norman Rockwell slice of life, the sun was coming through the kitchen window, reflecting off the vinyl table where baby Scott looked at me as his mother spooned applesauce into his mouth. It was such a peaceful scene, so detached from the chaos only miles away. An open milk bottle was on the table. The California sunshine filtered through white café curtains. And a child who couldn't take his eyes off me held his mouth open for another bite.

Ironically, even though my radio material would "carry the network coverage," I did not get to do the video that afternoon. With a guilty verdict two weeks before, the Manson trial had entered the penalty phase, and Charlie was back on the stand. There weren't many people who could step in on that story. So Sandy Socolow, the executive producer of the Cronkite show, assigned the Manson story to me, and correspondents Bill Stout and Terry Drinkwater covered the earthquake. They did a great job.

# ELEVEN

# Angela Davis

I left Kansas thinking that a combination of a law degree and journalism could be a powerful foundation for "specialty" reporting on legal issues. At the time, that was little more than a pipe dream—I could have counted the number of network legal correspondents in the country on one hand. But the stars aligned, and six years after leaving home and heading for Chicago, I was assigned to my fourth high-profile case—the trial of Angela Davis.

When I was assigned to cover the trial, I had to get up to speed. The case revolved around a high-profile crime that had taken place *inside* the San Marin County Courthouse on August 7, 1970. Under normal circumstances, it would have been inexcusable for a West Coast correspondent not to have heard about one of the worst crimes that had ever occurred within the walls of a courtroom, but I had been busy that day, transfixed by Linda Kasabian's testimony in Los Angeles. My bureau chief excused my ignorance, and I started my pretrial research. Once again, the lines between legal expert and court reporter blurred.

The San Marin County Courthouse was hardly among the French Victorian buildings sprinkled throughout the nation as models for the courts of the land, with beautiful but "old" pointed towers and gabled windows. Frank Lloyd Wright had offered a new design to house a temple of the law. In his signature style, he blended architecture and environment and created a breathtaking structure spanning a ravine in San Marin County, California. It was the most spectacular courthouse in

America, perhaps the world. Actually, strike "courthouse." I thought it was the most spectacular public building in the world.

Because of the architectural beauty, I found it almost sacrilegious to think of what had happened there.

Three Black inmates were in the courtroom of Judge Harold Haley, on trial for the murder of a prison guard at California's Soledad Prison. Civil unrest had swept through California's penal system, and tensions were escalating. One of the men known as the Soledad Brothers, George Jackson, had become a noted revolutionary. He had founded the Marxist-Leninist Black Guerrilla Party, and his book *Soledad Brother: The Prison Letters of George Jackson* had become a manifesto and bestseller.

The work of the court was proceeding quietly within the pink stucco walls and circular prosecution and defense tables when suddenly seventeen-year-old Jonathan Jackson, the brother of inmate George Jackson, who was still at San Quentin, brought a satchel full of weapons into the courtroom. Jonathan Jackson gave the weapons to the three defendants, and they took hostages.

They taped a sawed-off shotgun to the neck and under the chin of Judge Haley and then bound the prosecutor, Deputy District Attorney Gary Thomas, and three female jurors with piano wire. Their mission was to use the hostages as bargaining chips to force the release of George Jackson.

The group was herded into an elevator outside the courtroom, and when the door opened on the first floor, they faced a crowd of photographers, reporters, and curious gawkers. Jonathan Jackson said to a photographer, "Go ahead and take all the pictures you like." He led the group to a rental van in the parking lot, intending to drive to a radio station to make their demands public. Another report said they were headed to the airport.

But as the van pulled away with Jonathan Jackson driving, one of the defendants fired out the window. The police fired back and may even have fired first. Eyewitnesses contradicted each other. Johnathan Jackson was killed, but not before he pulled the trigger on the shotgun that killed Judge Haley. In addition to the shotgun blast, Judge Haley was hit in the chest with a .357 Magnum shot fired either by the kidnappers or by someone else inside the van. Two of the three inmates/defendants were also killed, and one juror hostage was seriously wounded.

Defendant Ruchell Magee, who was also wounded, was sentenced to life in prison. Prosecutor Thomas, one of the hostages inside the van, took the .357 Magnum from Magee and fired it. A point of confusion is whether Thomas hit the judge and Magee, but he is credited with stopping the kidnapping. Thomas said he witnessed the judge's face being blown away before he took the gun and fired it. Magee would be incarcerated for fifty-seven years before being released in 2023. He died on October 17, 2023, eighty-one days after his release from prison.

After the shooting, it was discovered that the shotgun used to kill Judge Haley had been bought by Angela Davis a couple of days before the attack in the courtroom. She had also purchased several of the other weapons. Davis was a leader of the Communist Party USA and was involved in the civil rights movement, specifically with the Soledad Brothers and the Black Panther Party. She was romantically associated with Soledad Brother George Jackson. She disappeared after the shoot-out. A warrant was issued for her arrest for supplying the weapons used in the takeover. The FBI listed her on their Most Wanted list, the third woman to make it there. She was arrested two months later on October 13, 1970, in New York City at a Howard Johnson's Motor Lodge.

This was where my assignment picked up and my lawyerly instincts started to kick in. If ever there was a case that I thought was a total slam dunk, it was Angela Davis. I looked at the facts. She had bought the guns. She had ridden with Jonathan Jackson for several days prior to the attempted takeover. She had fled after the smoke had cleared. Guilty as charged. Open and shut.

Or so I thought.

I joined the gaggle of reporters when the trial started on February 28, 1972. After a change of venue out of San Marin County was granted, the trial was moved to San Jose in Santa Clara County, tucked at the southern end of San Francisco Bay. For the first time, I myself felt like a prisoner. For obvious reasons, extreme security precautions were put in place. Twelve-foot-high fences were erected around the courthouse, and a television system was installed so the overflow of reporters could watch the proceedings in a room adjacent to the courtroom. Metal detectors and personal searches were conducted every time someone went in or out.

CBS News was not going to cover it wall-to-wall like the Manson trial. Neither the public nor the network had the appetite for this case that they had for Manson. Part of the reason was that the case seemed so clear. And from where I was sitting, watching the proceedings on a closed-circuit feed in an annex adjacent to the courtroom, I knew the coverage I could provide would be limited anyway. We could report on the process, but we couldn't read facial expressions, subtle emotions, and everything that gave these trials the electricity that I chased. So most days, I would go through security, take my assigned seat and watch the feed for as long as I could, go back through security, write my report and shoot it outside the courthouse, and then drive the film to the CBS station in San Francisco to meet my deadline for the *CBS Evening News* with Walter Cronkite: 3:30 p.m. Pacific time for Cronkite at 6:30 p.m. Eastern. Crawling along Highway 101 from San Jose to San Franciso in bumper-to-bumper traffic, I cursed the East Coast Bureau and their comfortable deadlines. I sure missed my quick jaunt to Carol Burnett's soundstage two years before.

The most important key to Angela's defense was jury selection. That was tied to the change of venue. In San Marin County, public opinion would rather have avoided a trial altogether and favored a straight line to the gas chamber. But in Santa Clara County, there was one big advantage for the defense: the jury pool included Stanford University, surrounded by its liberal community.

The defense organized an advisory panel of psychiatrists to study the jury list and recommend potential jurors who would be most inclined to believe Angela's story. The final jury started out "on her side." Volunteers from the defense team researched every name on the voir dire list so they knew the politics, education, and background of every potential juror before they were chosen or rejected.

Defense attorney Leo Branton Jr. also used experts to advise him for the cross-examination of witnesses. It seemed innovative at the time, but it has become standard preparation for trials in addition to using mock juries to test various arguments.

Branton also took advantage of his client's strengths, recognizing that Angela Davis was no shrinking violet. Aside from her political involvement, she had completed a doctorate at Humboldt University of Berlin and was active in the feminist movement and the antiwar movement against the Vietnam War. She was an assistant professor of philosophy at UCLA, among other academic positions. Support for her innocence grew throughout the nation and world. Protests filled the streets in major European cities based on the US civil rights movement and Angela's Communist Party involvement. More than two hundred local committees worked to free her! John Lennon and Yoko Ono wrote a song, "Angela." Other celebrities kept the movement alive with fundraising concerts.

By now, California was ground zero for highly publicized trials, and I was fortunate to fit the assignment perfectly. I often thought, *Hey, if Ichabod Washburn could see me now.*

Opening arguments started with prosecutor Albert Harris. He relied on the standard outline in a criminal trial. He offered to prove that Angela Davis had a motive, to free her lover George Jackson; she had the means when she bought the shotgun used in the crime; and she had the opportunity by spending several days prior to the kidnapping with Jonathan Jackson, the initial perpetrator. Harris also used her flight after the shooting as evidence of her guilt.

In most criminal trials, we ask if the defendant is going to testify. More often than not, the answer is no because they will be subjected to cross-examination. It's a risk because jurors might think, *Well, if she's innocent, why doesn't she say so?* and want to hear from the defendant. On the other hand, cross-examination can be brutal as it pounds the big three—motive, opportunity, and means—into the jury's mind from the prosecution's perspective.

But Branton had a clever strategy. He asked the court to allow Angela to represent herself. He would share the defense table with her as cocounsel. That way, Angela could deliver the opening statement. This would give her a chance to personally declare herself innocent but not have to expose herself to cross-examination. The unique request would require accommodation from the judge, Richard Arnason. He was regarded as an extremely liberal judge, but he did not bend to the criticism of being too liberal. He granted the request.

I perceived the opening argument by Angela as an astute situational analysis by Branton. Most defendants who want to represent themselves are not professional speakers. But Branton recognized whom he had as a client. When Angela Davis stood tall and spoke boldly and directly to the jury, she declared herself a politically persecuted Black woman and laid down a challenge to prove her wrong.

Her opening statement echoed throughout the courtroom: "I, Angela Yvonne Davis, now declare publicly before the court, before the people of this country that I am innocent of all charges which have been leveled against me by the state of California. I am innocent and therefore maintain that my presence in this courtroom is unrelated to any criminal act.

"I stand before this court as a target of political frame-up which, far from pointing to my culpability, implicates the state of California as an agent of political repression."

It hit the national media like a howitzer. Suddenly the prosecution was under pressure to put up or shut up. The jury, already predisposed to fight then governor Ronald Reagan, was ready to give Davis the benefit of the doubt.

It also gave those of us in the media an extra reason to cover the trial wall-to-wall. It was Angela Davis, Black liberator, versus the white nation. I had found that people tend to follow trials if they identify with the personalities involved. *Will Angela win or lose? How will her friends and family react?* In many ways, it becomes like a football game.

The prosecution's case started with the shoot-out. Among the first witnesses was Gary Thomas, who had been permanently paralyzed in the shoot-out and needed to be rolled into court in a wheelchair. He testified that he had watched the right side of the judge's face pull slowly away from his skull when the shotgun went off. In Marin County, Thomas was a hero, and he made a very sympathetic witness.

On cross, defense attorney Branton tried to show that Thomas's recollection could have been "fogged up" by the shooting and that when Thomas had grabbed the gun from one of the kidnappers, James McClain, and fired from the back of the van, he might have hit Judge Haley. This attempt went nowhere. Thomas had actually fought off one kidnapper to grab his gun and shoot back. Branton should have passed on any cross-examination.

The task of the prosecutor seemed simple enough: What did Davis think the shotgun that she had bought prior to the shoot-out would be used for—hunting rabbits? How many shotguns did she routinely buy? Branton argued that she had bought the weapons because she had taken up target practice and feared for her safety.

There was a diary of eighteen pages in which Davis described her love for George Jackson, Jonathan Jackson's brother incarcerated in Soledad Prison. Wasn't that proof of motive to kidnap—to free her lover? But it did not include any mention that connected her to the kidnapping and shoot-out. There was no confession and no notes. Branton sold it to the jury.

The defense attorneys called twelve witnesses to support Davis's claim that she had been targeted because of her work as a communist and radical figure. That was where the jury selection proved important. The jurors were liberal thinkers ready to believe Davis's claim of being hunted because she was Black and radical and hence a political prisoner.

I remember one phrase that was used to counter the flight argument of guilt. Why had Angela Davis run away? "If you were a Black woman in America, you'd know well why she ran. Because of the history of injustice all Blacks have endured."

Angela Davis credited Branton's closing argument with winning her case. He held up a drawing of Davis bound in chains and then ripped off the page to reveal another one under it, showing her freed from the chains.

Branton said, "Pull away these chains as I have pulled away that piece of paper."

Time has given us a rare insight into the defense strategy. Fifty years after the trial on January 28, 2012, ninety-year-old Leo Branton was sitting on a couch at a holiday party in Los Angeles and commented about the trial, starting with jury selection. It was captured by someone on home video and put on the internet.

It was like examining the thoughts of the key defense attorney. Branton's admission went like this: "There were things that happened in that case that happened for the first time in American history. For example, our case was the first case that had what we call jury profiling. We had psychologists who sat in during jury selection who told us what they thought would be a good defense verdict or prosecution verdict, and this had never before happened. And after we tried it and we had volunteer psychologists who sat in . . . about three months later, John Mitchell, the US attorney general under Nixon, paid hundreds of thousands of dollars to get somebody to come in and do the same thing for him. "

Branton continued on the home video, "We were the first case to be able to call experts on eyewitness identification. Most people believe that because you have an eyewitness, you have a defendant dead to rights. But eyewitness identification is not as good as people claim it to be. A lot of people are on death row and executed because eyewitness testimony has been wrong. The reason I tell you these things is that we would not have been able to put these things before the jury except for people who went out and got statements from witnesses and who did all the brief writing that had to be done . . . people like that. They should be given great respect for what they did."

To say *the fix was in* would be unfair. Branton was using years of experience to shape Davis's defense. He didn't bribe anybody or pay anyone off. That would have been too easy. Through hard work, he got the best panel of jurors possible, and then he sold it to the jury. Was it favorable to his client? Yes. Is that against the law? No. It's being a good trial lawyer. Was it unique? Absolutely.

Judging from the technique that is now commonplace among trial firms, the use of model juries to test the weight of complex theories is universally accepted. Political surveys are constantly probing the feelings of voters, week by week, to reduce the risk of certain arguments. Television producers use focus groups of a dozen potential viewers to gauge which plots are most popular. Ad agencies want to know what ad spots are most effective.

To use the tool in a high-profile legal case was a breakthrough, indeed. Without Branton at the helm, my initial conclusion that the trial would be a slam dunk would probably have been accurate. A trial is a fragile device to find the truth, but it is the best one we have.

As for the decision not to put Angela Davis on the witness stand, author Earl Caldwell said Branton made the decision on the fly during the defense presentation of witnesses. He reasoning that he didn't need the risk of putting her under cross. It turned out he was right.

On June 4, 1972, after thirteen hours of deliberation, Angela Davis was found not guilty of murder, kidnapping, and criminal conspiracy.

After the verdict, there was a gathering, let's call it a "wrap party," across the street. The blues were playing, beer was flowing, and Davis was smiling that big, toothy grin. This was all new to me. It was the first trial I had covered where the defendant was not frog-marched away in handcuffs. So I danced with her, something I had not done with Charles Manson or Richard Speck. After months in a high-pressure situation where lives were at stake and freedom hung in the balance, I threw the neutral journalist's role to the wind for a few brief, shining moments. My reports had already been filed, so the pulsing beat of a bass guitar didn't sway my opinions.

The victory was a mixed feeling of enormous relief, which I admitted was impossible for her or me to put into words. That said, feelings were still confused. The racial and political arguments had prevailed. But what Davis had not believed could happen also came true. An all-white jury believed her story instead of the prosecution's. The American system of justice had worked for her. It was not so corrupt after all, although she was quoted as saying the only fair trial would have been none at all.

The judge, Richard Arnason, was the polar opposite of Julius Hoffman in the Chicago Seven trial. Arnason was open to letting the trial take its own course and allowing the rules of evidence to do their job. In his final comments as he dismissed the jury, he left a valuable instruction in a quotation from G. K. Chesterton:

> Our civilization has decided, and very justly decided, that determining the guilt or innocence of men is a thing too important to be trusted to trained men. If it wishes for light upon that awful matter, it asks men who know no more law than I know, but who feel the things I felt in a jury box. When it wants a library catalogued, or the solar system discovered, or any trifle of that kind, it uses up its specialists. But when it wishes anything done that is really serious, it collects twelve of the ordinary men standing about. The same thing was done, if I remember right, by the founder of Christianity.

Some might say that Leo Darnton had found a way to put a finger on Lady Justice's scales of justice. It was the perfect jury for Angela Davis.

It was my fourth "trial of the century" in six years. Maybe the phrase "trial of the century" was starting to be overplayed, but I was still proud to have covered it.

# TWELVE

# Juan Corona

I never minded being awakened by a work call. Waking up to the phone ringing sent adrenaline pumping through my veins and questions racing through my head. I was about to find out about something big that had just happened, and they wanted me to cover it.

That was the case when a 3:00 a.m. phone call woke me up in my favorite San Francisco hotel, the Miyako. "How soon can you get on the road?" John Harris asked. "I'll get Larry Mitchell rolling too."

"I'm on the road in half an hour. Where do I point the car?"

"Sacramento. Turn left and head for Yuba City, about an hour north." He paused. It was early. "At least I think."

"Whatcha got?"

"I've got twenty-five bodies buried in a peach orchard. They've arrested a guy. The sheriff is waiting at the courthouse."

I knew that ABC and NBC were also scrambling their correspondents, but those guys would be flying up from LA. Once again, I was in the right place at the right time. Okay, so I was going to be the first guy in, but how was I going to get the first story out?

This assignment became a classic example of how we had to cover the news in those days. It was a time before mobile phone service and internet access. Everything we did was hardwired analog. Get to a phone booth to call in the jury's verdict live on the air. Drive physical photographs and rolls of film to the nearest TV station—or sitcom soundstage. At every turn, we had to get creative, figure out how to be the first and the fastest in a slow-moving world. It was hard to do anywhere outside the network studio, whether we were two blocks away on the street or in a city two states away. But breaking news way out in the boonies, like in Yuba City, California, was a whole different challenge.

Yuba City is in the middle of "delta country" in California, a vast farm belt of rice paddies, almond groves, and, yes, peach groves. Pretty much any crop that a farmer had a hankerin' for could grow there.

Harvest was made possible with transient laborers who hopped freight cars into Marysville and then met with contractors who took them to the fields, including those around Yuba City. The history of Yuba City goes back to 1849, when gold was discovered nearby at Sutter's Mill and the call of gold spread around the world. These days it was "green gold" in the fields that drew a mix of men showing up for harvest and then moving on, hopping a freight to farms that were hiring.

The sun wasn't up yet when I pulled onto the lawn by the office of Sheriff Roy Whiteaker in Yuba City, California. Sure enough, the sheriff was standing there waiting for me. I was the first of a wave of reporters, cameramen, and soundmen who would descend on the scene of any story when the word "bodies" was heard. In this case, twenty-five bodies meant more crews and network correspondents than usual. I was glad to get any advantage because it would take an hour to get the film back to Sacramento for the switch to New York.

With the sheriff all to myself, I enjoyed the conversation with one of the most impressive law enforcement officers I'd met. By that, I mean he imparted information that was helpful but didn't jeopardize a fair trial.

"So, Sheriff," I said, "why have you called this meeting so early in the morning?"

It was a nice way to start, and since I didn't have to compete with the horde that would soon be there, I used a relaxed approach.

He smiled but got straight to the point. "The crime scene is on the Sullivan Ranch north of town. We got a call from the owner that he found a hole in the peach orchard that looked like a grave, freshly dug. Strange thing is, the next day it was filled in."

The sign of a good story comes in different ways. This one came in a shiver.

"And he called you? I know you don't want to prejudice a jury, but please tell me what you think you can."

That put the sheriff on my side.

"My deputies went out and dug it up. They found a fresh corpse about three feet down, mutilated, sexually assaulted, stabbed, and his head was split open with a machete."

"So how did you get to twenty-five?"

"By digging, and I don't mean research. Another farmer called in. He'd found the same thing. Fresh hole. And inside, the body of an old homeless fellow. We get a lot of them coming through, looking for jobs during harvest. This one had a name, Charles Fleming. He'd been sodomized, stabbed, and mutilated with a machete."

By now, hardly able to hold my breath, I wanted to get out to the orchard before the others, so I asked, "Sheriff, could one of your deputies take us out to the scene?"

"Well, I've got a bus standing by for the press, but they're not here yet, so I'll have someone take you out now."

If ever the early bird got the worm, this was it. I was quietly thrilled. And it was warranted. For the next three days, we managed to stay ahead of NBC, ABC, print, and local TV in a head-to-head national competition to get the story first and accurately. We had not yet even heard of satellite trucks for news gathering.

I was already thinking of how I'd get the story back to Sacramento. That's one difference between TV and print. Print reporters, including those working for the hallowed *New York Times*, could pick up a telephone and make the latest edition. We had to physically get the exposed film to a processor, usually at a television station, develop it, and then take it to an editor, who would choose the right picture frames to tell the story. After cutting them together, we'd line them up with a narration track, put it all on two projectors, called A roll and B roll, and then "switch" it on the coaxial cable to New York. All by 3:30 in the afternoon Pacific time.

Every part of that sequence was difficult by any standard, but it was the final step that caused ulcers. A local director would be assigned the job of "calling" the process. A double chain (two projectors) meant both projectors had to roll at the same time and the director, looking at my script, had to instruct the technical director to "take" one projector; at the precise moment that called for changing video, he would switch to the other projector and then back if necessary.

Tricky, huh? And nerve-racking. Remember Mortimer Adler said *luck* was necessary to be successful? This process qualified.

In those days, correspondents were their own producers. That would change as the electronic game came into the picture. Instead of risking life and limb to carry film back to Sacramento, in a few years, live satellite trucks would be able to roll into Yuba City for a live broadcast from the scene.

There was a lot I would miss without the "chase." CBS New York hired a Huey helicopter to pick up the film (and me) around noon from Yuba City and make the one-hour trip to Sacramento. We flew low over rice paddies freshly flooded with water as the sun glistened off the square ponds. As far as we could see were crops and orchards, some with fresh blossoms in white and pink. Those images and the familiar *whoop-whoop* of the rotor blades made it easy to get lost in thoughts of Asia and Vietnam.

Over two days and two attempts at "switching" our piece to New York, the local technician in the projector room made some mistakes that caused me some blood pressure spikes. But we managed to show a little patience and coax the projectionist through the moment.

I was looking forward to several more days of stories here, and I didn't want to suffer through two more mistakes from the technician in back. So I did the next best thing. I took him a nice big bottle of Johnnie Walker Black. Next day, he smiled when he saw me coming. It's called motivation cultivation.

After two days, the story had run its course unless I could add one more day. OK, Bill. Be a reporter. The question almost flashed in neon: How could twenty-five men disappear without a trace or being noticed by relatives or friends?

First, there were no relatives in the area. Most of the men were gone during harvest, and their families were used to not seeing them for months. Second, the killer had a lot to choose from—mostly men from Mexico or the barrios in the big cities.

We followed the deputies for a couple of days but ran out of story on the third day and were ready to tell the Cronkite show that we were empty. We'd told the story. We had led the show for two straight nights and were well ahead of our competition, but I was concentrating heavily.

What was I missing? Then it came to me. Where *had* the men come from? They had jumped off the freight cars, hobo-like, and slept on the street or camps in Marysville, a well-known mainline pass-through established over a long history of railroads that reached back to the gold-rush days.

I pitched it to show producer Sandy Socolow, and he said go for it. "Let me know when you're close."

It was a reach. More than once over the next couple of hours, I doubted my decision. But as we rolled down the railroad freight yards, I saw groups of men smoking, lingering, waiting for rides, work, or a drink. I thought, *Damn, I was right.*

"Stop. Let's get out of the car, and Larry, follow me into the crowd. Keep rolling. I want to use surprise to keep it looking spontaneous and not give them a chance to work up anger and kick us away."

I chose the biggest group and walked up to it, picking a man aged about fifty or sixty, bearded, hair blowing. His Farmer John overalls were worn through at the knees and elbows, and his face was furrowed by a thousand days of outside work in the fields. None of the men were happy to see us, but the conversation stopped only momentarily as they looked straight at me alongside the camera. It was as if they had something they wanted to say.

The man I had picked started, "They say those men who died didn't have any friends. Well, we're their friends! All of us. We know those men, and we care about them. They're family. We come in here for harvest every year, ride the rails, not to get killed and dumped like trash in a peach orchard. You think no one cares here? Well, we care! We're humans just like them. They deserve better."

Edward R. Murrow's *Harvest of Shame* documentary echoed in his words.

I could see eyes moisten and the crowd around him close in. They didn't mean us harm. We were the only ones who seemed to care enough to listen.

I stopped the interview after a couple more sentences because I knew it was valuable. In the business, we'd call it "gold." It was my own kind of gold rush.

"Let's get to the airport," I said to Larry Mitchell. I turned to the group. "We're going to show a lot of people tonight how you care about your friends. You've touched me. Thank you."

On the way to the chopper, I called New York. "I know you weren't expecting anything from us today, but something happened, and I think it's really good. We discovered the invisible people who pick our food and make agriculture work in this country. But no one sees them. They were the group where the killer picked up their friends. They don't feel human a lot of the time, and no one seems to care. They wanted us to know they *do* care. Very much."

Sandy recognized it right away.

"OK, we'll lead with it. You don't have long to get to the switch. Go with God."

Everything had to work. The chopper had to be waiting with rotors turning. It was. The film was in and out of the processor at KCRA, Sacramento, in record time. I knew exactly where I wanted to edit in and out, added some narration, and took it personally to the projector technician. I told him, "I need you today!"

It was 3:20 p.m. On the air in ten minutes.

Sandy called to check. "Will you be ready?"

I said yes. And took a big breath.

Under the headline that "Nothing is ever easy," I slid into the console next to the director. Wait a minute; the director had changed! It was a kid, a freaking kid. How did that happen? He rolled the B roll once and missed the cue. Rerack! Let's try it again! The second time, same mistake. The pressure was sky-high. No one said a word, not wanting to distract him for even one second.

I knew he was young, and when he said, "Let's get someone else; I can't do it," I said firmly but confidently, "Yes, you can. You're my guy. And if we don't make it with you, we don't make it."

It was a two-minute piece. The phone was open, and I could hear that Sandy was ready to pull us from the lead. I could hear the videotape machines getting ready to rewind and take us off when the kid called the last direction and a cheer went up. We were away clean.

I could hear the announcer introduction in New York: "This is the *CBS Evening News* with Walter Cronkite."

I knew they were still cueing up the videotape. If it made it, it would be just in time . . . by seconds.

"Tonight, Bill Plante in Chicago, Dan Rather in Washington, Bob Schieffer on Capitol Hill, and Bill Kurtis in Marysville, California."

Cronkite's lead-in continued as I held my breath. *Just give me a few seconds . . .* , I thought.

"The search for more bodies continued in the peach orchards along the Feather River today as authorities zeroed in on where the victims came from. Bill Kurtis found a likely place not far from Yuba City."

A one-second pause seemed like an hour until I heard the man with the famous mustache speak and realized we had made it. The videotape room had made it. The kid director had made it. The projector-room technician had made it. My camera team had made it. The chopper pilot had made it.

I was watching on a television set in master control and heard a cheer come from the studio, where a group of KCRA news producers, anchors, and studio crew was watching the Cronkite show and "their" story on the air a continent away, a product of so many working so hard, working for each other with a common goal, risking a great deal to produce a product we all believed in. That was the way it was, making television journalism in 1971. It could have been from Vietnam or Washington, but on this day, it was from a small town in California against great odds. It was history.

To put a wrap on the story, the killer was Juan Corona, a contractor who hired transient men off the streets of Marysville to harvest peaches and other crops. He turned out to be a serial killer with homosexual motives who killed his victims while their pants were down after sex and then struck them in the head with a machete, sometimes making the mark of a cross. Receipts were found in some of the victims' pockets, and many of them had been seen with Corona. A search of his home turned up a tablet with seven of the victims' names and the dates of their murders.

Corona was ultimately convicted of twenty-five murders and sentenced to as many life sentences. But in 1978, an appeal was upheld on the ground of incompetent representation. His lawyers had not considered Corona's schizophrenia and had not pled insanity. But in 1982, a court upheld the original sentences. Juan Corona died on March 4, 2019, at age eighty-five, one of the most notorious serial killers in American history.

I learned, or maybe just realized, many lessons in covering that story. I attended the early part of the trial with Howard Brodie once again as my artist. We expected a big trial, but it was slowed by pretrial motions and never picked up the intense fascination that Speck or Manson had. But that's the job. It's only every once in a while (more often if you're lucky) that you catch lightning in a bottle and get the big story that grabs the nation by the shirt and holds people's attention for days on end. Far more often, you're just part of the daily news cycle and quickly forgotten, and that's if your work even makes it to air. It's funny how everything that made the Corona story *work*—the 3:00 a.m. phone call I got while I happened to be close to Yuba City, getting the right interview from the right guy in the eleventh hour, the young kid director at the local station—was nothing we could have prepared for. And when we got everything in place to cover what we thought would be another trial of the century, the story fizzled out. But it didn't matter to me that the Corona trial was a flop. I reported the news. I told the truth. And I'd like to think I did a good job. That's why we do it.

I also realized why I loved television reporting. I was having dinner with Howard Brodie during the Corona trial one evening when we started analyzing what we did for a living and *why* we did it. I told him about the thrill I get from matching the "perfect" narrative description with the visual playing on the screen. A television writer has to consider that viewers can see it for themselves. Television writing should supplement the information coming from the picture. Imagine yourself as the viewer. You are taking in two streams of information, one visual on the screen, another by audio. Sometimes that's enough. Remember, it's called tele*vision*. So what's left for the reporter, announcer, sports play-by-play, or weatherperson watching a tornado? It's not to repeat what's happening on the screen but to add something we don't know, something that marries the visual's natural flow without interrupting the viewer's concentration. What's the best way to join audio and visual to create something more than the sum of the two parts?

It's hard work to get there, but with time and practice, it becomes second nature. It's taking a walk in the woods, hand in hand with your wife, enjoying easy conversation and natural beauty at the same time.

# THIRTEEN

# A New Kind of News

It's hard to appreciate history when you're living it. During those early years in Topeka, Chicago, and Los Angeles, I was chasing my passion and my dream. I was living in the moment, taking every day, every story, every news cycle as it came. Only when I had time to catch my breath and look back did I realize I hadn't just been chasing a dream; I had been chasing history.

There's a beautiful harmony to our life stories that only time and perspective can reveal. In hindsight, the path from my first job at KIND with Nelson Rupard to the Topeka Tornado to the 1968 DNC to Charles Manson looks like a perfectly sensical straight line, as if a higher power had drawn my path from beginning to end. The arc of one's life isn't usually clear in the moment, but every once in a while, you can catch a glimpse of it while it's happening. Such was the case when I was called out of my correspondent's role in the West Coast Bureau to come back to Chicago to help change the course of how television journalism told Chicago's story.

Chicago was a newspaper town from its inception in 1833. As many as four dailies chronicled the city's growth in a traditional manner, using words printed on a page. Broadcast news was late to the party, and for years, an assignment editor would read the papers to find out what the "real" journalists at the newspapers had chosen as the news of the day. Then we'd go film it.

In 1973, two executives from CBS News were sent to WBBM-TV to change that, in addition to raising the ratings, which translated into more profit. Bob Wussler and Van Gordon Sauter represented a different approach to local news. They were newsmen first instead of being strictly salesmen. The change in emphasis was important. Wussler was a wunderkind at the network who had produced major news specials: the race to the moon with Walter Cronkite; political conventions; Nixon's famous trip to China; and the funerals of John Kennedy, Bobby Kennedy, and Dr. Martin Luther King Jr. Sauter had made his journalistic bones in Chicago newspapers and been baptized with CBS News as the Paris bureau chief.

Their analysis was to establish the basic journalistic principles that newspapers took for granted but which had yet to be fully embraced by the television shops. Television news organizations were still applying archaic technology to the practical workings of journalism. The television reporter had to herd a three-man team of cameraman, soundman, and lighting man into position before capturing useful footage that matched the content of the "sheets." The cameramen were from a different era, the newsreels with familiar names like Movietone and News of the Day. My first encounter as a street reporter was with genuine masters of cinema who had worked their entire lives in 35-mm film, riding the tops of panel trucks big enough to carry a small studio. Their résumés listed the great Ohio flood of 1938, the wheat harvest in Kansas. They were our eyes and ears of World War II, with their films shown weekly in theaters. *The March of Time* with Westbrook Van Voorhis of the extreme deep voice and narrators Ed Herlihy, Ted Husing, and Harry von Zell became household words.

By the time I was on the street in Chicago, the 35-mm film had shrunk to 16-mm, a saving of money and size that made it easier to get quickly on the scene and back to the lab for developing. The newsreel studios along Michigan Avenue were slowly emptying. And the grand old cameramen who could estimate exposure settings without looking at the light meter were retiring.

History was changing as time rounded the corner of the sixties.

The newsreelers transferred their black-and-white world of cinema to the new generation. Shoulder-held Mitchell cameras and Cine Pros were adapted from the larger 35-mm and became kings, now changed by the demands of the street for smaller tools and faster processing.

In 1966, I had to make sure the exposed footage was transported to the lab about four blocks from the WBBM-TV studio. A processing run was about forty-five minutes through a soup of chemicals. Always desperate for speed, we would dress our motorcycle couriers in black leather jackets and blue helmets that just happened to be the uniform of the Chicago police. Finally, we got a lab within the building. A young man named Buzz Hannan made his career running the film through the machine as producers and reporters stood like dogs waiting for a butcher to finish trimming fat from a rib eye.

And yet time was still the hungry master in one final step—editing. Add forty-five minutes to the time when the celluloid strip comes out of the chemicals so the editor can slice it, glue it, or Scotch-tape it, using a variety of ways to stick the frames together to tell a story.

Then and only then is the film put into a projector and literally shone through a lens into a television camera.

That's a long way from the pencil and phone required for newspaper reporters. It may look easy, but it takes the fun out of journalism.

Wussler and Sauter wanted to break this routine. They brought with them electronic news gathering (ENG) and minicams. Now cameramen were more technicians than artists, but the picture was stunning. Gone were the fading colors of film, replaced with images so sharp it was like you were looking out the window.

The revolution was afoot. Mind you, it was not successful yet. The equipment was too big and too heavy and required large batteries, but the future was clear: ENG was here to stay. The next step was to actually transmit from the location of the story to the station, bouncing the signal off the canyon walls of buildings until it reached the receiver. New York City was maddening in this piece of the puzzle. Union crews staged their own protests.

I took a crew and the first videotape to Africa, and it was like shooting the world all over again. The grand wildlife photographers were vocal in their dislike of the new pictures, but the electronic look brought reality and immediacy to the experience of watching a lion pride feeding.

All this filled the Wussler/Sauter grab bag of innovation, most evident in a new newsroom. They moved the anchor desk into the working newsroom. The writers were clicking their electric typewriters, and producers were detailing story notes on charts on the wall. Behind the anchor desk was an assignment area where crews and reporters were dispatched at the sound of police radios. The ratcheting sound of teletype machines labeled "AP" poured words, headlines, and text into the newsroom not far from the main desk. It all contributed to the energy of the space inside a factory where a television newscast was made.

The bosses were walking revolutionaries. The news director, Van Gordon Sauter, had a personality that matched the new wave. He liked Scottish and Irish herringbone tweed vests, which gave him an avuncular look, friendly as a panda, and when you left a conversation, you'd swear he cared only about you. In his office, one was greeted by a very real parrot straight from the rainforest hanging above his desk, a sure sign that this was an eccentric person in a wild new operation. Newcomers left his office with a brain full of thoughts. Was it their imagination or a Disney mock-up for the next movie?

At one point, Chicago's Second City comedy troupe asked to use the newsroom for a skit. Bill Murray, later to rise to fame in the entertainment world, played a confused weatherman who couldn't keep his scribbling straight.

CBS had designated a Buick for the new general manager's company car. Wussler bought a Mercedes. Other staff around him were aghast at the bold defiance of company policy. Wussler answered, "I was sent here to change the image of a station running in third place. Why should I buy a third-rate company car? That's why I bought the best, because we're going to be the best."

The final touch was to gather just the right people to inhabit the new space and attack the most difficult challenge in any newsroom—the anchors. They had persuaded the wise men in New York City to allow me to return to Chicago as one of two anchors. I was the network correspondent, now worldly from my work on the streets of the world and in courtrooms. My coanchor, Walter Jacobson, was the Chicago connection who was given the assignment of writing a daily commentary or editorial analyzing the events of the day.

At first, the combination was like a forced marriage from the old world. Put two competitive, ambitious types together every day at 6:00 and 10:00, and one would expect sparks to fly. Maybe that was what the execs were hoping for. But we were smart enough to realize that our partnership was stronger together than in forced combat. In fact, we rarely if ever quarreled. And years later—decades later, really—we remained the closest of friends, having grown together in the crucible of hot klieg lights.

The result was a nine-year triumph that changed the nature of local television news. We were determining our own definition of news. We had broken the ceiling.

Adler's luck was at work. Right experiences. Right time. Right place. Right management. Innovation was rewarded. Ready for success—and success came soon enough. It wasn't long until CBS caught wind of what was going on in the Windy City. The bigwigs called Wussler and Sauter to New York to tell the rest of the company how local news should be done. Wussler would become president of CBS Sports and, in 1976, president of the CBS television network. The showman had arrived back in New York City.

In those early days of change, a group of us were squatting in Bob's large office at WBBM, and he mused that "one day we'll look back on these days as the golden days." He was right, and I'll never forget that. For all his endless ambition and flashy showmanship, the simple idea of changing local television news for the better was still golden in his heart.


In the list of ingredients in the recipe for a successful newsroom, the anchors are the couple on top of the wedding cake.

Walter and I were very different people. He was terribly committed to researching and writing a commentary of some ninety seconds. In fact, it was the primary and perhaps only thing in broadcasting that he truly treasured, and he dedicated every day and every show to making it the best possible observation of politics and life in the big city of Chicago. I learned to respect it as remarkable.

However, before and after his ninety seconds, he molded a cavalier use of broadcast skills into an interesting character, a role that became attractive to an audience and provided a contrast that made my midwestern sincerity more interesting. It was the unexpected quality he injected into a staid newscast. It might be snickering when he read the name of the planet Uranus or provoking Johnny Morris, our sports man, into singing the Chicago Bears fight song at his anchor desk. But his core value was his commentary, and it was consistently the best I've ever heard. We became the national standard for local news. He was Mr. Inside to my Mr. Outside. Most of the time, we'd see each other for the first time when we sat down at the anchor desk. As the happily joined couple, we had plenty to talk about during the commercials. After all, we were on the same mission.

I don't think the Wussler/Sauter duo had this vision in mind when they put us together, but it turned out to be a stroke of genius.

For my part, I was straighter than an FBI agent declining a bribe. My whole demeanor, honed through the "trials of the century" and correspondent work, was straight down the middle. It turned out to be the perfect pairing. Without planning, we slipped into a complementary duet with mutual respect for each other's abilities and a realization that we were stronger together than apart. I don't remember a single quarrel during our fifty years of working together, with a few gaps of employment in our careers, of course.

After enough time behind the desk, Walter and I came to realize what it really meant to be an anchor. We were invited into living rooms and rec rooms every weeknight until we were as familiar as a photograph on the wall. The viewers regarded us as members of the family. We were there for good news, like a World Series triumph, and for bad news, like death in a faraway war or a shooting close to home. But somehow, because it was us, the trusted friends delivering the news, it didn't seem as bad. Our viewers, our extended family, knew that we would be there tomorrow and things would return to normal. They saw us in our familiar setting and knew the world was still turning. It's like a lawyer building a client base with one successful case after another or a doctor establishing a practice by serving patients who recommend him or her. That's why bedside manner matters.

A journalist serves a community. But what about the dream to make the *world* your community? I managed to find a way to do both by anchoring with Walter Jacobson, who *was* Chicago, and by covering international stories connected to a global city. As the world got smaller and the global marketplace got bigger, a market like Chicago had multiple economies flowing intravenously and was connected to every part of the globe. That was what I wanted to tap into. That was where I saw news going. That was where I wanted to be. And I chased it down as fast as I could. But those stories will come later.

Okay, so 'BBM had new anchors. But all the skill and charisma in the world can't carry a news program alone. The reporters and writers, the camera crews and editors, even the person who answers the phone should "get it" and feel part of the cause. The theme that we had abandoned the slick television look for a gritty from-the-newsroom look, where real journalism was valued, was real. Executives struggle with how to communicate a mission that brings all the employees together as a team. Some are smart enough to hire the best people they can and let them do their jobs. With that formula, WBBM-TV would establish some historic benchmarks starting in 1973.

In our growth, we upset the journalistic protocols in a newspaper town. There were four newspapers when I arrived. They set the daily agenda for defining the news. Print reporters occupied the front-row seats at news conferences. Television assignment editors would read the morning paper to determine which stories to cover that day. We knew that to achieve real change, we had to start breaking our own stories and become real journalists. That meant independent research, following up feedback with our own viewers, and getting a story on the air first and fast.

The news team was the entire newsroom, absorbing what we were trying to do, united in our cause and dedicated to establishing local television journalism as the future.

Always full of surprises, Bob Wussler brought a surprise from CBS News called ENG. This was cutting-edge technology, and the network trusted us enough to give us first crack at it. In New York, the technicians' unions were resisting this move from analog to digital, fighting every step of change. "We can't get a signal. All these buildings are in the way!" they would call in to the assignment desk. But we folded it into our spirit of innovation, taking it in stride as a tool of the future that we would make work.

It would take a few years for the minicam to replace film as the primary mode of television reporting. But when the cameras were made smaller and easier to use, the product was sharper, the editing was faster, and soon ENG tools would become the standard.

On paper, it seemed like the ability to transmit live video without having to first process and edit it would immediately transform news gathering forever. This was the jet fuel that would carry us into a new age. But there were growing pains.

Chicago is famous for the Loop, the rectangular elevated train track around the downtown shopping and financial district. The noisy metallic *clack-clack* is so familiar that pedestrians hardly look up when it passes overhead. On February 4, 1977, when we were getting familiar with the new electronic gear, history rode the rails as an El train tried to make the ninety-degree turn at Lake Street and Wabash. The driver of one set of four trains was going too fast and blasted into the back of a Ravenswood train. The collision sent four cars off the elevated train; two of them fell into the street, and two were left hanging off the tracks.

It looked like a basement display of a model railroad gone awry. Eleven people were killed. More than two hundred were injured.

It happened at rush hour, 5:30 p.m. Walter was just getting off the air, and I was getting ready for the 6:00 news. The natural journalist's instinct is to head for the sound of the guns, so to speak. As we waited in the newsroom for on-scene reports—it was only seven blocks away—they didn't come. Within half an hour, we learned that our crews hadn't made it to the accident yet. So I turned the anchor desk over to Harry Porterfield and headed out the door.

It doesn't happen very often that an anchor has to bolt from the desk to do his own reporting, but in this case, it was warranted.

In only ten minutes, I arrived at the spectacle of two elevated trains hanging off the rails and two others on the ground or headed there.

When I arrived, firefighters and police were busy pulling riders out of the cars. It was that fresh. All first responders seemed to be having the same problems, climbing through the wreckage to reach the injured.

I found our truck a block from the scene. Our reporter seemed stunned at the calamity and frustrated at a problem with his new minicam. We were still at an early stage of developing the electronic substitute for film. It required a cable connection between the shoulder camera and the recording device in the truck. The new task of spooling cable on the freezing street for one block had shut down our capability of covering the story.

We didn't have a long enough cable. What the hell were we going to do? With this new tech, our analog instincts had gone out the window. And in the heat of the moment, surrounded by chaos, so had rational thought. But all it took was a deep breath and a few logical thoughts to realize that we just needed another spool. Soon enough, someone was on the way from the station with cable looped over their shoulders. The connection was made, and I helped drag the extension up to the cars dangling from the elevated tracks.

We were late, but we were there. Our competition was much closer to the scene than we were. They could practically shoot out the window of their studio, at least so I thought.

I managed to reach the open end of a train car that was hanging at an angle down to the ground. Somehow I talked my way into climbing aboard to get a point of view of the world turned upside down. Above me, lines of riders who had escaped injury were stretching along the elevated tracks to find stairs heading down.

We missed the 6:00 news, but when the pictures finally came in, we broke into regular programming. We quickly caught up with the statistics: eleven dead, more than two hundred injured, the worst El train crash in Chicago history.

It was one hell of a test of the new electronic gear. The freezing temperatures caused one difficulty, and the restriction of needing cable lines seemed to call for the old joke that it was like talking through two cans and a string.

We were one step behind the first responders. Be first. Be accurate. Be good. And work with what you've got. As far as the minicam replacing film? We were almost there.

FOURTEEN

# The Last Days of Vietnam

We were making good progress in climbing the ratings, but by April 1975, the fate of the Wussler and Sauter experiment was not yet assured. Everyone at 'BBM was working to make this new way of news work, including we anchors. "Walter's Perspective" was an original segment for a local newscast that set us apart from the usual formula of headlines, weather, and sports. As for me, I got to continue what I loved, the work of a network correspondent able to choose my stories from the headlines around the world. As long as they had a connection to Chicago, that is. By my estimation, I was the first foreign correspondent for a local television station. Newspapers across the country had been sending their correspondents after international stories for years. Robert Cromie and William Shirer traveled the world for the *Chicago Tribune*, for instance. But America was still figuring out what to do with television news—especially *local* television news. Luckily for me, Wussler and Sauter were crazy enough to let me follow my passion wherever it led. So I hopped on a plane and kept chasing history.

The Vietnam War was almost at an end. The North Vietnamese divisions were moving down Highway 1 along the coast. When they were just outside Da Nang, Bruce Dunning, CBS News correspondent, turned in one of the war's iconic reports. He and cameraman Mike Marriott were covering the airlift of civilians out of the Da Nang airport on March 29, 1975. But the orderly loading of families onto a 727 World Airways jet flown by Ed Daley was suddenly interrupted when South Vietnamese

182

soldiers rushed onto the plane, forcing themselves up the back stairs, pushing past women and children in their desperation.

People were hanging on the stairs, men piled on top of one another in the seats. Daley knew he had to go before the runway became too crowded to take off. He screamed to his crew to raise the back stairway, turned the jet onto the main runway, and pushed the throttle forward. With people hanging onto the landing gear, he pulled off the ground and headed for Saigon. Some fell off the plane on the way.

I watched Bruce's report and knew I had to get to Saigon as soon as I could. I just had to make the story relevant to Chicagoans. My local news peg was the Catholic Church in Chicago, which was taking up collections at every parish for Peter's Pence, a fund that was at the cardinal's discretion to use as he saw fit. His choice was to send it to Saigon to help the refugees flooding into the city before the North Vietnamese took over.

A trip in the last days of the Vietnam War fit our plans to inject some different coverage into the local station. It was an ambitious move for an ambitious station, and it scratched my correspondent's itch. I was overjoyed to make the trip.

Since it was a personal expense, I thought I would take my dad along. It was my gift to the general, and apparently it was a good one, since he would talk about it for the rest of his life.

I was carrying a Scoopic, a relatively new 16-mm camera that took four-minute rolls. It was made mostly for home movies, but the simple setup made it perfect for me, as I would be running a one-man-band operation. There was one caveat: every frame counted. No home movies on this trip.

As usual, the view of Vietnam from thirty-thousand feet was much different than the impression from television. The airliner dodged bulbous white clouds that highlighted the same cobalt-blue skies as back home. Hawaii came to mind, not a country torn by ten years of war. Even Tan Son Nhut airport was relatively quiet. Most of the airlines had left, anticipating the worst. A few fighter planes landed on individual trips to support South Vietnamese troops.

I caught a cab into central Saigon, where we would be staying at the Caravelle across from the Continental Palace. Both hotels were of historical significance to me. The Caravelle had served as CBS headquarters during the war and offered a delightful rooftop restaurant where you could survey the city and listen to the artillery *whumps* in the distance. They were like artfully placed sound effects in a Graham Greene novel that added texture to place and time. Over ten years, the grainy film reports had so saturated my brain that the reality was suddenly in strangely sharp focus with bright colors. World War II black-and-white newsreel footage has the same effect when it's played in living color.

Across the street, the Continental Palace hotel had an outdoor veranda that bordered on Tu Do Street. To continue the Graham Greene theme, it was where the lieutenants of the French Foreign Legion drank gin and tonics into the night before visiting local opium brothels. The location jutting almost into the street was perfect to watch the most unique parade of color and costumes imaginable. Young Vietnamese women were dressed in traditional ao dai dresses slit up the sides with long, trailing ends almost reaching the ground that seemed to form wings when they rode on the back of a motorbike.

My dad was captivated too as we plunged into traffic like dolphins in a school of colorful tropical fish.

I had an appointment with Father John McVeigh, then director of Catholic Relief Services (CRS) in Saigon.

Chicago Cardinal John Cody's Peter's Pence gave me some clout in these waning days of South Vietnam. It was a special collection among the archdiocese's flock to help a charity of the cardinal's choosing.

Father McVeigh set me up with a visit to a CRS orphanage near Tan Son Nhut and then the first orphan flight scheduled since the tragic crash of the C-5A on April 4. The giant aircraft was part of Operation Babylift, which was airlifting orphaned children out of harm's way. That first flight had 328 people on board but when it reached twenty-three thousand feet, the rear cargo door broke loose and with it control of the hydraulic systems. There wasn't an immediate crash. The crew had a few minutes to turn the aircraft and try to get back to Tan Son Nhut, but two miles from the runway, it dropped into a marsh and skidded for a thousand feet before bouncing into the air again. It made it across the Saigon River and then hit the ground a second time, where it broke into four parts. Most of us had such a sickening feeling in the stomach that we didn't listen to the rest of the story, fearing total disaster. But while the bottom compartment of the C-5A was crushed, the top section was intact when it hit the ground. There were 178 survivors out of 328 on board.

When we arrived within days of the crash, the faces still reflected the horror of what had happened. Everyone knew the inevitable was near: the North Vietnamese would soon take Saigon. But the crash with so many children on board seemed to be one final reminder that we shouldn't have been there in the first place, that even an act of kindness would end in terror and heartbreak.

Father McVeigh had arranged a visit to Go Vap Orphanage to observe the work of Catholic nuns before we put the last orphan on a C-130. These orphans at Go Vap would not be leaving Saigon.

They played in a compound some twenty feet square, about fifty of them ranging in age from three to eight. According to the mother superior, they would probably not leave the orphanage for several years because there was no one to take them out, even for a walk. She was sympathetic and very caring but pragmatic as well. She had to care for two hundred youngsters. It was up to her to make sure they were fed and clothed. There was very little time for holding one child to her breast. Better they quickly learn the ways of the compound and that if they cried, no one would come. The older children had learned by experience and exhibited a rough and aggressive manner, the product of institutional living where love is parceled out to a hundred at a time and very little trickles down when one is lonely at night.

The experience of standing in the small compound with the high-pitched chatter of three- to seven-year-olds has not left me in all these years. They held their arms straight up as they screamed incessantly. It was a cloud of deafening noise that heightened the shock of their faces yearning desperately for one simple thing—to be held. The touch of a human being. Not knowing that the basic power of a hug to communicate a human emotion of love would never come, perhaps in their whole life. That was life in the orphanage. I thought maybe the takeover by the North Vietnamese would be their salvation. This holding center was not.

There was little that we could do except pray that the coming occupiers would embrace their own children here without recrimination.


We were waiting for word that the last group of CRS orphans was leaving for the United States, but until then, having only five days in country, the reporter in me wanted to squeeze in every story I could think of. There's a story around every corner and over every drink in the wretched final hours when the fate of a country hangs in the balance. It felt like watching a wave come in from the sea, building and building, the crest rising higher until it finally tipped over itself and came crashing down.

CBS cameraman Mike Marriott had told me to go for drinks in the lobby of the Caravelle, where I'd be sure to run into the flight crews running loads of rice to Phnom Penh. "Buy 'em a drink and they'll let you ride along." That would be a ride-along in a DC-8 four-engine transport with a hold that carried fifty tons of rice. Our Caravelle conversation also included a Chicago connection who would serve as my "news peg." His name was Salty Walls from Hammond, Indiana, just outside Chicago. He had volunteered with other veteran flight crews to fly Flying Tigers airliners and keep the capital of Cambodia alive with an airlift similar to the Berlin airlift. Like Berlin, Phnom Penh was surrounded. In Phnom Penh, it was Khmer Rouge soldiers who had cut off normal supplies of food and transportation. Only the big silver birds were keeping the city alive with fifty tons of rice to a flight.

Salty was the flight engineer with a crew of other volunteers who were grabbing one last adrenaline rush under the headline of doing something good before their time was up. Maybe like my dad.

I found the Flying Tigers jet moored on the Tan Son Nhut flight line, riding the heat waves shimmering off the concrete ocean at high noon. A Vietnamese crew of cargo handlers was laboring with large wooden pallets packed tightly with sacks of rice, lifting them aboard a track of spinning rollers, then pushing them far inside the endless cargo hold. They called these DC-8s Stretch-Eights because their silver fuselages seemed to extend forever.

It took more than an hour to load the rice, an amusing fact when compared with the *un*loading time—nine minutes. The difference was motivation. The workers in Phnom Penh lost one man a day to exploding shrapnel from enemy rockets lobbed toward the airport. The longer it took to unload, the longer they were exposed.

Salty's crew seemed glad to have my company and jovially handed me a flak jacket and steel infantryman's helmet. This suddenly put everything into a combat perspective. Salty flashed a big grin as he tried to snap a protective vest over his large stomach. The vest was short by about six inches. He shrugged and said, "Things have changed since World War II."

The whine of jet rotors turning over sent the handlers scurrying out of the plane. We were underway before Salty had even closed the side hatch.

American air-traffic controllers had left Tan Son Nhut, and the result was a mess. It wasn't that their Vietnamese counterparts were that bad, but even the most experienced would have been challenged by the various kinds of aircraft making demands on the airspace. Giant C-5A air transports were followed by fully armed A-1 Skyraiders (propeller Vietnamese air force) fighters heading north to support South Vietnamese troops, which were trying to hold off the inexorable North Vietnamese advance.

Into this chaos we ventured, all eyes searching the skies for stray aircraft. Pilot Don Edwards pushed his right hand forward on the throttle, and the plane lumbered like a battleship on wheels, trying to pick up speed but having a lot of difficulty. It shook and rattled and protested with disquieting noises of metallic strain until it finally allowed its nose to lift into the air. Then, with the greatest reluctance, the rest of its aching body followed.

Green palms passed under us, then sampans on a river and the brown of harvested rice fields. We were up to stay. There were a hundred pictures to get, and I was bedazzled trying to adjust the exposure on the Scoopic from the harsh full-sun (22 f-stop) exposure of the outside light to a wide-open 1.6 f-stop inside the cockpit. I wanted to get the droplets of sweat that poured down the copilot's temple.

Salty put a hand on my shoulder and shouted above the engine, "Should be OK for a while, 'bout half an hour."

The scars of war were visible below in the miles of crater-pocked landscape that followed the Mekong River northwest of the Cambodian border. That was our reference path as well, our highway into Phnom Penh.

"Takes about as long as a flight from Chicago to Peoria, about thirty minutes!" Salty yelled. His steel helmet bounced with emphasis as he spoke, and his chest hair heaved and struggled between the zipper edges of the protective jacket. "We were told to watch for a SAM [surface-to-air missile] base up north, but we've had no trouble so far. But every trip, we keep looking."

I needed close-ups of the pilots and pictures of the terrain and the cargo hold packed with rice sacks. For audio, I set a tape recorder on a ledge behind the pilot to take in the ambient sounds of the cockpit and flight radio. I'd sync it with picture back in Chicago.

It seemed only a few minutes before Edwards was cutting power and banking to the left over the Mekong River as it sliced through the center of the capital. "That's the palace over there," he pointed, "and the race-track." He gestured with his head toward a large blown-out bridge and one of its spans lying in the water. "That last span went the other day," he said. "Sappers got it." Near the banks of the river, a freighter lay on its side, exposing its rusted iron bottom to the sun. I zoomed the lens down toward the ship and picked out frail brown people running in and out of the stern.

Edwards leaned back to tell me, "We don't want to abort this first approach. That exposes us to the ground fire on the other end of the run-way. The Khmers advanced last night, and we don't know but what they just might be near those trees." He pointed to a stand of eucalyptus and rubber trees at the far end of a strip of white pavement.

Flaps were hydraulically extended, wheels lowered. The air drag cut our forward speed until it seemed we were hanging in the air waiting for the landing strip to come to us. I peered over the pilot's shoulder and felt the heat from his perspiration. We were all wet with sweat, and my eye-piece needed constant wiping. The seconds were suspended as we waited for the familiar screech of tires on pavement. Instead, the radio spit out the news that the plane scheduled to leave before we landed hadn't been cleared yet.

"Damn," went the cry. It meant another pass. We were so close, just a few hundred feet off the runway. Full power.

We seemed so vulnerable, our huge bird turning slowly in the sky without the security of speed or altitude, awkwardly sliding into another lazy circle around the airfield, all the while exposed to ground fire. It didn't come.

Within sixty seconds, we were again dropping rapidly toward the earth, landing roughly with an impact that threatened to tear the wings off. The copilot turned around, professionally embarrassed, and said, "It may not be pretty, but we're here."

We taxied past a burned-out cargo plane that had been hit by rocket fire several days earlier, then turned toward a small corrugated iron hut barely peeking out from behind a hill of sandbags. A tall American in a purple jumpsuit stood with his hands raised, waving us in as the Cambo-dian workers rushed to unload.

"Bravest men we'll see today," Salty said, referring to the skinny young men who clambered into the aircraft like buccaneers raiding a brigantine.

Edwards added, "That's the Purple People Eater," looking at the smiling giant behind sunglasses who was holding both thumbs in the air. "He's a crazy son of a bitch, gonna get the hell blown out of him one of these days. He just keeps standing out there. There was a rocket in here just five minutes ago."

The pace was fast. Both pilots kept their hands on the controls and the engines fully powered. That was one reason our position was so dangerous. The sound of incoming rockets couldn't be heard over the high whine of the jet engines.

"Don't get off the plane unless you want to stay," they yelled at me.

"Don't worry!" I yelled back.

We were there nine minutes—not eight or ten, just nine. The plane turned away from the man in the jumpsuit even before the hatch had closed.

There was a moment's delay for a Cambodian fighter to taxi by. I could see Cambodian soldiers run behind the traffic-control hut to hunch under the protection of the sandbags.

Then, when we were only a hundred yards from the main runway, Salty shouted, "Rocket to the left!"

A plume of dirt still hung in the air as my camera rolled. The rocket had landed only thirty yards away, eerily without sound.

"That's what they look like," Salty said. "First time under fire?"

I nodded. No time for a longer answer. We slipped onto the main strip and picked up speed with the lightness of a Piper Cub. The absence of the fifty-ton payload gave the craft new life, and it lunged forward like a stallion anxious to get back to the barn. We cleared the runway within seconds and banked to the right to avoid the run over dangerous territory, reaching for altitude to escape ground fire. I knew we were safe when the pilots loosened their jackets with a holler of relief.

There's an exhilaration in cheating the devil, a cockiness that sets in with false assurance. But the flight was not yet over.

During the thirty-minute trip back, I relaxed, taking casual shots needed to complete the story: activity within the cockpit, the relief shown in the easy smiles and conversation as the three men lapsed into stories of past close calls. Before I knew it, the time had almost slipped by and I still needed a picture of the empty cargo area, an "after" shot to illustrate the return. So I unhooked my seat belt and moved through the cabin door into the empty hold. A cargo net stretched between ceiling and floor as a safety precaution against a loose load sliding toward the cockpit. I rested my camera in it for stability while I rolled the Scoopic.

What I could not see ahead was the chaos of the Tan Son Nhut air traffic. It was like an air show where a pilot had to pick the best path through a crowded sky while screams from a strange language filled his earphones.

Suddenly we were seconds away from a near midair collision with another jet beginning its rice run to Phnom Penh. The pilots heard no warning on the radio; their first signal of anything wrong was the sight of a huge Stretch-Eight looming in front of them. Reacting swiftly, they plunged into a drastic dive.

Still in the back, I was lifted into the air, suspended in a weightless state. I had no idea of what was happening. But I grabbed the cargo net and pulled myself down. Images flashed through my mind of astronauts moving weightlessly in their space labs. There were other images, too, of being splashed off the plane's bulkhead.

As I gathered my senses enough to crawl back into the cockpit, it was obvious that the crew was not thinking about *me*. Salty's face was splotched with red, the copilot was cussing wildly, and Edwards was saying nothing. It was still quiet as we landed and the jet engines whirred to a stop. Probably five minutes passed before the pilot broke the silence by apologizing for the sudden dive.

"It kinda gets crowded up there sometimes," he said.

Perhaps later, at the bar of the Caravelle Hotel, the men would let the conversation drift across a few beers to this story, and it would be embellished over years of retelling. And sometime, during their elaboration of that moment, one of Salty's crew just might wonder what happened to that crazy journalist caught in the empty cargo hold of their Stretch-Eight.

Two days into my five-day trip, and so far, I had two good stories—one full of adventure, the other dripping with emotion. I was waiting for a call from Father McVeigh, who had promised to set up the final orphan babylift with a surprise passenger—a six-month-old baby headed for his or her new home in South Bend, Indiana. It wasn't exactly a last-minute rescue of a random child given up by a scared mother, but it was the story I was given.

A note from Father McVeigh was waiting for me at the Caravelle. The first flight since the tragic crash would be leaving the next day. It would also be the last orphan lift before the North Vietnamese entered the city. Although I didn't know it at the time, this story would become so much more than I ever could have imagined.

We started at a halfway house near Tan Son Nhut airport. Nuns were placing babies, probably four to six months in age, in cardboard boxes, the kind you'd find in a grocery store with the brand of Petergen nutrition sweetened condensed milk. I guessed at about thirty babies, all fitted in Dr. Denton full-body pajamas. Some boxes had two babies, a few just one.

The nun explained that this was not an official babylift. These babies had adoptive parents waiting in the States. President Ford's babylift was looser, a come one, come all project. The CRS had vetted and cleared these adoptees with the Vietnamese government.

The nuns didn't want to leave the babies very long in the steamy building. Yes, it was hot, Saigon hot, in April. At a signal, a little army of nuns each lifted a box and marched toward the front door, outside which a bus was waiting in the street. They were careful with the precious cargo. A smiling Vietnamese officer ushered the group onto the bus, and I joined them. I was standing at the front door as the bus inched along the serpentine dirt street between airport buildings and then directly out onto the tarmac to a waiting C-130. This old veteran cargo plane would get the babies safely to Clark Air Force Base in the Philippines before they changed to a bigger jetliner for a direct flight to Chicago.

I was following one particular box in which a pink-suited baby named Phan Thi My Hoa was reclining with her foot resting casually on the edge. It would be a clue to her life starting outside the nation at war in a quiet suburb of South Bend, Indiana. I contacted my assignment desk at WBBM-TV, Chicago, to schedule a crew to film the arrival.

At O'Hare International Airport, the crew quickly found the soon-to-be parents and stood with them as a nurse carried the tiny baby in the pink pajamas down the plane's exit bridge. There was no band playing, no confetti or welcome signs. Just a family waiting for their new daughter. Their smiles provided a glow that was all the welcome needed.

Phan Thi My Hoa would become Pamela Jean Harris, a remarkable little girl who possessed more energy than a dozen other babies. There wasn't an honor class or achievement that she didn't churn through with colors flying. She was small with an olive complexion and beautiful Vietnamese features, which didn't seem to faze her until one day when friends mentioned that she didn't look like them. It planted a seed, and so began the adoptee's quest to find out who she was and where she had come from.

She had been told about her journey on the last babylift from Saigon and the reporter who was there when she was carried onto the plane. In a strange way, I knew her origin story even though I'd spent only half a day with her in the steamy heat of South Vietnam. I would occasionally invite her to sing "The Star-Spangled Banner" to open veterans' meetings in Chicago. It was stunning to introduce her as a living Miss Saigon (from the stage musical) and see the tiny, elfin Vietnamese figure materialize as an American, a confirmation for those who had fought in "country" that we had done some good. *Look at what we saved* was the thought.

Pamela's singing talent was considerable and might have led her to Broadway if she hadn't made a few different choices. Perhaps fueled by her excessive energy, Pamela Jean sowed some wild oats. She exchanged the national anthem for the blues and headed for California with a blues band and husband.

Everyone who follows the show business dream eventually has to face the reality that is having to make a living while pursuing your craft. Luck plays a bigger role on this path than on most. It seems that every time you are ready to break out, someone else comes along with either more talent or a more marketable gimmick.

Things happen. Life happens. Pamela had the advantage of intellect in case things didn't work out and decided to attend night school on the side to become a lawyer in Long Beach. I lost track of her for the next few years until I got a call wondering if I could help her find her Vietnamese parents. I said, "In VIETNAM?"

It wasn't that outrageous. Veterans had been going back for years and found they were welcomed not as oppressors but as close friends returning from a trip. Pamela explained that there was a hole in her memory that she now obsessed about.

"It's the adoptee's curse," I said. "You have a wonderful family who took you in before you were off the bottle. Has anything changed?"

"No, not at all," she said. "But who am I? And why did my parents give me away?"

There it was, the eternal question.

It was a great story, but finding her biological parents in Vietnam would be about as likely as the US sending troops back in.

She agreed but was pleased that I said we'd try, and she could go back with our crew if things worked out. It was more a hope than a promise. I knew I'd probably never have to keep it. I mean, really.

I needed help and asked one of the great producers at Kurtis Productions, Sharon Barrett, if she'd like to give it a go. If luck prevailed, the trip back would be terrific. I could give Pamela a full narration of what had happened from her birth in Saigon to being born again in America.

Sharon said yes, she was *in*, before she thought about it. She might also have thought I had more information than I did. Basically, I had a color photograph and a four-minute piece for a television newscast.

From that, we'd have to locate the CRS workers who had been standing around the boxes with babies, waiting to carry them to the bus and then to the C-123. It had been thirty-two years.

I remembered Father John McVeigh, who had been in charge of CRS in Saigon in those desperate few weeks before North Vietnamese soldiers entered the city. He had been thrilled to see someone from the States, and especially someone interested in his final task of shipping orphans out on the last orphan lift. I'd had dinner with him the night before I went to Tan Son Nhut to accompany the babies. Almost forty years later, I received a phone call from Father McVeigh as he was passing through O'Hare Airport, but I was out of the office. It was too late to reach him. He died in 2016. That contact would have been too easy.

Meanwhile, Sharon was pursuing a more traditional path using a journalist's well-worn tool: the telephone. She found a Sister Susan McDonald who had been a nurse at the Good Shepherd Orphanage in Saigon in the 1970s. On April 26, 1975, she had boarded the last babylift plane with thirteen other caretakers and two hundred children, among them a six-month-old baby girl dressed in pink.

The puzzle was coming together. While the years had made complete accuracy difficult and obscured the faces I had passed in the strain of the final hours, Sister Susan McDonald, sixty-one, was a breakthrough. She was still committed to the babies she had cared for all those years ago, and she started making calls to old contacts in Vietnam.

Sister McDonald blitzed the country (the new Vietnam) with advertisements in newspapers and television explaining that we were hoping to find the family of a baby girl who had been on the last orphan lift out of Saigon in the spring of 1975.

One of the seductive thrills of journalism is "chasing the lead." Sister Susan called to tell us that a CRS worker in the hill town of Da Lat, a favorite French getaway to escape the steamy heat of Saigon, had brought a baby to Sister Susan's orphanage.

It gave Sister Susan hope that the ads were paying off. But that works two ways. The Vietnamese government was sensitive to anything that brought back memories of the war and made it clear that they didn't like the daily reminder of the ads. Sister Susan said we had to tread lightly.

It was good news, but it brought us face-to-face with a delicate question that could mean the end of our quest. I call it "the plateau." It seems that in every story, you reach a point where you're at a dead end—story over, box canyon. The question before us was what if we did find someone who claimed to be the mother or father? Wouldn't there be hundreds or thousands in Vietnam living in poverty who would claim to be Pamela's folks? We might be stuck.

The modern answer to that question and one that we instantly thought of from our *Cold Case Files* series was—DNA. That certainly would settle any question.

But it meant that we'd have to ask the person who answered the ad if they would provide a saliva sample so we could analyze it. Then, we would have to compare it with a sample from Pamela Jean. And if we were going to use it in the documentary, we'd have to shoot it too.

But first we needed a family. Fortunately, that didn't take long. Sister Susan called to say that a family still living in Da Lat had answered an ad and claimed to be Phan Thi My Hoa's family, and they had a birth certificate to prove it.

That was incredible, if true. The family agreed to a DNA swab, and so did Pamela Jean. We taped her swabbing her mouth and putting the cotton-tipped stick into an envelope. In Vietnam, we hired Red Bridge

TV & Film Production Service to do the same with the family that had answered the ad. They mailed the swab to us.

Sharon put in a call to Cellmark, a leader in genetic testing, to schedule a DNA test, which they agreed to do.

The only hiccup was with the Vietnamese family. They produced a contract, obviously engineered by the Vietnamese government, saying the purpose of the filming would be to help an orphan find out more about the country that still held a warm place in her heart. The story we told would not malign the Vietnamese government in any way. And what we filmed would not be used for illegal and/or sexual purposes. We had come this far, and frankly, that was our intention anyway, so we agreed to sign.

Now it was a matter of waiting for the results of the DNA matching.

In the gap, Sharon talked with Pamela Jean at least once a week. Even not knowing if the match was positive, Pamela was having second thoughts about how her search would be taken by the Harrises, the only family she'd ever known and to whom she was still committed. They had encouraged it in the beginning, which might have been expected given their kindness and compassion.

The Vietnamese family was still living in Da Lat, but the mother had died several years earlier. Before we received the DNA results, Pamela's father told the story of why Phan Thi My Hoa had been given up for adoption. During the war, Pamela's mother had been with a Vietcong lieutenant and become pregnant. She didn't want to bring shame on her family by taking the baby home. Because she was Catholic, adoption through CRS was an option.

The mother had several other children in Da Lat with children of their own. They knew the story and were anxious to find a new sister.

Months passed until Orchid Cellmark finally sent word to Pamela, who passed the final score to Sharon. Remarkably, it was a 97 percent match. Bingo! The needle in a haystack had been found!

Now, Pamela Jean had to make a choice. Did she still feel deeply enough about finding her biological family to make the trip to Vietnam?

In a telephone interview, she confessed that she had changed her mind the closer her question came to being answered.

She had returned to Indiana, where she practices law and, I hope, reflects on how lucky she was to be scooped up at random out of the jaws of war, one of millions of stories from Vietnam, but one that ultimately had a happy ending.

But it didn't make the decision any easier. She thought she was too immature to meet her blood relatives. She didn't know them. She didn't know Vietnam. What she knew was a family of four who lived in a small town in Indiana with parents who hung their handmade ornaments on a Christmas tree every December, went to every one of her recitals, and always welcomed her home. "My life," she told Sharon, "has been lived here."

I didn't try to talk her into going. In the years after the babylift, I had stayed in touch with the Harrises. We had become friends. I had invited Pamela to several singing appearances in Chicago, visited the Harrises over the holidays, and followed Pamela's career search to Los Angeles. Of all the calls I made on a regular basis, and there were few, there was always one to check in on Pamela Jean Harris. When I last heard from her, she had chosen to stay and honor the family that took her in and loved her.

The Vietnam War, and everything left in its destructive wake, has drawn me back for many career-defining, life-changing stories. But that baby on the last lift out has always had an especially strong hold on me.

# FIFTEEN

# The Phone Call

A journalist's life is spent chasing history; getting to the news of the day when it happens, where it happens; and telling people why it's important. This chase leaves little time for a family life. That's why the career path of the network correspondent is littered with heartbreak, divorce, and broken families. The way that I broke that cycle was to become an anchor. I wasn't a transient correspondent spending two-thirds of the year on the road. I anchored the evening news at WBBM-TV, and I anchored my family to Chicago. They provided love, support, and stability and at times were the only thing keeping me tethered, keeping me from being completely lost in the whirlwind.

In local broadcasting, if you're good at your job, the longer you are in the market often translates to the station seeing more success in the ratings. Better ratings and more viewers mean advertising dollars for the station and stability for the anchor.

But even the most well-adjusted anchorman still misses weeknights around the dinner table. And because I could never shake my correspondent's instincts, I traveled far more than the common anchor. So when I returned home from Vietnam in May 1975, I needed to be with my family. We all needed a break from the news cycle.

I wanted to see the Rockies again, so I tucked Helen, Mary Kristin, and Scott into a car for a classic camping trip. I had in mind spending nights in a tent by a rushing mountain stream warmed by a fire while looking up at the stars.

I chose Yankee Boy Basin in Colorado, at 10,800 feet known as the Switzerland of America. Late spring was a time of wildflowers and roaring waterfalls. Perfect.

I found a campsite beside a stream full of snowmelt in a bowl surrounded by snow-capped peaks. It was late by the time I got the tent up. Helen was not keen on spending the night outside, so I and the two kids stretched out on air mattresses and sleeping bags while she stayed in the car.

As we often hear, darkness fell, and with it came a transformation of the mind that turned everything outside the tent flaps into a sinister world full of threatening sounds, each one signaling monsters on the prowl for a meal.

What I didn't know was that the sinister world was inside the car.

Near morning, I left the sleeping kids and knocked on the driver's-side window. Helen was awake. I climbed in behind the wheel to check on her night compared with ours, ready to roll out an exciting tale. But her face, even in the dark, looked concerned.

She said, "I was doing a self-examination during the night on my left breast, and I found a lump."

I wasn't ready for something like that. A veil of shock seemed to fall over me like a blanket, draining breath from my lungs and color from my face. It pinched my vocal cords into thin reeds as I tried to maintain some composure for a question, hoping for an easy explanation.

"How big is it?"

"I don't know how to measure it, but it seems big, like a cherry pit."

"That is big. Did you notice it before?"

"No. I just had a mammogram six months ago that was all clear. Don't know how they could have missed it. Maybe it means it's benign."

"Does it hurt?

"No, not at all."

It was the weekend, and we were scheduled to be home in Oak Park, Illinois, on Monday.

"First thing Monday, let's go see the doctor. Frankly, I'm always hearing about benign growths or cysts. I'll bet that's what it is. But we'd better start back now."

And so it began, without a lot of drama, only a heart-stopping realization that Helen had entered a sorority of women whose lives change suddenly with a single touch. The sorority is big: nearly 300,000 women a year are diagnosed with metastatic breast cancer. Even fifty years after Helen's discovery of her cherry-pit-sized lump, more than forty-two thousand women will die from breast cancer every year.

That's enough to cut short a camping trip.

The breast-cancer journey has been traveled many times. Helen's doctors were caring, sensitive, and well rehearsed in the sequence of steps on the journey that every patient or potential patient faces.

First is to find out if the lump is really cancerous. As good as doctors may be, as experienced and highly trained, they can be sure it's cancer only if they take a biopsy. That requires a small incision in the breast to retrieve a piece of tissue from the lump, also small, that can be further examined by a pathologist. While the patient is still under anesthesia, the tissue is sent to the on-site pathologist who will examine it and render a judgment on whether it's cancerous.

At this first step, Helen and I were babies at the mercy of our doctors. From the first reveal in the Colorado woods to the end of the journey, our emotions were so inflamed that logical thinking was impossible. Choices were patiently explained, but we always took the doctor's advice. It was Russian roulette with a human being.

The biopsy was scheduled to be done in a hospital under the care of two surgeons. They explained that it was routine; however, if the biopsy showed that the lump was cancerous, they would like permission to remove the breast. No need to panic, but speed was a concern. And she would be prepped and ready, under anesthesia, so why wait? Helen and I agreed, never thinking it would be anything but a cyst.

Helen had told her mother, Frances, about the biopsy operation late, not wanting to put the family through days of worrying while waiting for the outcome. The postoperation phone call to Frances would be left to me.

There are a few moments that remain in the memory, seared into the brain like cattle brands that never go away.

It was supposed to be short: go in, look around, and then close. The doctor told me it would take about half an hour. But after the first hour in the waiting room, I sensed that it was more than just a quick look around.

I went out into the hall, shiny from daily overnight scrub-downs. The hospital smell hit me, clean but antiseptic. I thought, *What do I expect, roses?* It was strangely empty, this suburban hospital where Helen's doctors practiced. Had I made a mistake in choosing them? One was a friend of a friend, highly recommended. But what did I know? Wild thoughts entered my mind. Come to think about it, what do *they* know? There's no cure. Treatment is to cut, poison, and burn—surgery, chemo, and radiation. To me, that suddenly said, *We don't know what the hell to do. We'll go in and hope for the best.*

Doctors, nurses, dressed appropriately in white uniforms to say "Trust me" in a nonverbal way. Maybe they're just human beings like me, playing a dress-up game to make the families feel better.

An hour and a half passed, and the worst thoughts came to the surface. *It's got to be bad. It doesn't take this long to get a piece of tissue.*

At the two-hour mark, two figures in surgical gowns appeared through doors at the end of the hall—a long hall, a long wait. When they got close enough, I could see their faces. Somber. One of them couldn't look at me, almost ashamed that he had given me any hope at all.

"We have some bad news. The lump was cancerous. We tried to get all the cancer cells, but they had already reached the lymph nodes under the arm. That means it's fast growing. The pathologist also tried to be extra careful and took time to make sure he was right."

The other doctor, the friend, said, "I'm very, very sorry, Bill, to bring such bad news. We recommend an immediate protocol of chemotherapy. There are promising new drugs that give us new hope. It just means we're into stage two."

"Can I see her?"

"She's recovering right now. You can go in in about an hour."

Slowly, my voice scratching, I said, "Well, you have a difficult job, and this is the worst part, having to bring such bad news. I appreciate your efforts and concern. I'll make an appointment in a day or so, and let's start."

They turned and headed back down the hallway as I watched. Cloth surgery booties muffled their steps, which seemed to fade into the tiles that lined the passage. It was theatrical, a stage exit, and I was left alone with the phone call.

It was a pay phone in a black box hanging inside a glass enclosure with folding doors for privacy. Standard. As I pulled the doors back and sat down, I waited, afraid to make the call. What did I say? What could I say? *Your daughter has breast cancer?* Or *I'm sorry to say things didn't work out as we had hoped. The news is the worst that we feared?* I thought, *There is no good way to say it. Just do it. Now.*

I didn't have change, so I called collect. Frances answered, accepting the call with an anxious tone.

I said, "Well, I'm sorry to have bad news. The lump was cancerous."

Frances had no answer. My hand was shaking, and my voice was caught in my throat. Two people separated by a black box of wires that enabled one of the most important calls of their life. The pay phone came to represent death and misery and years of depressing news as we worked toward an eventual end that we could not avoid.

No need to linger on several years of hopelessness, waking up on a sunny morning to a new day until the reality of living with a terminal disease catches up with you. The children, Mary Kristin nearing the age of ten and Scott close to six, knew Mommy was sick but not how serious it was.

The time flew and dragged at the same time. Everything had been flipped upside down. Going to work had become the stabilizing force, while everything outside the studio was caught in a violent, chaotic storm. Each chemo session held reason for hope when there were signs of a remission and then a crashing repetition of "It's back and growing again."

Helen Marie Scott was a small-town girl from Independence, Kansas. Her father was a union carpenter who left his fingerprints on many a house in the midwestern Kansas town. It was idyllic in many ways, a safe place to rear kids, with good schools to launch them anywhere they wanted to go. The universities and colleges of Kansas were world-class.

Helen was a cheerleader. I was a quarterback on a remarkably successful football team. She was a homecoming queen and loved acting in school plays, as did I. She was on the honor roll both in high school and when she enrolled at Pittsburg State in Pittsburg, Kansas.

We were "steadies" in high school and maintained a relationship in college despite the two-hour distance between Pittsburg and the University of Kansas in Lawrence.

Our two children were her focus during thirteen years of marriage. During our time in Los Angeles, I wondered if she would be happier back in a smaller town like Independence (population ten thousand) instead of moving cross-country as job slots opened up. That option was being discussed when I was on the verge of going to the bureau office in Saigon.

When Helen contracted breast cancer, we were living in Oak Park, a suburb just outside the Chicago city limits, birthplace of Ernest Hemingway, home of Edgar Rice Burroughs of Tarzan fame and Frank Lloyd Wright, who had used the little suburb as his primary "gallery" of homes in his formative years. Among the arching elm trees was a combination of culture and comfort that appealed to Helen until her world turned dark.

One image has stayed with me. Each visit for chemo required us, Helen and me, to sit in the oncology department's waiting area. Lined up on either side of a small room were patients who had come for their shot of chemicals, a vial full of poison and hope, a last chance on the inevitable slide of a disease with only one outcome. The forced smiles revealed a depth of concern, worry, and searching... for understanding. And always there was a hope that maybe *they* would be different, the one in a million for whom the chemicals would magically work. The miracle.

Factored into our visits to Chicago's Rush Presbyterian Hospital was a parallel course to stay afloat in the highly competitive world of local television. The work was actually a godsend to me, a break from the perpetual sadness.

Helen was supportive of my desire to travel abroad and arranged for family members to be with her when I was away. On one such trip, she planned to visit her sister in Council Bluffs, Iowa. I would travel to Africa for a series of reports.

The early chemo reports were positive. The treatment was stopping the growth and even reducing the tumor. But within months, the mood changed. The cancer was growing again—fast. She was young at thirty-seven, but instead of having a healthy body able to fight the horror inside her, her system was fueling this type of cancer more rapidly than normal. The cancer began to show up elsewhere in her body, and even melanoma appeared.

I was in Africa when I got a call to come home quickly: "Helen's gone into a coma."

It was a long trip from Nairobi to Chicago and then to Omaha, Nebraska. Helen had been hospitalized at the Creighton University Medical Center. Scott had been with her at her sister's home in Council Bluffs, and I made arrangements for him to get to Independence and the grandparents.

Here's another tip. The chaos of the fight is like fighting a war, with good news on some fronts, defeats on others. The grandparents were life-savers and bounced the kids back and forth between my parents and Helen's. Both couples lived in Independence. Neighbors brought meals over when Helen was convalescing. We tried to keep Mary Kristin in school as long as we could. Anything to stay normal.

One mistake we made was to keep the children in the dark. I guess we thought they couldn't understand that their mother could die or that they were too young to process it. We vastly underestimated their intelligence. They deserved to be informed along with the rest of us, to be treated like part of the family working toward recovery. Instead they were left with the image of a mother in bed all the time; losing her hair; unable to dress them, feed them, comfort them. Relatives were taking her place, making decisions that broke the normal "chain of command" within a family. Trust was broken, which left them wondering what would happen to them. Worst of all, they had to guess about their mother's illness.

Later in life, Mary Kristin told me, "We knew all along."

And then there was the change in personality. Chemotherapy alters one's being. Helen was struggling to stay normal under the chemicals designed to kill the uncontrolled growth within her body and reduce her pain at the same time. The quiet soul who lived a life that was outwardly happy and caring, who kept her problems private to protect others, was drowning in the soup of medication, the only answer her doctors had for possible recovery.

For these reasons, some people choose to avoid overmedication. They change their diet to healthier food and try to maintain a positive attitude, hoping the shock to the system will suppress the foreign invaders in their cells.

Helen's journey took two years, and before convalescence during a short remission, some friends asked her to join them for a trip to Great Britain. She was searching for answers about both her health and her spiritual being. She'd heard about a group called White Eagle that some had spoken highly of as a support group with answers to cancer victims' questions.

But when Helen got to London, White Eagle turned out to be nothing of the kind. It was an alternative religion. Helen came home to the comforting environment of her Christian roots. She was disappointed, but the change of environment had been good for her.

I found her sleeping in her hospital bed. She woke happy to see me, asked about Mary Kristin and Scott, but asked not to talk about treatment and chemo and pain. The time had come to think of other things, pretty things, pleasant things.

Over the next week, I read to her, which she enjoyed. She would stay awake as long as she could and then close her eyes.

Once she woke up from her drifting consciousness to whisper to me, "I'm dying."

I said, "I know. Don't worry about the kids. Everyone has been great. It will all work out."

And then, while I was holding her hand, she passed away in her sleep. The hospital staff seemed to know to the minute when life would end. They stepped in and led me to a room for some privacy. On the way, I saw a pay phone in the hall and remembered I had a call to make—to her mother.

# SIXTEEN

# The Massacre

For all the women who will die each year from breast cancer, the impact will be measured by the pattern of a pebble thrown into a pond. It touches children the most because they haven't yet developed a way to understand the natural cycle of life and death. Or at least that's what we think. Sometimes children figure it out better than we do. Relatives, coworkers, schoolmates, distant relations, random friends. We observe the loss and honor the life with formal funerals in churches, memorials in great cathedrals, after which the congregants go on with their lives with only the memory of what was and what might have been. Such is the way death is observed in Western civilization.

For me, life changed dramatically. One set of relatives offered to take the children and raise them in a more civilized lifestyle than in the scary wilds of a metropolis like Chicago. When I told Mary Kristin and Scott that I was keeping them with me, they actually cheered, saying, "We were afraid we were going to be orphans."

It would be a new life for everyone.

One of the few things that stayed consistent during those difficult months and years of finding a new normal was my television work.

I kept working to provide for the kids and to keep myself sane. It was hard trying to rebuild our home base while also pursuing a demanding career. Thankfully, I had plenty of help from grandparents and close friends.

I would also continue my travels for the station, and my next trip was to Africa, where we'd shoot a series of stories using electronic video. Our early access to digital technology opened up new ways of capturing life in Africa that few news reports or nature documentaries had. It would be the only way I could clear the tears and move forward. I would again take my father, this time for support. Little did I expect to find a remarkable lesson in how another culture deals with loss, and has for thousands of years. As a journalist, I try to follow the facts before making conclusions, but the events that would appear in front of me seemed like a spiritual epiphany.

This was my first trip after Saigon had been taken. We had five days in Kenya, and the first four were charming and magical. Africa is the mother of us all. As soon as your feet hit the ground, you feel an ancient pull toward the land as if the umbilical cord is still attached. The human culture, the great animal kingdom, the transfixing beauty of Mount Kilimanjaro. There's something deeply, viscerally human about being there.

But I wasn't there for majesty. I was there to find a story, and it was looking like I'd be heading home empty-handed. My Vietnam reports had been a great success, but a failure in Kenya could mean the end of my dream to make WBBM-TV the first local station to have a foreign correspondent on staff.

Moody Bible Institute was headquartered in Chicago and trained missionary pilots to ferry supplies to various missions throughout Kenya. It was my last hope for a story with roots in Chicago.

On the last day, we were flying north from Nairobi, following the Great Rift Valley to a drought-stricken area near the northern border of Kenya where two missionary doctors were tending to villagers in the barren, arid hills. We were to meet them at a particular tree that "you can't miss." The people gathered there in the shade to wait for the doctor.

Arnie Newman of the African Inland Mission was our Cessna pilot, who had been trained in Chicago at the Moody Bible Institute. It was a different view of Africa. Below us were vast game preserves that spread raw and untouched between quilted swatches of tea and coffee plantations. Herds of elephants plodded slowly along, in the words of Isak Dinesen, "as if they had an appointment at the end of the world."

Beyond the jagged peaks of Mount Kenya, the land looked prehistoric as steaming geysers puffed from seemingly fresh beds of lava spawning rivers of fluoride that cascaded down the sides of the valley.

We were using one of the new electronic cameras, the same ones CBS used at political conventions. I think it was the first time to use them in East Africa, a new spin on the traditional National Geographic films.

My cameraman, Peter Bertolini, was videotaping the escarpment below while Chuck Meyer watched the controls of the large, early-design ENG camera that hangs over the shoulder. I pulled the microphone up front so Arnie could describe the terrain below.

"There are still bandits in those hills and various tribes who come out of the mountains to raid other villages," he said.

Suddenly he was interrupted by a squawk of the plane's radio, the timing so uncanny that a more religious man would certainly have called it "the finger of God." The voice broke with hysteria.

"Arnie, is that you?"

"Roger. Affirmative. Go ahead."

"We've had quite a time down here at the Finnish mission. A Pokot raiding party came through about an hour ago and massacred the Turkanas. We've got thirty or forty dead, more wounded . . . mostly women and children. Can you give us some help with your plane—take some of them to Kapedo and that hospital up there?"

There was no need to answer. The Cessna tilted into a slow downward spiral, passing rough lava formations on one side of a river swollen brown and ugly by spring rains. A village soon passed beneath us, its thatched-roofed huts looking like giant beehives against the rocky soil. Bodies littered the ground between the huts.

"That's the mission!" Arnie pointed to a cinder-block building about a quarter of a mile from the village. Most of the bodies seemed to be strewn across the dirt just off the building's back porch.

The plane landed hard on the crushed volcanic rock that covered the tiny airstrip. Arnie wheeled sharply toward a car pulling to a dusty halt.

"Don't have room for all of you," the driver yelled as he swung open the door, "but I'll make two trips. There's no time to lose. We've got some bad cases."

We heard the mission before we saw it. There was a strange buzzing noise, like the sound of a big crowd in the distance. As the car pulled to a stop, the buzzing became a mixture of children's screams and the death wails of their mothers. The droning sound provided a frightful clue to what lay beyond the cool hallways leading to the rear porch.

Our first view was of bodies under a bloody sheet, the feet extending out of the covering like a photograph in a macabre gallery. The pairs of feet were either large or very small, those of adults and children.

Behind the mission, tribeswomen washed the native hairdressing, a mixture of cow dung and grease, from the ocher-colored heads of the wounded Turkana women. Next they cut the hair down to the scalp to prevent infection. Some of the bodies flopped like dead weight in the hands of the tribeswomen who laid them prostrate in the sun.

Other Turkanas who had escaped the slaughter stood in a circle watching the futile efforts to save their tribe. The men were wearing colored feathers, their skin ornamented with facial scars. The women had row upon row of bright beads around their necks, the mark of beauty among unmarried women. Their faces were not twisted in grief at the spectacle before them; instead, they showed signs of shock, looking dazed and emotionless.

We could begin to discern the injuries. Many of them were knife wounds; spears and arrows had also been used. The nurses threw beads cut from the victims onto a steadily growing pile in the center of the yard. I realized that all of the injured were women and children. Those around me were too busy to venture an explanation.

Indoors, a young Finnish missionary doctor was working in a stream of sunlight at a simple but clean operating table set up on what normally would have been a first-aid station. Two helpers maintained battle stations against hordes of flies, sweeping handheld fans in broad gestures across the woman on the table. A metal ring sticking through her earlobe bounced upon an ebony cheek when her body moved, creating a queer scene.

Here, Western man was reaching back to an ancient culture. The young doctor's blond hair fell over his glasses as he leaned toward his sutures. He had no anesthetic to deaden the painful stiches. But when he pulled them through the skin, his patient made no sound.

Others who seemed less seriously wounded were taken to a waiting car for the short ride to our airplane. I carried one child in my arms only to have it die by the time I reached the car. I remember thinking there was no quiver, no mystery as the life passed from the small body.

We wrapped the adults in blankets to make them easier to carry. Too often the doctor waved us away, pronouncing the victims dead.

Two poignant scenes I shall never forget. Two Turkana women held a third as she died; they looked into her lifeless eyes and wailed their emotional goodbyes. Then, within seconds, the sound cut to a dead silence. The women placed their friend's body on the ground and turned away quickly as if to escape the reach of death's fingers.

Another Turkana woman, dressed in a Western skirt, peeked cautiously into a shed that was being used as a morgue, fearful of what she might find. Her head jerked upward as she recognized a small child, perhaps her child. She began to run in circles, waving her arms and screaming hysterically. Friends held her close until she slumped to the ground, sobbing.

Gradually the wounded were transported to the Cessna and taken to Kapedo, thirty minutes away. Its facilities were more modern than the mission's but still nothing to compare with anything in the United States or even Nairobi.

The dead were prepared for immediate burial. Families seemed to know just what to do, using large animal skins to carry the bodies away. Children watched their elders dig the graves. There was no ceremony. The process seemed quite matter-of-fact, as if the Turkanas were much more aware than we were that death is a natural consequence of life. These people seemed to be a part of nature, blending into the cycle of life and death so apparent around them on the African plain.

I was so busy recording every visual image, jotting notes, and gathering the elements of a story to tell later that I glazed over the obvious. What obligation did I have as a journalist who happened to be a witness to the horror here? Should I drop my notes and help drag bodies or assist the young doctor suturing knife wounds? It wouldn't be the first time I had broken the journalist's barrier. I had befriended Tokyo Rose. I had danced with Angela Davis. I had helped Pamela Jean search for her past. But in this moment, it was clear that my few minutes of help wouldn't save lives. There's a rule that a journalist shouldn't become part of the story. We're observers. But I reasoned that if I was at the scene of a story and could possibly prevent harm or save a life, I should break the rule and enter the fray. It's common sense. That was my rule, learned from experience. But the incident was dialing down, and the last victims were being carried into the corral.

The next lesson was that I could do more good by telling the story to someone who could effect change and perhaps prevent such an occurrence in the future. So we worked. My camera crew, sweating in the unfiltered equatorial sun, said not a word, leaning into their gear and the giant metal camera on Peter Bertolini's shoulder. We were almost afraid to speak for fear of touching off a vengeful emotion. It was like drifting invisibly through these lives at a time when they were too stunned to even acknowledge our presence.

As we walked the short distance from the mission to the village, trying to re-create the scenario of attack for our camera, I asked an English-speaking mission worker what had happened. He was a tall young man whose brilliant white teeth shone against his obsidian skin as if designed by an artist. His English was quite good, suggesting effective education at the mission.

"The Pokots came just before dawn," he said. "They stretched a hundred in one line and moved this way," pointing toward the village. It was exactly the kind of assault tactic taught in the Marine Corps, a skirmish line designed to get full firepower up front and trained on the enemy. In this case, there were only a few guns. The primary weapons were bows and arrows, spears, and knives, the kind of war-making arsenal that had been used for hundreds of years.

"They went through, killing only women and children," he said, "maybe because the Turkana men heard them coming and ran away or were getting ready to defend themselves. Then the Pokots ran into the hills, looking for the cattle or the men who ran from them."

"Why did it happen?" I asked.

"Maybe for cattle and sheep. Maybe not. Maybe because this Turkana tribe did the same thing to the Pokots last year."

The scenes in the village were straight out of the Iron Age. Men sorted through weapons on the ground. Their arrows seemed thin and brittle, but when tipped in poison, they could bring down an elephant. Warriors held their spears close as they whispered in small groups, discussing future protection or revenge.

As we were walking between the small conical huts, I noticed a tall, handsome young man carrying a bow and arrow. He would have been intimidating if not for his smile. He said that his name was Isaiah. He was anxious to talk to the strangers, perhaps using his mission training in English.

"Will the Turkanas make a raid on the Pokots?" I asked.

He replied with the innocence of an adolescent, "Oh, yes. You can be sure of that."

"And will you go to kill Pokots?"

He hesitated, lowering his head before he answered, as if he were ashamed of his feelings. "The others will kill. They like to go and kill. But I will not go; I don't like to kill."

Isaiah lived in two worlds: that of the Christian mission, from which he received his education, and that of his village, to which he owed his life and loyalty. We finished taping in the village and walked back toward the mission with Isaiah trailing us, practicing his English.

There in the baking afternoon sun, the four of us were dazed by the experience. It would take several days before we realized just how much of an impact it had made. But for now, we had a sense of mission, of journalists doing our job. That carried us through without allowing our own emotions to catch up with the shock of witnessing a human slaughter.

Weeks later, an official Kenyan government report said that some new weapons—rifles—had been smuggled into the northern border area from guerrillas fighting in the Ogaden, a region of neighboring Ethiopia. The introduction of guns into these old running quarrels had tipped the balance of power in favor of the Pokot people, who had moved to take advantage of their new strength.

Looking back, the events of that dramatic day seem to have knitted together too smoothly, as so many of my stories do in hindsight. The flight at the last minute. The interview with our pilot while our camera was running and the interruption on the radio. Then the diversion of our flight to a massacre in a land of belching volcanic vents and hot fluoride springs seemed like a time warp beyond our imagination. Finally, as the Cessna was gliding in on its final approach over the village to pick us up— an image that would be the final shot needed to complete our story—our last battery would run out just after recording the shot.

If we didn't have the videotape, we might still be wondering about what really happened on that brilliant landscape in northern Kenya, where twentieth-century humans got a privileged glimpse of an age-old struggle for survival and how a different culture handles loss.

The camera separated us from the reality of what we had experienced. It was a barrier between two worlds, ancient and modern. But that barrier faded with time, and I came to appreciate what I had witnessed in a deeply personal way. I returned to Chicago, where my family was still in mourning over our own loss. As we processed our loss and grief together, I often thought back to the Turkana women holding their fallen friend. I thought of their loud, unashamed screams of agony and loss, which then fell silent, as if all the sound had been pulled out of the world. They laid their fellow tribeswoman on her back and walked away to tend to more immediate needs.

Survival required instant action. For the living, life carries on, forever changed but always moving forward. But memories live forever. And those left behind will always live alongside us.

# SEVENTEEN

# Saving a Life

The realization that broadcasters have the power to save lives, the realization that came to me in the destructive wake of the Topeka Tornado, was the thing that ultimately drove me to the profession for the long haul. But I never expected that I would save a life as personally as I did in Marquette Park during the summer of 1976.

Marquette Park is one of the green jewels on Chicago's southwest side. It's dotted with meadows, trails, lagoons, and small ponds for fishing or cruising model boats.

It is also historic as one of the sites where Dr. Martin Luther King Jr. led a civil rights march on August 5, 1966, to promote open housing. The decision to bring his movement to the northern cities led to a surprising result. The hate on the faces of seven hundred whites gathered that day in the park erupted into throwing rocks, one of which hit King in the head. The *Chicago Tribune* reported, "The blow knocked King to one knee and he thrust out an arm to break the fall." He told the press, "'I've been in many demonstrations all across the South, but I can say that I have never seen, even in Mississippi and Alabama, mobs as hostile and as hate-filled as I'm seeing in Chicago.'" Many regard it as a turning point in the civil rights movement, emphasizing that racism was even more intense in the North than in the South.

All of which were good reasons to do a follow-up story ten years after the history-making march.

Chicago city planners following the Columbian Exposition in 1893 hired the Olmsted Brothers to design and landscape three hundred acres, with promenades and meadows strategically placed as islands of oasis and during hot weather as cooling centers for people to escape from the hot, festering neighborhoods. Marquette Park was one of the largest of the ring of parks built around the city's core.

When I arrived with my crew—George Case was the cameraman—it looked like a prairie paradise compared with what we'd just left, the television headquarters in the crowded, noisy Streeterville section of the city.

Astrologists would point out that the date of June 8, 1976, was exactly ten years to the day (and almost to the hour) after the tornado disaster in Topeka.

Homemade kites were flying, trailing knotted tails of underwear tied together with twine. Young mothers and babysitters were chasing toddlers across the great lawns. Chicago red hots were being hustled under the trees, even then served only with mustard, not ketchup.

I took my suit coat off in the steamy summer heat and was looking for some shade when I spied a lagoon, or pond, where some teenagers were sailing their small electric boats. *That's an interesting visual for a stand-up*, I thought, and motioned for George to follow me.

We got there just as seventeen-year-old shirtless Bob Vosatka, standing knee-deep in the water at the lagoon's edge, was launching his boat. The motor seemed strong, as it left a tiny wake in its journey toward the middle. His buddies were cheering on the shore, their voices skipping off the water in the absence of throwing stones.

If ever a scene spoke to the moment, it was this one. It said, *A Chicago summer day in the park*. If I could have mimicked Seurat's painting at the Art Institute, I would have included the constant rumble of young voices with one volume: loud. Tittering girls watching the boys, hoping they would return the attention, responding if not to the female voices then perhaps to the skimpy skirts and tight shorts. And knowing the girls' eyes were on them, the young boys were displaying at the water's edge with a hand splash now and then before turning back to their nautical venture.

As I was formulating a paragraph in my head about the change since Dr. King had marched here, I heard the cheers turn excitedly urgent. Something had gone wrong. I turned as Bob jumped deeper into the water and started swimming toward his boat, about forty feet away in deep water. What else could he do with his summery world watching? His boat had flipped over. Bob's style in the water was a *form* of swimming, the arms stretched out to either side and chopping at the water, evidence that he had not been formally instructed.

I thought, *Great visual, but this kid isn't going to make it with a style like that*. What if he got tangled with the weeds on the bottom?

The shouts changed to a darker tone. Bob's friends were beginning to panic. I said to myself, "This is serious. I can see the headline: 'Anchorman Stands on Shore While Youngster Drowns.'"

Two of Bob's friends jumped in, but they couldn't swim any better than he could. You couldn't see algae from shore, and certainly not while swimming, but the underwater growth reached up like green tentacles to clutch and hold flailing feet.

For me, it was a critical decision. I knew a journalist should not get involved in a story, but surely it didn't mean ignoring a life-and-death situation, especially if I was in a position to help—maybe even save a life.

I expected others to join the friends trying to help. But at least a dozen people stood paralyzed, as if watching an accident in slow motion.

I could see Bob dip under the water twice and knew a third time likely meant he was so exhausted he wouldn't be able to come up. I kicked off my shoes and in suit pants and white shirt with my tie still knotted dove in, a shallow dive to avoid the bottom. The water was warm and would have been enjoyable under other circumstances. Funny how the brain reacts. Every swimming lesson and Boy Scout lifeguard instruction came back from years in deep storage, the kind of thing you learn but tuck away, not expecting to ever use it.

*Keep your eyes on the swimmer ahead*, I remembered. So I kept my head out of the water, letting the strokes and kicking carry me. Instinct added to the lessons. Before I realized it, I was there by his side. Again, I remembered that the victim might struggle and pull us both down, so I went underwater, turned him around, and wrapped my arm over his chest. It worked perfectly. There was no struggle. Bob had no strength left.

His friends who were swimming toward him trying to help barely had any energy left themselves. I said, "I've got him. Try to make shore." They turned back.

It all happened within less than two minutes. Bob floated behind me while I used my left arm to stroke to the lagoon's edge, where I could get my footing. Others finally jumped in to pull Bob up to the concrete walk around the edge.

The joyous shouting had stopped. It was so quiet I could hear a speaker with the Temptations singing from across the park. The young faces told the story. Their color had drained at observing the brush with calamity, as if the reality of life had intervened to remind them of its fragility. Someone had called the fire department, and two men in uniform came out from under the trees. The firemen seemed to have expected the worst and appeared relieved to load their gurney with Bob Vosatka and bounce it back over the green lawns to the red ambulance. They'd call his parents from the hospital.

One asked if I'd like to go to the hospital, but I declined. Frankly, the adrenaline was a burst of energy, so I felt better than ever. When George came over to check on me, I said, "Why don't you take the video to the station? I'd better go home and change." The siren punctuated the moment with a theatrical conclusion, and suddenly I was aware of my dripping-wet dress shirt and still knotted tie, as if ready for an expensive dinner.

There was a flurry of excitement back at WBBM-TV, and Walter and I had a good discussion at the anchor desk. It was hard for many, especially the competition, to believe that the rescue hadn't been set up for publicity purposes. But two things helped put those thoughts to rest: the front-page story in the *Chicago Tribune* and a Chicago Medal of Merit from Mayor Richard J. Daley awarded to me in front of the Chicago City Council.

The *Tribune* article quoted Bob as saying, "I didn't think that I was going to make it. I knew what was going on, but I was unable to move anymore. And my friends, they were tired and were pulling me down by accident. Thank God that Mr. Kurtis was there and willing to help me."

The American National Red Cross awarded me a Certificate of Merit, and President Gerald Ford wrote a note commending me for the rescue.

Bob Vosatka kept in touch a couple times over the years. I think of Bob every time I see Seurat's *Sunday Afternoon on the Island of La Grande Jatte.* And it always reminds me of an important lesson in journalism: be ready for anything, because anything is what usually happens.

# EIGHTEEN

# Agent Orange

The most persistent story to come out of the Vietnam War has been Agent Orange, the defoliant used by the US military to clear the dense jungles in enemy territory. By the end of the war, some journalists, including me, were already asking questions about Agent Orange. Most reporters were concerned about the environmental impact of the herbicide, which we thought qualified as biological and chemical warfare. Reporter Thomas Whiteside wrote one of the most well-known of these stories in the *New Yorker*. But I was asking questions no one else was. I was looking for answers in places where no one else was aware. And I found a story no one else did: proof that Agent Orange had harmed American soldiers. My investigative team broke the story in the spring of 1979 with an hour-long documentary on WBBM-TV, Chicago. Agent Orange still makes the headlines today and stands as the biggest story of my career.

I got the tip from a whistleblower while I was writing a story at my desk at WBBM-TV for the ten o'clock news.

Maude DeVictor, a veterans' representative in Chicago's Veterans Affairs regional office, sent me a list of twelve names of veterans whose medical symptoms could not be explained. They had one thing in common—they had been in contact with a chemical that the US Air Force had sprayed on vegetation to destroy crops and clear a free-fire zone around bases. The list came in a manila envelope tossed down by Phil Ruskin, a studio director at the station who also taught at Columbia College in Chicago. That's the way a lot of stories come to you: a random tip that someone thinks might be newsworthy, that is then passed from desk to desk until someone decides it's worth looking into.

Within moments of opening that envelope, I felt my mind begin to race with the implications of this story, if it were true.

This could be far more than just a weed killer. Was the US using chemical weapons? Wouldn't that be in violation of the 1925 Geneva Protocol? How much of this did the Pentagon know about? Was it ignorance, or was it a cover-up? Which would be worse? If it hurt the Americans who deployed it like this, what of their Vietnamese targets? After reading those twelve names over and over again, I came to the sickening realization that after all the Vietnam veterans had endured, they might have to bear yet one more burden—a time bomb dropped on them by their own government.

This all seemed like a worst-case scenario, though. I figured I should do a couple of initial interviews to see if there was anything there and drop the story if it was a dead end.

My first interview from the list was with Ethel Owens, whose husband had been an air force sergeant with Operation Ranch Hand, the military name for the mission to spray an herbicide over six million acres in Vietnam. Her husband had worked in the flight office and would have been a great eyewitness if he hadn't passed away only a month prior to my visit. But he had told his wife that sometimes the mist caused by the C-123s that were carrying the defoliant looked like smog in Los Angeles. That description was immediately seared into my brain. My reporter's instincts snapped to attention at the stunning visual image, and although I couldn't go to court with it or even build a story on it, it was the kind of mental picture that followed you to bed and in the morning sent you to the next interview.

The second name on Maude's list was Milton Ross of Matteson, Illinois, not so far away that I couldn't make it there and back between the 6:00 and 10:00 newscasts. He had complained to Maude about psychological problems and loss of sex drive. He was stationed with a Special Forces unit in the Central Highlands operating out of Pleiku, one of twenty-two advisers working with two hundred Vietnamese troops. He said, "I remember being sprayed out of helicopters for bugs and vegetation and to keep the perimeter clear."

His son, Richard, was about five years old. He came into the living room where we were doing the interview and put his hand on his dad's knee with his small fingers hanging down. One of the fingertips was dangling by a piece of skin that looked like a birth defect. It didn't seem to bother him. I looked at my cameraman, and he nodded that he saw it too and zoomed into a tight shot of the little finger.

I didn't know it at the time, but that shot would "sell" the Agent Orange story to Congress and break it open for veterans around the country.

Investigative reporting is filled with dead ends, blind leads, interviews that aren't quite how they were described. This story had such huge potential I was expecting a land mine at every turn, expecting that one slap to the side of my head that would say, *Sorry, pal, you missed the obvious; go home.* When you're looking from "outside the tent," a lot of investigative reporting is disappointing.

But it only took those first two interviews to answer the question: should we pursue the story? The answer was yes, in a Chicago minute! But where to start?

As an investigative reporter, I gathered facts, tested them, and handed them off to people who could do something about it. Lawyers do much the same thing when building a case, and I had the advantage of walking in a lawyer's shoes, knowing what the "best evidence" rule is, and standing my ground when under fire.

As a reporter, I always tried to get my story to the place where it could stand up in court before I put it on the air. That's more than is required in journalism, but it's the safe bet. Especially here, where we'd be poking the bear—in this case, five of the biggest chemical companies in the country.

It was clear that we had to build a strong case.

We had three things to prove:

1. Verify the symptoms. Were they real or psychological? Were there possible explanations of the veterans' symptoms other than exposure to Agent Orange?
2. Had the complainants actually been in contact with the herbicide or within a reasonable distance? We eventually had veterans tell us they had passed under trees dripping with white liquid sprayed from a plane.
3. If they had been exposed, was the defoliant harmful to humans, and what harm could it do?

Each of these questions could have stopped us because the chemical companies had a body of research that claimed the opposite of what we were trying to prove. In investigative reporting, there's always a point at which the journey leads to a cliff that looms as a dead end. The barrier came quickly. There was a stack of research that reached back forty years, studies of farmers that had found that the chemicals in the farming application of the herbicide, if mixed properly, were harmless to humans.

In fact, when I was in high school, my dad wanted to clear some pastures with that very herbicide. It was a mixture of two chemicals: 2,4-D and 2,4,5-T. I rode in the back of a pickup truck with a fifty-five-gallon drum full of the mixture. A small motor fed a pump-and-spray unit that produced a stream of the white, milky liquid strong enough to cover trees. They were regarded as invasive weed trees called Osage orange or hedge trees that spotted pastures that should have been cleared for grazing. I certainly couldn't see into the future that the mixture would later be labeled Agent Orange and used in Vietnam. We were drenched by the blowback. But I knew my dad was careful to follow the instructions, and we showered when we got home (and not just for my dates). Although he and I were dizzy at times, we shrugged off the exposure. Little did we know that one of the chemicals, 2,4,5-T, contained a contaminant from the manufacturing process called dioxin, often described as one of the most poisonous substances made by humankind.

During the Vietnam War, the US sprayed twenty million gallons of herbicides in at least 6,542 Operation Ranch Hand missions, covering about 12 percent of South Vietnam. The average concentration was thirteen times what the USDA recommended in the US. Studies in Vietnam found concentrations of dioxin in soil and water hundreds of times greater than the level the EPA considered safe. But did the greater concentrations harm humans?

One statement that we ran into repeatedly was a report by the USDA and Department of Defense that "there is *no* evidence to show that 2,4-D and 2,4,5-T are harmful to humans." A lot was riding on that statement. Drawing on my legal background, I faced off with lawyers for Dow Chemical and Monsanto who threw that statement at me. I responded, "A more careful reading shows that '*no* evidence to suggest' is much different from 'there *is* evidence to suggest *no harmful effect* to humans.'" The tests simply hadn't been done.

Lawyers and conservative columnists also liked to claim that only "ten pounds of dioxin was actually sprayed over one-third of Vietnam."

The herbicide expert for Dow Chemical, Dr. Lewis Shadoff, said that dosages should be roughly two pounds per acre on rangeland. But the Vietnam use was roughly fifteen pounds per acre, and the herbicide was repeatedly sprayed over the same areas.

We all asked, "If it's harmless to humans, why not provide all the military wanted in combat situations?"

The answer was that militarized Agent Orange in Vietnam was stronger than the version for farm use. Agent Orange was the military designation for what they called the Rainbow herbicides with names like Orange, Purple, or Blue. Each had a different mixture or different strength for a different use.

When Chief of Operations Admiral Elmo Zumwalt ordered more of the Rainbow herbicides, he was told that it was beyond the chemical companies' capacity to produce with their current method of production, which was safe. But money talks, as does the need to fight a war.

When the chemical companies told their scientists they were going to speed up manufacturing, the answer they got was that more of the chemicals required more heat, and more heat would produce more of the contaminant—dioxin. Turning the herbicide into a weapon of war meant it was not the same product farmers used. Now it *was* deadly to humans.

One veteran said he knew the hormone-based product was supposed to take two weeks to work through the growth cycle. But his troops had seen leaves falling off trees in two hours.

The answer to the escalating criticism was always "Who cares? It's war! We're saving American lives."

Our research continued. At the end of three months, we had good evidence that US troops had been exposed to the herbicide and that it was dangerous.

We discovered that Agent Orange had the possibility of causing birth defects. One of our experts, Dr. Val Woodward, a geneticist at the University of Minnesota, declared for us that dioxin is a teratogen—a generator of deformities in fetuses—and very likely a cause of cancer and birth defects that could be caused by males. Monsanto scientist Barry Commoner theorized that dioxin could have been stored in the fatty tissue of a veteran and released into the body when he lost weight, even many years after exposure. At that point, I realized that this ticking time bomb had a long fuse, and we'd be hearing about Agent Orange for years, even decades, to come. Finally, Dr. James Allen, who had conducted extensive studies of the effect of low levels of dioxin in monkeys at the University of Wisconsin–Madison, shared his findings that trace amounts, measured in parts per billion, were carcinogenic and deadly.

We were ready to go public. But how? This was too big even to be the top story on the ten o'clock news. Instead we produced a one-hour documentary. *Agent Orange: Vietnam's Deadly Fog* ran at 10:30 p.m. in November 1978, following the ten o'clock news on WBBM-TV, Chicago.

Local stations aren't really equipped to produce documentaries. It's a different kind of production that requires its own camera and sound teams and a healthy budget. But when management at WBBM-TV found out what we had, they stepped up and said let's go for broke. General Managers Dave Nelson and later Ed Joyce along with News Director Jay Feldman realized this kind of story was why we had all chosen journalism as our life's work. And these stories seldom come along, if ever.

I headed the investigative unit, the Focus Unit, with executive producer Donna LaPietra and associate producers Brian Boyer and Rose Economu.

Our collection of veterans and some farm families had been complaining of the herbicide for years, all without scientific background because no one was willing to go beyond the chemical company's statement that it was harmless to humans.

We had worked so quietly that few in the newsroom had any idea of what was coming. But the veterans knew what we were talking about. And after we hit air, within days the Vietnam veterans network began pulsing with this new story. They were eager to say to their families, "See, we're not crazy after all; we do have problems. It's Agent Orange."

I knew that the story would take on a life of its own once we put it on the air. I was expecting that reaction and wanted to take advantage of the rush by sending a transcript and videotape (three-quarter inch) to every senator and member of Congress in Illinois, just in case they hadn't seen the broadcast at 10:30 p.m. *after* the newscast, so they could answer inquiries from veterans.

I hit the jackpot with Congressman Abner Mikva of the Tenth District in Illinois. He was a liberal champion of the Chicago political scene. He graduated from the University of Chicago Law School; served five terms in the Illinois General Assembly; and was elected to the US House of Representatives, where he served five terms on the Judiciary Committee and the Ways and Means Committee. He was appointed by President Jimmy Carter to a judgeship on the US Court of Appeals and served fifteen years before working for President Bill Clinton as White House counsel and receiving the Medal of Freedom from President Barack Obama.

He watched the broadcast and asked his friend Congressman Don Edwards to schedule a presentation before the House Committee on Veterans' Affairs.

In the meantime, the Associated Press had picked up the story, and veterans around the country were gathering to watch the video in their own meetings. By the time we arrived in Washington, the word was out that a major development had surfaced concerning the Vietnam War. The room was filled with representatives of agencies with vested interests in veterans' issues. The Veterans Administration had already let it be known that there was no evidence linking defoliants with health issues in US veterans. After all, they implied, it was only a *local* TV station that had broken the story. If it was really big, the networks would have carried it.

In the stately House hearing room, Congressman Mikva introduced the documentary, the lights dimmed, and the audience simmered down except for groups of staffers used to attending such events as substitutes to "show the flag" for their congressmen.

Then, about ten minutes into the presentation, the camera zoomed in to the fingers of Milton Ross's son, Richard. There was an audible gasp that brought the audience to a dead silence. Breathing seemed labored, and heads leaned forward as if suddenly alerted to why they were there. For this standing-room-only crowd, the lightbulb went off. Could it be? Could the US military have injured its own men? How many? Birth defects? *That usually doesn't happen with males, but* we had found enough evidence that it could presumptively cause birth defects. What kind of compensation could they get?

The dead silence continued until the end as if the oxygen supply had sprung a leak.

To be honest, although we had done the best we could with production, the film had a rough, unfinished look. The graphics did not have movie or network sophistication. But no one in that room or since has questioned the quality. Because we had the truth.

That was what Congressman Mikva said when he stood up while the credits were rolling and began to criticize the VA for not responding positively to what everyone had just seen. Before he could finish his remarks, the representative from the VA interrupted and listed ten things they planned to do for veterans, from recognizing likely diseases that may have been caused by Agent Orange to starting an epidemiological survey of veterans to determine who might have been injured. He said they would guarantee that every veteran who was suffering from the unknown symptoms would receive a full examination.

The drama in the room was a testament to what I believe journalism is all about: our job is to communicate problems to intelligent people who can solve those problems.


Those intelligent people got to work to solve the problem—which is not always the case. I did my best to keep up with the flurry of investigations, reports, and hearings that began shortly thereafter, but it was clear that this was no longer *my* story. Yes, my team and I had broken the story, but it soon became a national story that belonged to all of us. Pandora's box was open.

A class-action suit against the five chemical companies was settled for $180 million to help several thousand veterans. However, they never had to pay it because at the same time, Congress went into action in response to the overwhelming pressure brought by veterans. It supported surveys of several hundred thousand veterans to once and for all determine who was hurt, what kinds of diseases were most likely to have been caused by Agent Orange, and how best to compensate those affected. The survey concluded that there was a significant increase in soft-tissue sarcomas among veterans who had served in Vietnam.

It was clear that Congress should shoulder the burden of compensating the Agent Orange veterans through the Veterans Administration, although the massive bureaucracy, while appearing to want to do the right thing, still applied help haltingly. One reason may have been that there was never a definite answer to whether the defoliant could have caused the illnesses, much like the difficulty in proving the causes of cancer.

Among many journalists and experts who picked up the Agent Orange torch, Dr. Gil Bogen served as president of the Vetline Hotline, a nonprofit in Illinois that treats Vietnam and other veterans. He found that the herbicide used in Vietnam was much more powerful than the one used by farmers, like the one my father and I had used.

The following passage from his book *When the Lion Roars* details what happened when the government investigated the effect of weaponizing Agent Orange.

> According to a memo found during Admiral Elmo Zumwalt's [chief of naval operations, 1970] investigation, the US government knew of the defoliant's toxicity. Dr. James R. Clary, a former senior scientist at the US Air Force Chemical Weapons Branch who designed the spray tanks for Operation Ranch Hand, wrote in response to a Congressional investigation into Agent Orange:
>
> "When we initiated the herbicide program in the 1960s, we were aware of the potential for damage due to dioxin contamination in the herbicide. We were even aware that the military formulation had a higher dioxin concentration than the civilian version due to the lower cost and speed of manufacture. However, because the material was to be used on the enemy, none of us were overly concerned. We never considered a scenario in which our own personnel would become contaminated with the herbicide."

There it was at last. Part whistleblower, part relentless crusader, sixty years of struggle. Finally the pieces of a complete answer were in place.

It seemed like the lid from a sixty-year-old bottle of toxic liquid had popped off, releasing truth and allowing the final steps to help the veterans.

A personal survey revealed that some Vietnam vets were compensated after landing only once in a helicopter in Saigon during the war.

A list of diseases and conditions that are presumptively associated with Agent Orange is breathtaking: amyloidosis, chloracne, Hodgkin's disease, Non-Hodgkin's lymphoma, B-cell leukemia, type 2 diabetes, multiple myeloma, Parkinson's disease, ischemic heart disease, peripheral neuropathy, porphyria cutanea tarda, prostate cancer, respiratory cancers, and soft-tissue sarcomas.

Nearly sixty years later, the VA has reduced its exposure requirement to veterans who "served *anywhere* in Vietnam between January 9, 1962 and May 7, 1975. They are presumed to have been exposed to herbicides, citing the Agent Orange Act of 1991."

"It wasn't easy to admit we were wrong," Senator Patrick Leahy, one of the early advocates for US Agent Orange/dioxin assistance to Vietnam, explained in a statement to the Senate:

> On the one hand, the government of Vietnam for years blamed Agent Orange for seemingly any case of birth defects in the country, no matter how farfetched. On the other hand, the US Government consistently denied causation between Agent Orange and birth defects in Vietnam and refused to accept any responsibility for the alleged harm. For years, the issue remained a contentious one for our country. It would be hard to overstate the importance the Vietnamese give to addressing the needs of people who have been harmed.

By the end of the war, nearly five million Vietnamese had been exposed to Agent Orange, resulting in 400,000 deaths and disabilities and a half-million children born with birth defects.

It wasn't until recently that we took a major step to right the wrongs of the past and reckon with our sins. Between 2007 and 2021, Congress appropriated nearly $390 million to address environmental and health damage in Vietnam and to Vietnamese people attributed to Agent Orange.

In the immediate wake of our documentary hitting the airwaves and while our country was reckoning with the sins of its very recent past, I moved on to chase the Agent Orange story elsewhere.

In 1980, I accepted an invitation from an internationally renowned doctor in Hanoi, Dr. Ton That Tung, the private physician to Ho Chi Minh. He had been collecting examples of birth defects that he felt had been caused by Agent Orange. The samples were preserved in bottles of formaldehyde. His hospital, Phu Doan (renamed Viet Duc), was an old French hospital with nurses in pressed white uniforms scurrying around the famous doctor. The windows were iron-framed squares shining their light on gleaming tiled hallways. His real area of expertise was a radical operation for liver cancer that extended survival for six months. News of his breakthrough had swept through the medical profession worldwide after an account was published in the *Lancet*. He wanted us to film the operation for him, which we did. That too is journalism, tit for tat—we would film the liver operation if we could also film the alleged Agent Orange evidence.

The fact that we were allowed in in the first place was newsworthy. My camera crew and I were the first American journalists to be allowed into the country after the end of the war.

It was only five years since the US had left South Vietnam, and Hanoi showed great poverty from fighting a multiyear war. A war museum had been created with the tail section of a B-52 sticking out of a pond in front of the building. Spider holes were open to tourists as an example of how people had survived the B-52 bombing in the tiny one-person holes in the ground. They looked like manholes for fixing the street, but they had provided perfect protection except when directly hit.

Meat was on the menu only once a month. Malnutrition was rampant. We were taken into a storefront restaurant for dinner, and the menu was walked in front of us on a leash. We passed on the dog but chose a live turtle for soup. Electricity was turned on for only a few hours a day. Without refrigeration, the living menu was the only way to assure freshness.

It was clear even in 1980 that the Vietnamese were very concerned about the damage to the country and citizens caused by Agent Orange.

Our communist "handlers" took us to an American helicopter base in Tay Ninh province, previous home, as best as I could make out, to the 187th Assault Helicopter Company. They felt it would be the best place to see what remained of an Agent Orange defoliation. It was one strip of asphalt embedded in the green jungle. Standing alone on the flight line, I could conjure up a column of Hueys (UH-1 helicopters) boarding troops, rotors starting their slow turns as they got up to speed. I could feel the squall pushing against me from their downdraft and the loss of hearing from the *chop-chop* sound building to takeoff. Multiply one chopper by ten in the most dangerous province in country, and you had an aerial ballet with the chorus line lifting off in unison, leaving trees bending in its wake.

As I stood on the edge of the asphalt looking at unexploded ordnance in a drainage ditch alongside, I realized the regrowth that looked like jungle was really a ten-year grow-back from a circle surrounding the strip. The vegetation was less than half as tall as the main forest. Something had cut the field down to the ground for half a mile on all sides.

I pointed to the circle and asked my handler, a former Vietcong soldier, a two-words question: "Agent Orange?"

"Yes," he replied. "Before Orange, I could crawl up close and watch GIs taking showers."

"That close?"

"Yes. Until they poisoned the trees and plants and the soldiers could see us easier, even at a distance."

In one respect, I was proud of the US technology, adapting to tropical warfare by taking the jungle away. Having been a grunt in the Marine Corps, I would have used whatever was available to reduce enemy cover. But now, eight years since Agent Orange had been banned after scientists had responded to South Vietnamese complaints that it was harming their people, I had new insight.

We were also taken into the Mekong Delta region, where the Saigon River irrigated 270,000 acres of mangroves, worth a fortune in lumberyards before the war. But there were no trees visible, only mudflats. I sank up to my knees as I walked to what remained of one tree that had been cut down and sawed up for firewood. It looked like the last tree in the world, stripped of its limbs and standing alone in endless mud. They were trying to replant new mangroves, but the tide kept washing the tiny saplings away.

The United States would not consent to a peacetime agreement to work together on anything.

The research of Dr. Ton That Tung may not have met the medical standards of the great scientific institutions of the world, but it was the best he could do in a country at war. If we had studied his work then and there, we'd be forty years ahead in learning the terrible potential of dioxin poisoning and rebuilding a relationship with Vietnam—a relationship that came fifty years later, in 2019.


One would think the explosion of stories about Agent Orange over the last sixty years emanated from a single point of origin, the journalistic equivalent of a nuclear blast. Instead it started with a whistleblower and a few interviews. It didn't have to break as the lead story on *60 Minutes*. It was the hard work of investigative reporters that turned out to be the biggest story of our lives. It should be a lesson to young journalists that truth can come from the smallest source. Be accurate; check it out from every angle; and if it is true, you can change the world.

From those humble beginnings, other journalists picked up the story, found more of the truth, and added it to the pile. Veterans formed not-for-profit groups that helped identify and guide veterans who thought they had been harmed by Agent Orange. But the story was not as easy to solve as it appeared sixty years later.

The chemical companies were fighting the possibility of having to pay millions of dollars in compensation, and the Department of Veterans Affairs also had trouble accepting liability. The admission of poisoning our own troops implied an embarrassing violation of international law, and there was that nagging claim, established years earlier, that the defoliant was harmless to humans.

I was lucky to have had the support of WBBM and CBS in chasing the story as far as I could follow it. And as history has shown us, it's still ongoing. That's why I started this chapter by saying the most persistent story to come out of the Vietnam War is Agent Orange.

It was the biggest story of my career.

# NINETEEN

# American Faces

I'm always looking for stories. It's just how my mind works, and it's why I enjoy my career so much. Many years of reporting and investigative journalism have taught me that there's always another story hiding just around the corner, waiting to be found. It's the reporter's job to sniff out those stories, but whenever WBBM-TV sent me overseas, I knew I had to look extra hard. It wasn't enough to get just one story out of an international trip. Our pioneering operation in Chicago had put a lot of faith—and money—behind me and my scheme to add international reporting to the local news, and I had to deliver. I squeezed every story I could out of my first trip to Vietnam in 1975 and my trip to Kenya after that.

So when I received permission to enter Vietnam in late 1980—the first American allowed in since the end of the war—I was ready for anything. My first priority, of course, was Agent Orange. After all, it was the reason Dr. Ton That Thung had invited me in the first place and the reason the new communist regime had allowed me to enter the country. Of all the costs from the war, the Vietnamese government felt most strongly about the herbicide defoliation that they claimed had caused birth defects and diseases without cures. Everyone from the top military officials to the most rural peasant communities had seen or felt the effects of Agent Orange. When we left Chicago, we were ready to shoot a follow-up documentary, *Agent Orange: The View from Vietnam*. Our contacts with the Vietnamese government made it clear that this was all we would do. But still, I had a feeling that it wouldn't be the only story we'd come back with.

I was thrilled to be the first American journalist to return to Vietnam with a television crew. We felt like the first GIs into Tokyo after World War II. The US Embassy in Bangkok said they hadn't seen inside Saigon since April 1975. No American was allowed into the country for more than a quick touchdown at the airport. From Bangkok, it was like looking at a dark forest without lights at night.

From our first moments in Saigon, now Ho Chi Minh City, I was grateful to see that the city was just as beautiful as it had been five years before. Bougainvillea still splashed its purple, white, and red colors over stucco walls that separated French architecture from boulevards shaded by plane trees and eucalyptus. But a closer look was a whiplash from the past. US military jeeps drove past with uniformed Vietnamese drivers. The television station was showing a live performance of traditional dancing, but when I walked into the restroom, it still sported the best of American-made urinals. It was like a turtle had crawled into a familiar shell where everything worked, but to a veteran, everything seemed out of sync and no longer a turtle.

The Caravelle Hotel was exactly the same as it had been during the war, not a table or chair out of place on the rooftops where correspondents had listened to the *whump* of artillery in the distance. Vines of bright flowers crawled over the walls, just as they had when Walter Cronkite had eaten here.

Across the plaza in front of the National Assembly Building, the Hotel Continental was like an old dowager trying to hide the years with makeup on a craggy face. The once rich and shiny mahogany staircase was dried and cracked. A Vietnamese restaurant had replaced the French restaurant overlooking old Tu Do Street. I watched the street sign changing to Le Loi Boulevard to satisfy its new occupants. Words like "freedom" and "revolution" were everywhere.

Our handlers set our itinerary, scheduling trips to see Agent Orange damage as far away as Vung Tau on the coast and up the Saigon River into the Mekong River Delta, where 270,000 acres of mangroves had been destroyed by Agent Orange. The Vietcong had used the river like a cloistered highway into Saigon.

But between these trips out of the city, we were free to walk the streets, go wherever we wanted, and talk with whomever we wanted. For the reporter on a three-man television team, it was paradise. One day, as I was crossing Tu Do Street, just across from the Caravelle Hotel, I watched a gaggle of dirty street kids panhandling for money. I was instantly thrown into the past, reminded of my earlier trip during the last days of the war, when Vietnamese street children had chased GIs down the broad sidewalks, begging for a quarter or for a cigarette as the Americans slipped into bars and brothels on the trail of women in colorful ao dais. Pulled back into 1980, I caught a glimpse of a young face in the pack of youngsters wrestling over an orange. It was haunting in its clarity and quite distinct from the Vietnamese faces around it. There was no mistaking: it was an American face. I realized in that moment that I'd found my unexpected story: the children of the war.

A woman was selling British and American cigarettes from a small tray alongside a grating that was pulled shut across a storefront. A young boy stood by her side, watching me. Dressed in casual tropical khakis, I looked different than the clusters of Vietnamese pedestrians on the sidewalk. His stare had locked on my face. The boy was different too. He had a round face, olive complexion, big dark eyes, and straight hair black as night. I couldn't tell his age, especially here on the sticky streets of Saigon—oops, Ho Chi Minh City. It was his smile that cut through the Asian street culture: it was American. His look seemed to say that he hadn't seen anyone like me before either.

This wasn't the Agent Orange follow-up we'd come for. But we were the first American reporters admitted back into Vietnam in five years, and I was like a kid in a candy store.

The boy glanced at me with the look of one who has just noticed his reflection in the mirror, then moved closer to his mother.

"Father American?" I asked her.

She answered, "American MP."

Unquestionably this child of about nine was a scrap of the American war. I tried again, asking about the boy's father, his background, but the woman was obviously nervous, glancing about, seemingly looking for someone she expected to be watching. She spoke in choppy Vietnamese English. "I'd like to talk with you, but I be careful."

I took the cue, looked away, and retreated across the street, taking a picture as I walked toward a curb. The scene was familiar, a tropical urban clutter of colors, with children playing on the sidewalks and shoppers standing and looking at a carpenter's team changing the sign of the street on a lamppost. No longer Tu Do, now it was Le Loi, the name of one of the first emperors of Vietnam.

She was right. Not far away, an ever-present handler from the government was watching.

Past the center square, a young girl was selling steaming food. Her American face stood out like a beacon. She too worked alongside her mother. The child's name was Linda.

Yes, the mother said, her father was American.

Here she was, an American girl of eleven or twelve, speaking only Vietnamese, laughing nervously like a schoolgirl among friends. But her mother said she hadn't been going to school for five years, not since the "liberation."

The picture was slowly coming into focus, and my mind was jumping from those images of the GIs who used to walk on this street looking for escape to these children who were doing the same thing.

I had discovered what had happened to the children of American GIs when the US left Vietnam suddenly in 1975. Some fathers were caught overseas and couldn't get back to pick up their families. Others simply left their girlfriends behind, typical of GIs serving overseas looking for sex.

Reflecting on my story about orphans in 1975, I wondered what had happened to them, especially the US citizens. Those with Vietnamese mothers and US fathers are called Amerasian children. When the Americans pulled out, there was worry about what would happen to these living reminders of the war. The answer was clear; the evidence was around me. They had become the street children of Ho Chi Minh City. It was chilling.

There were an estimated five thousand Vietnamese American children in and around Ho Chi Minh City. US State Department officials confirmed that they had received entry-visa petitions for more than six hundred children of American citizens who had been left behind in the confusion of the American departure. These petitions were among more than fourteen thousand that had been filed with the State Department by both Americans and transplanted Vietnamese who still had family members in Vietnam.

When the mothers on the streets of Saigon realized that we were Americans, the first they had seen in five years, they unleashed a torrent of woes. After the Americans left, they said, the new government denied them jobs and even rice rations, and they were forced to make a living by working in the black-market economy. Their children accompanied them, turning the streets into their playground each day, for the mothers said the children had not been allowed to attend school since the North Vietnamese takeover. Although the official Vietnamese policy is that all children are to receive the benefits of education, it was clear from the evidence before our eyes, from the testimony of the mothers, and from information from international relief organizations that there was educational and employment discrimination against these women.

After we had spent three days at the old Rex Hotel—now the Ben Thanh—we noticed that the park across the street seemed to be filling up with these children. The children's mothers had stationed them there to watch for the Americans.

Soon, each time we came out of the hotel, the children would carry letters to us, pressing them into our hands as secretly as they could. If we walked any distance, there would be signals from them to meet them around the corner out of public view.

They were frightened of "monitors," men and women assigned to watch the citizenry—the invisible sentries of Vietnamese society who had been given the job of making sure the populace met the government's rigid requirements. In Ho Chi Minh City, there were harsh strictures: permission was needed to spend the night with a friend or to travel from one section of the city to another. Those who resisted such measures experienced a loss of individual freedom that was tantamount to living within a prison. Hundreds of thousands of people risked death in small boats on the open sea trying to escape these repressive conditions.

Vietnamese people animated by desperation were now thrusting messages into our pockets. The notes were carefully written in English and addressed to the United Nations or Red Cross. Personal photographs were attached to many of the narratives, and most of them told much the same story of separation and privation.

One afternoon, half-a-dozen mothers gathered in a park one block from Tu Do Street, clustered among some twenty of these Vietnamese American children. The youths were dressed in the best clothes that their mothers could find, showing themselves to be presentable, even attractive prospects for acceptance by their relatives in far-off America.

The mothers and children spoke quickly about the harsh conditions.

One young boy read a speech that had been written in poor English by his mother. It told of the killing of his American father by the Vietcong; this had left his mother alone with four children, struggling to provide for them in a city that regarded their welfare as among the lowest in its list of priorities. One mother found it hard to speak of her feelings about her children having been out of school for five years. She knew what would happen to them, lacking an education in a country where they were objects of hate.

Despite our efforts to hide these people's contacts with us, there were too many letters, too many obvious attempts to pass materials to us even though we said, "No! People are watching; keep them."

Still, the mothers and children pushed documents into our hands, their faces reflecting their fear of missing their only chance to escape.

Our actions were reported. The night before a scheduled departure, it was customary to hold a dinner to thank our monitors and guides, who in this case had accompanied us from Hanoi. I had some clout because of the Agent Orange story rather than from flashing the big CBS "eye" and promising nationwide coverage. They didn't care about that. What they wanted was a story showing the vast damage and human defects left behind.

We were sitting at a long table on the rooftop of the Caravelle, drinking French wine with chilled spring rolls, shrimp, and bean sprouts with peanut plum dipping sauce. Speeches from both sides, soaked in the alcohol, made us sorry to be leaving until our favorite handler leaned across the table and whispered, "The authorities notified us that they know you have the letters. If you try to take them out of the country, it could be very bad for you at customs. We do not control them and can't help you there. We will pick them up tomorrow morning at 8 a.m. We have had a successful trip, and you have a very good story. Please don't ruin it at the final stage."

Numbness changed my face to reflect Mike Tyson's favorite retort that everybody has a plan until you get hit. We were in the winner's venue, and there was no US military to come rescue us.

By a quick count at the hotel, we had accumulated close to one hundred letters, including complete dossiers of personal identifications, birth certificates, pictures, histories, and addresses. What had begun as an intriguing glimpse of a closed society behind a communist border and a discovery of the existence of a hidden American legacy had turned into a moral dilemma edged with fear.

The ethical questions were clear. Did we turn the letters over, possibly condemning these people to further abuse? Or did we resist, risking the inspection of our sixty videotape cassettes, our two hundred pages of notes, and our fifty film canisters—all filled with potentially incriminating information about the children and about those who had given us leads to other stories of life behind the bamboo curtain?

I promised to turn over the letters in the morning if one of the monitors would come to our hotel room. After dinner, we debated the alternatives through long hours into the night. We decided that our first step would be to photograph as many of the letters as we could. We used the concealed shower stall of the bathroom so that the bright light wouldn't alert a monitor who might be watching our hotel window. My cameraman, Skip Brand, and audio man, Don Reynolds, closed the curtains and began shooting each letter in the shower stall. One by one, we taped each letter to the wall in front of the video camera on the tripod. Sweat drenched us as if the shower had been turned on.

When the task was completed, we had a record of the letters, but it was still unthinkable to turn them over to the authorities. But how and where could we dispose of them? The monitors would see us walking to the river if we tried to sink them underwater. We had no access to a fire. And we didn't know anyone who could hide them for us.

Finally we came up with a strategy. We decided to offer the Vietnamese authorities two letters since we believed that they didn't know how many letters we really had. One letter included no pictures but contained information about Vietnamese people who had relatives in the United States. The other letter was about a small boy—too small, we hoped, to be the subject of retribution.

At 8:00 a.m. sharp, our government interpreter from Hanoi knocked at the door. Immediately he asked for the letters. I objected to being used by the government to obtain material about its citizens, but ultimately I gave the interpreter the two letters. He seemed relieved. He expressed appreciation that, in the spirit of our good relations during the past week, we could now avoid unpleasant moments. The two letters seemed to satisfy him. I will admit to using a typical Chicago trick. I slid him a side gift of a hundred dollars in cash. It works every time, especially in a country where a hundred dollars is equivalent to a gold bar.

When the interpreter had gone, I filled my leather camera bag with the remaining letters. Swinging the bag over my shoulder and hanging a camera about my neck, I left the hotel, hoping to give the impression that I needed to take a few last tourist shots of Saigon before our departure at noon.

It was a walk of four blocks to get to a group of consulates (or former consulates) near the former US Embassy. As I rounded the second block, a woman sitting on a bicycle pulled alongside and asked when we were leaving and if the letters were safe. As we talked, I noticed that there was another woman watching from across the street; then she turned her head. I kept walking, and she followed. Each time I slowed down and turned, the woman looked toward the street as if she were waiting for a bus.

I had to wait in the courtyard of the former French Embassy, now the only working diplomatic office in the city. As one would expect, the place dripped with class. French louvered windows framed the brightly colored tropical flowers growing throughout. A few minutes later, I was taken into the office of the French consul general, the only diplomat remaining in country, who was surprised and pleased to have another Westerner to talk with. During our opening conversation, he said, "Although it's beautiful," pointing to the arched windows that opened onto a magnificent walled tropical garden, "it's a bit of a prison. It's hard to travel. I need to get permission to visit my citizens. It's not like I can jump in the car and drive to Vung Tau for a swim. And the great Saigon restaurants have yet to return. You know they knew how to prepare French dishes better than in Paris before the war. I'll be happy for another posting."

When I told him of my dilemma with the letters, he quickly said, "Of course, we get them too. I'll be happy to deliver them in the diplomatic pouch to the UN officials in Bangkok."

On the way out, down French Victorian stairs, we passed under a wall hanging under glass that must have been ten feet high. It was a siege map of Saigon during its ill-fated Indochina War. Drawn by hand, it detailed everything, even the ditches and creeks that led into the city. To this day, I've coveted that map.

I thanked the guards at the gate and pointed toward the Hotel Ben

Thanh by a park in the city center, four blocks away. With the letters taken care of, a great weight lifted with them, and for the first time I enjoyed Saigon's wide boulevards, tropical trees, and plantings. I was almost skipping as cyclos (tricycle taxis) passed by.

The former US Embassy next to the French looked like it had been frozen in time at the exact moment when helicopters had lifted the last embassy personnel skyward, headed for a carrier off the coast.

The war was over. And so was my journey as the first American reporter to see behind the bamboo curtain in five years.

As I literally swung my camera bag and took a few pictures, I turned the final corner to where I could see the hotel. I was concentrating on a tennis court where US officers and their wives had once played that was now filled with Vietnamese military. I mused about how things changed but also remained the same.

When I looked back, there was the woman who had been tailing me before I went into the consulate. She stood some fifteen feet away. Her face was sullen, and she was staring at me. I moved ahead, but she was approaching me. As she got closer, she reached into her shoulder bag. Should I run? The hotel was just a block away. The distance between us was now only a few feet. My mind was jammed with thoughts. So close to leaving, was this the final opportunity to stop us?

I watched her arm, as if in slow motion, reach into her purse. But instead of a weapon, she pulled out . . . another letter.

The airport exit went smoothly. We were out. No veterans leaving Vietnam had ever felt better than I did.

I looked back, thinking I could feel the bamboo curtain closing again. It would remain closed for many years. But I had a story to tell, one reason you should never let a journalist into your country if you want to keep something secret. I would do what journalists always do: tell stories to people who can do something about them. In this case, I needed a big gun to get directly to the opinion makers and those who had the power to pry open the tight rules that kept the Amerasian children on the streets.


Since we didn't have the footage to tell this story on the air, I decided to write it. I took a wild swing and sent the fully written story, uninvited, to the *New York Times Magazine*, the most prestigious journalistic publication at the time, where it sat for six weeks until editor-in-chief Edward Klein gave it life. It had been so long that I had forgotten about it until one afternoon, while I was sitting at my desk in the WBBM-TV bullpen, our telephone receptionist called across the noisy newsroom, "Bill, *New York Times* on one."

I didn't react. Could be anything, I figured. On the line was a former Chicagoan working as an assistant editor at the magazine. "Hello, Bill? This is Michaela with the *New York Times Magazine*. Did you send us a story about six weeks ago about children trapped in Vietnam?"

I said, "Yes, I did, on spec." I figured it was a nice way to decline with a personal call.

Michaela said, "We'd like to put it on the cover."

To this day, I regard that moment as a highlight of my journalistic career and maybe the beginning of a trend toward high blood pressure.

"The cover?"

"Yes. You sent some slides. Could you send everything you shot? We want to print it on March 2. In a few days, an editor, Glenn Collins, will call you to go over the copy word for word. It will take a couple hours, so you'll have to set it aside. If there's anything you want to add or change, now's the time to do it."

"I understand," I said, trying to be cool while I was having an out-of-body experience hovering above the desk looking at the newsroom, my life, my future.

The experience of hitting the jackpot in print journalism after climbing the journalism ladder strictly in television and radio is hard to communicate. We in television had been "second-class" pretenders among our print colleagues. A lot was jealousy. They could see it coming: television was growing in strength and popularity and had a great advantage in deadlines. We were breaking stories without waiting for the newspaper editors to determine what was news. But we were still seeking respect. This was a ticket in that direction.

As with our original Agent Orange story, the first story, the original, was only the first leg of the relay race. The baton passed to other reporters and then to those in a position to act on the truth. I was glad to pass the baton with the publication of my *Times* article on March 2, 1980.

Working through the State Department we found that an estimated eight thousand Vietnamese American children had been left behind when the US had pulled out of Vietnam on April 30, 1975. Six hundred petitions (a number that would later increase dramatically as word spread) had been filed with the State Department to have them transported to the US. They were American citizens, but the US had no way to verify their identity or to claim them. On the Vietnamese side, there was a diplomatic standoff, and they were unwilling to exchange diplomatic representatives until the trade embargo was lifted. Under pressure from Congressman Stewart McKinney, who was inspired by the *New York Times Magazine* article, Congress passed the Amerasian Immigration Act in 1982, allowing the children to begin coming to the US by classifying them higher on the immigration list, part of the Orderly Departure Program of 1979. There was one last catch: Vietnam objected to the children and relatives who accompanied them being classified as refugees. With that issue corrected, a flow of children began. By 1989, the Amerasian Homecoming Act, sponsored by Senator John McCain and Representative Robert Mrazek, was enacted.

While I shifted my focus elsewhere soon after my article was published and the documentary hit the airwaves, history continued to march forward. Tens of thousands of Amerasians and their relatives have immigrated to America under the homecoming act. It never gets old, seeing my stories develop a life of their own and effect real change. It reminds me that news becomes history and that reporting the news can change history.

# TWENTY

# *CBS Morning News*

By the early eighties, WBBM-TV had become the gold standard for local stations, with high ratings (and income) and a respected community reputation. For those lucky enough to touch the 'BBM "magic," it was all they needed to advance up the corporate ladder. In my case, Van Gordon Sauter had become president of CBS News, and when the beloved Charles Kuralt stepped down from anchoring the *CBS Morning News*, Van had a vision for a new kind of morning news on CBS and started politicking to bring me to New York City. It was the second time I'd leave the 'BBM for a national gig. Kuralt and I were friends from my earlier days in Los Angeles, and I was honored to take his seat. Whenever he'd come to town, we'd share a mutual favorite pastime: a good meal and good wine. There was a feeling that our great experiment in Chicago could take care of itself now. After all, my coanchor, Walter Jacobson, was still at the helm.

Every television journalist (at least every one I've known) dreams of becoming a network anchor. Murrow, Brinkley, and Cronkite were gods among men and the inspiration for us all. So in 1982, when Van tapped me to leave Chicago to become an anchor on the reimagined *CBS Morning News*, I didn't hesitate. It wasn't the evening news, but it was still the big league. We were competing with the very popular *Today Show* on NBC and *Good Morning America* on ABC. I had accumulated enough experience and reputation within the CBS ecosystem to be seriously considered for the program, a live two-hour broadcast five days a week. I had also proven that I could be the face of a new kind of news, and while Van wasn't reinventing the wheel at *CBS Morning News* as he and Bob had done in Chicago, the network wanted to breathe new life into its morning programming, and they needed a proven innovator on screen. To top it all off, they paired me with Diane Sawyer, a proven professional on a meteoric rise to take the business by storm and become the first woman correspondent for *60 Minutes.*

In a theatrical send-off with all the pomp and circumstance our local station could afford, I left Chicago and headed for New York City. My eastward departure for bigger things felt eerily similar to when I had left Topeka for my first job in Chicago. I sure wasn't in Kansas anymore.

But it was a rough entry into New York City. No one remembered me covering four "trials of the century" for CBS News ten years earlier. I was just a local anchorman who had taken over for the cherished Charlie Kuralt. Coming in from the outside, I was the disrupter before there was even a word for it. Diane and I worked well together, and the ratings showed it. But at CBS, the *Morning News* was always second to the *Evening News*, and whenever our ratings improved too much or too quickly, the boys at the *Evening News* and the network executives reminded us of our place in the food chain.

There was one other thing. Getting up at 3:00 a.m. to prepare and anchor a two-hour live national broadcast starting at 7:00 a.m. qualifies one to donate one's corpse to medicine. It's brutal. My world was upside down. There was no sympathy for our schedule and little appreciation for our work outside our morning crew. It was always a hard walk home after our show and eight or nine hours of work, passing the fresh daytime crew on the sidewalk.

Although it took me three years, I managed to earn my way out of intracompany Siberia and secured tenure and respect among the staff. We certainly had our good times, pushing the boundaries of what was thought possible for television news. The advent of live satellite coverage once again changed what was possible with television news. We were connected to almost anywhere in the world. Diane went on to *60 Minutes.* She absolutely deserved it, but it broke up the only chance the *Morning News* ever had to beat the highly competitive *Today Show* and *Good Morning America.*

After a series of trials with several other coanchors, Phyllis George became my new coanchor. A former Miss America, Phyllis was looking to grow her own career by slipping from sports into the news. Literally and figuratively, she was following the new path for women that Diane had created. She cracked the glass ceiling and showed that a woman could be both beautiful and brainy. Many would follow her lead. Every morning, I was witnessing history, watching in real time as my coanchors broke the status quo and moved our nation forward. It wasn't my story, but I was honored to be there.

TWENTY-ONE

# The Golden Leaf

In trade for the physical hassle of turning our workday upside down, Van Gordon Sauter assigned me to be the correspondent for three CBS Reports, the series of documentaries born when Edward R. Murrow left CBS News in 1962. It carried the prestige of Murrow's work and laid the foundation for using television and film to carry journalism to a new level. For me, it would become another milestone, an epiphany in mid-career pointing the way to my future.

The first was a deep dive into the world of smoking, which in 1983 was puffing its deadly way forward while killing more than thirty thousand people a year.

The act of ingesting an addictive poison into the lungs didn't need a new examination. Instead it called for a look at how, despite all the evidence, the practice had continued its uninterrupted journey in America based on choice: *It's your choice if you want to kill yourself; that's freedom.*

It taught me a valuable lesson in how democracy works. We called it *The Golden Leaf.*

Why did it take so long to restrict smoking, even in the face of over-whelming evidence?

The answer is politics, rock-hard southern politics in the states where tobacco was king. It was a $60 billion business. Any decline in tobacco would put a big dent in the economy, or so the senators and members of Congress from the southernstates wanted us to believe.

One drive through the beautiful state of North Carolina made a believer out of me. Newly plowed soil rippled to the horizon as it waited for

244

the seed planter. Larger plants on a later schedule kept a rotation going year-round.

I smelled the tobacco in the drying barns, and it was both invigorating and filled with a sense of history. Here was a plant that grew from first seed to harvest almost without need for fertilizer. For several hundred years, it had defined a territory and a culture and meant a good life for the tobacco farmer.

Was the cancer-causing poison of a cigarette within the plant or after harvest, when the tobacco companies added their "specialties" to enhance addiction, ensuring that a lifelong habit meant lifelong customers?

We found the answer within the democratic system, honed to perfection by southern politicians. I'd call it the dark underside of democracy, where manipulation of congressional votes is regarded as a virtue.

As Senator Thomas Eagleton described it, when tobacco was challenged, the tobacco politicians joined together to fight it. When it was not being assaulted, they compromised on other issues so that when they did need votes, they could call in their favors.

All these maneuvers happened with the full support of the giant tobacco and cigarette companies to build a "China wall," a fortress to perpetuate smoking even if it killed people. It was the politics of smoking versus the health of Americans that forged a tobacco-state barricade against any threat to change.

I had started with CBS News as a line correspondent covering the headlines of the day. The packages rarely lasted more than ninety seconds for the *CBS Evening News* with Walter Cronkite. The show was only thirty minutes long—thirty minutes to condense the news of the world, including the United States, for twenty million viewers. I remember pitching the prosecution's wrap-up in the Angela Davis trial to New York. My good friend John Lane, under pressure to squeeze the day's stories into half an hour for the Cronkite show, asked me, "Can you sum it up in ninety seconds?" A minute and a half to summarize a month's worth of testimony and arguments. But I did it.

For *The Golden Leaf*, an hour-long documentary was akin to writing a book. We had no excuses of not having enough time. It was also the reason documentaries never achieved the status of the *60 Minutes* magazine format. Hour-long documentaries require an hour's worth of attention, something the modern viewer is rarely willing to give. *60 Minutes* found the perfect format, holding its reports to roughly twenty minutes apiece with varied subject matter. It has won the fight for the viewer's attention longer than any other news format in television history.

We traveled through the tobacco barns of North Carolina. I sat next to Senator Jesse Helms in a limousine taking him from a tobacco sale to another appointment. There in the back seat, where he couldn't get away, I asked him if he had personally called the president (Reagan) to get his administration to go easier on labeling tobacco products.

"Did you make a call to him on the labeling bill? To get him to withdraw White House support?"

Helms gave me a knowing smile. "Did I make a call to him? The answer to that question is no."

I knew that Helms was holding back and suspected that he had something he wanted to share if given the chance. "But there might be something else there?" I asked.

"Well, I visit with the president with some frequency. And we discuss a variety of matters of interest to him and to me. It would be senseless for me to pretend I don't discuss issues of interest to him and to me. I discuss it at every available opportunity for the people of North Carolina."

Senator Helms confirmed that he had the ear of the president. And when he talked as the head of the Senate Agriculture Committee, he could speak for twenty-two tobacco states. His discussion was designed to perpetuate the economic interests of those states, in other words, maintain the status quo through a keen knowledge of how the congressional system works, call it compromise, trade, or threat. His goal was votes.

The senator didn't like my direction, but he couldn't escape. All politicians like publicity, and Jesse Helms was known for his clever ability to please the press with quotes like this reference to Duke University's liberal population: "Why build a zoo when we can just put up a fence around Chapel Hill?"

I think we surprised him. In terms of investigative reporting, we would call that interview "golden." It contributed to the investigative process of collecting meaningful evidence that in the end supports a conclusion.

I must admit that the documentary process is not as clear as it seems, looking back on it. A team of producer, correspondent, assistants, and camera crew, often working separately, pour their efforts into a pile that must be sorted. In the middle of it, I asked, *What do we have? Enough for a story, knowing that the tobacco industry is going to challenge whatever you broadcast?*

That's why my legal background was like a rudder helping me stay the course. Prosecutors face the same challenge and are often criticized for not spending the same energy to prove a suspect innocent as they do to prove their guilt. That winds up being the job of the defense.

So we went back to Washington and interviewed Surgeon General C. Everett Koop for the hard question of what Senator Strom Thurmond was bargaining to save—the status quo.

We got Koop to explain to Americans what was actually in a cigarette. It was far more than just natural toasted and cut tobacco leaves. "The terrible part about it is that when you analyze smoke, there's several thousand ingredients. And of course we can follow some of them, those that are carcinogenic, but we don't know everything about all of them yet."

*The Golden Leaf* showed the desperate attempt of the tobacco industry to keep America smoking while frustrated members of Congress and representatives of special interests worked individually to put their assault ladders against the battlements only to be pushed back into the darkness, having to wait until the next session to try again. But the compromise of the southern tobacco states devolved into a scorched-earth tactic of ensuring "*all* for me, even though it means that people will die." It's the science of how to use the democratic system to ensure that power stays in too few hands, often the wrong hands.

The good old boys with Big Tobacco were virtuosos at maintaining the strength of tobacco government support and keeping regulations at a minimum. A tobacco farmer could get a $3,000-an-acre subsidy from the government, ten times what a corn farmer could get, all because of "friends" in Congress. With influence, power, and money on the table, it was difficult and harmful compromises that kept Congress going.

One of the most important parts of long-form news like *The Golden Leaf* is the final stand-up, the closing moments when the reporter looks down the barrel of the camera, right into the eyes of the viewers, and brings the whole story home. I had to ask myself what facts, conclusion, and *feeling* I wanted to leave the audience with and then how to capture those with my writing, delivery, and production. Thankfully, I usually had help. For *The Golden Leaf*, I worked with executive producer Andrew Lack, producer Leslie Cockburn, associate producer Robert Hershman, cameraman Terry Morrison, and audio man Paul Oppenheim. It was an all-star team. In the final cut, we decided to add a version of Aaron Copland's resounding and inspirational "Appalachian Spring" that he had adapted especially for Murrow. It captured the emotional feeling I wanted to provide to the audience. But it also felt like the ghost of Edward R. Murrow giving us an endorsement for another documentary in *his* series. It makes me weak in the knees every time I hear it.

With Copland swelling to an American crescendo, the camera moved in on me for the final close-up. "From their advertising to the new warning labels about what's in a cigarette to what's wrong with cigarettes, the tobacco companies have successfully defended their interests over and over again. They have done it with powerful Senators and Congressmen who point out that tobacco contributes 60 billion dollars a year to the nation's economy. What is left out is 13 billion dollars spent on health problems related to smoking and another 25 billion on lost production and wages. If the politics of smoking comes down to a matter of dollars and cents, no one can deny Americans are paying a heavy price. For CBS Reports, I'm Bill Kurtis."


Edward R. Murrow's shadow loomed large during my days at *CBS Morning News* and with CBS Reports. I was standing on the shoulders of giants, and I tried every day to do good as part of their legacy. Not long after *The Golden Leaf* came out, I was screening one of Murrow's most important pieces for CBS Reports, *Harvest of Shame,* produced in 1960. In his opening stand-up, he stood alone in a field, his deep, thunderous voice reaching from the television set to grab the viewer by the throat. As I stared at this moment in history, I was struck by a deep irony in how the times had changed and how I had carried on his legacy. I realized that in his hand, held casually near his waist, was a cigarette. Did it signal "I'm holding this to make me look casually debonair"? "I need this for my addiction"? Or just "This is the accepted image of the day, as much a part of the American lifestyle as the latest fashion"? Now that I was looking for it, I saw the cigarette as a constant prop in Murrow's recorded life. I realized he was saying, "Smoking is as much a part of me as a suit and tie." I've never seen a cigarette used this way in my fifty years of broadcasting. And unfortunately, it killed him. Five years later, on April 27, 1965, he died of lung cancer at the age of fifty-seven.

# TWENTY-TWO

# The Plane That Fell from the Sky

Van Gordon Sauter, the president of CBS News, was captivated by TWA Flight 841. Several years before, on a cloudy night over Saginaw, Michigan, a Boeing 727 had plunged thirty-four thousand feet in forty-four seconds and miraculously pulled out of deadly dive. The crew and eighty-two passengers were saved by the pilot, Captain Hoot Gibson. But his heroic feat was colored by an investigation into why it had happened. A commission found the crew to blame for allowing the plane to roll over and then plunge straight down, headed for disaster.

While I was at *CBS Morning News*, several years after the historic near disaster, Van decided that he wanted to tell the story his way: to broadcast the drama and terror of the actual event. But how? We knew how to report chaos and were experts at it, but *re-creating* the whirlwind? That's a whole different ball game.

Van asked producers Paul and Holly Fine, one of the nation's best documentary teams from Washington, DC, to see if they could stay within television news standards to depict what had happened. He didn't want a flashy, exaggerated Hollywood treatment; he wanted to capture it as if his camera crew had been on the plane as it dropped out of the sky. If anyone could do it, it was the Fines. The producing couple had reenacted the attempted assassination of Ronald Reagan, a shining addition to their stellar work for *60 Minutes* on CBS and for other networks. But this job was a special challenge. How could they re-create the rapid descent of a plane that was falling out of the sky with the passengers on board?

I was assigned as the correspondent for the project, and Paul,

Holly, and I hit it off immediately. It was a match made in documentary heaven.

Paul and Holly had an idea to contact each of the passengers and ask them if they would travel to Burbank, California, and sit in the seats they had occupied during the drop. Burbank is in the land of moviemaking. Anyone with an aviation script needing to shoot inside a plane can rent the interior from a "junkyard" of aviation parts. The passengers who chose to come would indeed sit in their very seat to reenact their facial expressions and emotions during what they had thought was their last few minutes alive.

In order to achieve real-time accuracy, Paul interviewed each passenger separately so he could play their thoughts and feelings while he was filming a close-up.

Thirty-nine of the eighty-two passengers answered yes, they would like to do it. Their reasons varied. Some were still suffering from post-traumatic stress syndrome (PTSD), the combat syndrome of recurring memories of life-threatening events. Others wanted to see their fellow passengers who had survived the life-or-death experience. It had been the ultimate bonding experience.

Holly Wicker, an escort for orphan children immigrating from Calcutta, had been in her seat holding a child who was now four years older. As the chaotic re-creation played on-screen, we cut in sound from Holly's actual interview: "My attention at that point was focused on a five-pound baby on my lap who was turning blue." Between passengers' recollections and my voice-over, the camera panned through the cabin in slow motion. Van didn't want Hollywood, but he still wanted drama. A woman who had been making up in the lavatory was now sprawled unconscious in the cabin aisle. Other passengers screamed and strained against gravity to lift arm to face.

During the emotional discharge in the cabin, a separate story was unfolding in the cockpit: the story of he story of Captain Gibson, who heroically pulled the 727 out of its dive moments before tragedy. He was an acrobatic pilot in his leisure time. A bachelor, noted for his handsome features and magnetic effect on young women, Hoot was a pilot's pilot, exactly what was needed to break the descent of the plane that fell from the sky. Breaking the fall was precisely what happened. He was unable to control the plane's nose-down dive, which created slipstream pressure over the wings so powerful that it wasn't possible to create a vacuum for the airplane to achieve "lift." He tried everything he could think of until, from instinct, he put the wheels down for landing. The extension of the wheels broke the fall enough to create the vacuum over the wings and allow Gibson to control the dive, pulling out at five thousand ft above the ground.

The work of Paul and Holly Fine has rarely been equaled in taking facts, including recruiting the actual participants in a harrowing event to reenact the story. The word "reenactment" doesn't even come close to describing the herculean effort it required.

I was lucky to watch the Fines work. I got to the set to find thirty-nine passengers sitting in their exact seats in the fuselage. It became a "happening" for the passengers, crew, and pilots, an experience of reunion and participation. Napoleon is quoted as saying, "When your enemy is making a mistake, don't interrupt him." I would paraphrase that quote as "When your producers are operating brilliantly, don't interrupt them."

In the hands of the best in the business, Van's original obsession with this historic event and his moon-shot scheme to capture the story had actually worked. The re-creation of the flight was miraculous. In previews, one reviewer said, "The program is one of the most compelling reconstructions of a flight emergency ever to be filmed." Others thought so too, and in 1983, "The Plane That Fell from the Sky" won a Peabody Award.

I was privileged to add what skill I had to Paul and Holly's dream team. For all their technical vision and masterful execution, they were stuck at how to start the story. It seemed clear to me that the basic facts were the most dramatic part of the story. So with a shot of a jetliner landing at National Airport in Washington, DC, I began, "On April 4, 1979, a Boeing 727 fell thirty-three thousand feet in forty-four seconds. The eighty-nine people on board came within two seconds of crashing. Most of them thought they would die. . . . Tonight we're going to find out what happened during one of the most extraordinary flights in the history of aviation."

# TWENTY-THREE

# Muhammad Ali

As part of my three-year journey with CBS News in New York, I did a profile of Muhammad Ali for a new CBS News program called *The American Parade*. CBS executives were hoping to capture some of the *60 Minutes* magic with a spin-off magazine show focused on celebrity interviews. Sort of a "Whatever happened to . . ." show. I pitched a different perspective of one of the world's great personalities and, more importantly, a direct investigation of an issue that could have meant an end to professional boxing. A picture of Ali that was much different from the brash, loud, controversial figure most of us knew. The subject that no one wanted to talk about was potentially explosive in the world of sports: was Ali brain damaged?

As of my report, that question had not been answered. The piece that came from my three days with Muhammad Ali turned out to be another brush with history, and one that I will always be proud of. But it also offered me another glimpse into the thrilling, joyful challenges of this form of storytelling. My days as a legal correspondent had long passed, and I could feel my time as an anchor coming to a close. My time with Muhammad Ali reminded me of where one of my biggest passions was—with investigative and documentary reporting. While it may not have the flashy appeal of a murder trial or an urban riot, making this kind of news was just as thrilling to me.

~

Ali was forty-two, retired from boxing but still enjoying universal adulation as the most popular athlete in the world. I wanted to explore the shadow that had begun to follow him wherever he went: the trembling hand, the slurred speech, the slow gait. You couldn't help wondering whether boxing had damaged his brain. A confession would change boxing forever. If the Greatest walks down Queer Street, no boxer is safe.

There were plenty of opinions on the subject, but the official position of the Ali camp as represented by his manager, Herbert Muhammad, and the Nation of Islam was a bold no, even after sixty-one boxing matches. Herbert was emphatic: "Any shaky clues are not caused by boxing, and Ali is not brain damaged."

So what *was* the problem? I spent three days with the champ at his farm and his gym in Michigan, his mansion in Los Angeles, and several mosques for prayer to see him in different situations. My offer to Herbert was to either end the brain-damage rumors or find the truth. Ali looked forward to the travel as a break from the rhythm of his retirement. Put simply, he was bored and I offered something interesting.

We started on Forty-Seventh Street, Chicago, on the deep South Side. It's the most historic Black neighborhood in the city, with a dossier of famous entertainers like Nat King Cole; Louis Armstrong; poet Gwendolyn Brooks; businessman John Johnson, founder of *Ebony* magazine; Black-owned banks, corporations, and retail stores; and the core of Chicago's Black community.

But none were bigger than Muhammad Ali. When he stepped onto a street anywhere in the world, there was bedlam and love.

By the time he cleared the car door, Ali was swarmed, and he switched into his familiar faux boxing stance, throwing punches at kids jumping around him.

The love went both ways. While Ali was in this crowd, his pocket was picked for $1,500. When I asked him about it later, he didn't seem angry. He acted as if it was worth it, even expected.

This was home, Bronzeville, Chicago, one of many homes that we would visit. At this time, he spent most of his life in his rambling house in Los Angeles or in some hotel room with little to do. The constant entourage of fifty or sixty people was gone, his servants didn't live in, and his in-laws lived in a separate house on the grounds. Now he was eight thousand miles and eight years from the Thrilla in Manila. He would tell you that boxing was just a preparation for his real life to come, that his greatest triumphs were yet ahead. But when I was with him, I was struck by the silence.

I wondered if those who had been with him in the good years, like Angelo Dundee, who had known him for twenty-five years, felt the same way.

"I think Muhammad right now is a bored individual. I feel badly for him because he's not in the glow anymore, the limelight. How do you replace what he was? You don't."

Dundee should have known. And so should his third wife, Veronica, whom he had married in 1977. She said, "He doesn't have a real single purpose now. He makes appearances for charities and things, but he's not sure what he wants to do. He's adamant about his religion and wants to be a minister, but beyond that, there's no one thing that he has a schedule to follow and do and have a real purpose."

I was pursuing the champ's daily routine, looking for clues in his offhand comments, his facial expressions and body language, in what he did and didn't say. I was trying to search for a story and tell a story, all in real time and on camera. And it had to look natural, casual, effortless.

I was building the story as we went from location to location. We moved from his mansion in an old section of Los Angeles to the local mosque. As the imam prayed before a full house of congregants on their knees, Ali towered above them, his hands folded in a cup before him. He dreamed of building a mosque in every state in the Union, but for now, he contented himself with transferring words from an Islamic reader into his own hand and writing up a daily schedule that included down-to-the-minute times for daily prayer.

His manager, Herbert Muhammad, represented the church, the Nation of Islam, in his life. "I think the religious factor is the main thing that holds it together because in our contract, our agreement with each other was that if either one of us left the Nation of Islam, the contract was automatically null and void."

Herbert had scheduled the multiple destinations around the country, all Ali's properties, like his farm at Berrien Springs, Michigan. He was a son of Elijah Muhammad, a founder of the American Muslim movement.

The three of us, Herbert, Ali, and I, walked down a path in front of the farmhouse; on the right was a barn they had turned into a gym. Ali had been quiet during our time together, hardly the loud shouter I was used to seeing. So I offered a provocative comment to Herbert, hoping to get Ali talking: "There was a time when he was fanatical about separatism and the religion."

Ali jumped in, seeing an opportunity for a bit of humor at my expense. "In those days," he said with a smile, "you were the devil."

I bought the joke and returned, "The white man was the devil; that's right. Have you had a tough time changing? Has the religion changed?"

Ali was now alive, in focus. "No, sir, it was natural because I never really believed that people were evil because of their color."

I recalled a similar conversation we'd had at the mansion in LA and used the humor to open what is usually a touchy subject among boxers and their managers. Again to Herbert Muhammad: "It is commonly thought that Ali gave away all his earnings to the Muslim movement. In fact, just recently he donated his mansion in Chicago to the faith."

Ali answered, admitting that he needed the tax write-off of more than $1 million.

Herbert took the bait: "We got $8 million for the Thrilla in Manila, and we got $250,000 for training expense."

I said, "Joe Louis spent his life with nothing. How do you ensure that Muhammad Ali isn't that way, and what are the finances?"

It was a conversation among friends but appears aggressive in print.

Herbert replied, "Muhammad Ali is a multimillionaire right now; it's a fact. And the interest on that money, he lives off the interest on that money."


In the editing room, when the hard work of an interviewer is over and the hard work of a producer begins, I found my interview with Angelo Dundee to cut in a clean transition: "Money is not his god and never has been his god." That's the other fun part about cutting together these stories; you're not bound by time and place, as you are when reporting live. You can pull together sound bites and video clips from days apart and miles away to tell the most cohesive, interesting version of the story.

Now with Angelo, I pressed further: "But as far as you know, he kept the money."

"Muhammad is in good shape financially. There will have to be no benefits for Muhammad Ali. Muhammad Ali could make money by accident."

There was visible evidence of his wealth all over the country. A training camp in Pennsylvania. A larger development in Virginia Beach. And this farm in Berrien Springs, Michigan. It was formerly owned by someone else with a famous name.

Ali loved pranking: "It was owned by Al Capone."

My question: "Have you found any signs of Capone out here?"

"I found an old tommy-gun."

We both laughed as we continued our walk on the farm. At the southern end of Lake Michigan, where Chicagoans chose to pick up some rural flavor, it included some cultivated areas and a collection of outbuildings that looked more like a Kentucky horse farm than hardcore farming.

Ali hoped to make this farm and his development in Virginia Beach part of his future. He and Herbert wanted to train boxers and promote boxing matches. They said the promoters of the day didn't give their boxers a fair shake. But Angelo Dundee threw in some reality to quench the dream.

"If I'm trying to sell a fighter, the last guy I want around me is Ali. They won't even know I exist. Do you know they thought I was a mute because of Muhammad Ali? I couldn't get a word in edgewise. He can't be a trainer, a manager, because nobody wants to talk about the subject. They want to talk about Muhammad because he's such an interesting individual."

Now, exploring a new theme, I cut from the farm in Michigan back to Los Angeles, where Herbert had set up a horse-riding exercise with Veronica, an excellent rider. Ali was feeling better about having me around, more relaxed and teasing Veronica: "You get too much attention. Too much attention."

Veronica cautioned Ali, "They're very sensitive. Be careful; he might kick you."

That was gasoline on the fire with a master showman. Ali leaned down to put his head on Veronica's horse, playing with the horse. "They gonna say he's got brain damage. He's fighting HORSES!"

With that joke, I realized that the incessant rumors of brain damage were never far from his consciousness, and he was tired of them. They came from the media and people who had never met him; from those who owed him everything and his most casual fans; from his friends and loved ones, which was probably worse.

Ali couldn't help himself and mounted one of the horses to ride around the ring with Veronica. He was a big man and rode like one who'd had no lessons. The greatest athlete in the world couldn't stay out of the limelight. Fearless, confident that he could do anything, he was bouncing in the saddle with his hand on the pommel, chasing Veronica, who was tired of Ali turning her serious exercise into an exhibitionist performance. Living with Ali could be like that.

Before we let him ride off into the sunset, I thought it was about time we probed deeper. There were sixty-one matches for which Ali had deliberately trained by showing he could take blows to the head in sparring rounds. It was much like riding a horse with Veronica. Impulsive. Impetuous. Devil-may-care.

With the establishing work done, it was time to start building the case. First, we had to find out what happens to the brain when the outer skull is struck with an eight-ounce glove traveling sixty miles an hour. If the hit is to the front of the brain, the jellylike mass is battered against the rear of the skull. If the blow is to the side of the jaw, the brain ricochets from side to side, twisting the brain stem. The result may damage any part of the brain, from the outer layers to the deep midline structures. That can affect all human function.

Dr. Ira Casson was a neurologist who had done studies on the effect of chronic brain damage in boxers. He gave us a formal explanation: "Slurred speech, unsteady gait, poor coordination. Many of these people will look like patients with Parkinson's. They will have tremors, be very rigid, have trouble initiating movement. If it gets more prominent, they will have trouble with memory, with knowing what's going on around them. If it gets more severe than that, they will have frank psychotic syndromes, organic mental syndromes where they become confused, disoriented, not knowing what's going on about them. They won't be able to know things like who the president is. If they get severe, they won't be able to function in the world."

Ali had lived his life in a fishbowl. Many of us felt as if we'd known him all our lives. That was why when we saw his more recent interviews, we sensed something wrong. It started with his speech. You asked yourself, *Can this be the Louisville Lip, the brash kid who dazzled us with his oratory?*

I reviewed our hands-on, face-to-face opportunity to observe Ali: "If you're around him for a while, you notice an occasional twitching in his hands. Or a glaze in his eyes, and you wonder if ever again he'll float like a butterfly and sting like a bee. You notice his open briefcase with vials of medication in it, and you think maybe the rumors are true; maybe the American hero is brain damaged or punch-drunk."

And then, before our very eyes, Ali changed. Ali loved magic tricks to entertain kids. He showed us one and had us amazed.

I said, "LOOK AT THAT! There are no lies in the ring, but outside it, the Ali we knew was an illusion."

Angelo Dundee knew what I meant. "He knew how to create scenes. Ali always was the kind of a guy who could light up naturally. Turn that light out and he was dull city . . . turn it on and he was dynamite."

Back in Los Angeles. We were lying in the yard in front of his Los Angeles mansion in order to get a different setting for an interview. It also relaxed the champ, who repeated an oft-told story of where he'd got the idea of doing crazy antics to build up ticket sales.

"I got that from Gorgeous George," the famous wrestler. "I came to see him kill and see if he could back up his words. And twenty thousand people came to see it too. And I said, 'That's a good idea. I AM THE GREAT-EST.' That wasn't true, but I put emphasis on it. And people at ringside said that nigger needs a whupping . . . and I said, 'You paid $200 to see it . . . and I said, 'Ahh,'" laughing at himself as he let us in on his big secret.

Dundee remembered, "When he was young, did he slur his speech? He didn't slur his speech. He spoke low. A couple times I'd go, 'Eh?' I told my wife. She thinks I'm going deaf or something. But he would talk slow and quiet when he's by himself, yes."

Veronica on the subject: "I've noticed that sometimes he gets lazy about how he talks, and I say sometimes it sounds like you're mumbling, when I tell him, no wonder they say that, and he could perk right up and sound like he used to."

I asked Ali, "Veronica says sometimes you get lazy and talk slow and things like that."

Ali explained, "I talk to so many people, do so many interviews; I sign so many autographs, I try to take all the shortcuts I can. Now I'm concentratin', how do I sound to you?"

"GREAT. You sound terrific."

"I wish I could talk as pretty as you." And in a truly humbling moment, he dropped his register and matched my delivery: "Hello, this is Bill Kurtis, CBS News."

Veronica said, "I think people just want to have something to write about, so they take a little bit, and then there was a bad story over in London that we don't even know that he was brain damaged. . . ."

Ali explained further: "I got off the plane at 4 in the morning. I was slurring my words, I was dizzy, and the word got out I was on drugs. I was tired, like I was on heroin."

One way to look for brain damage is to look for small-muscle coordination. Ali's detractors pointed to his autographs, scribbled in a crowd, and then used that writing as proof of a problem. Angelo Dundee helped him learn how to spell.

Dundee was on point: "Slow. It would take him forever and a day. Today it takes him forever and a day to write out something. I've been with him. Takes forever and a day. Slow process with him. Not book smart. He's world smart."

I picked up the trail straight to Ali himself: "What about memory? Can you remember things? Short attention span?"

Ali never could pass up a joke. "What did he say? I forgot."

Herbert knew Ali's comedic timing well and stepped in to play the straight man. "You've forgot already."

We all laughed, but as the lightness of the moment faded, Herbert took the opportunity for a more honest explanation. "I think people . . . say, 'Ali, you remember me. I met you twenty years ago. I was wearing a green jacket and red shirt, you remember?' He don't know. He may have met a hundred people exactly like him."

As luck would have it, my crew had footage of the perfect example to back up Herbert's claim. We cut in a shot of Ali in a crowd, surrounded by people. One of them cried out, "I'm from South Carolina! I'm the one who brought you from South Carolina, remember that? I saw you at the airport!"

In a project like this that takes place over multiple days, it takes time to build a rapport and trust between the reporter and the subject. Once that's established, it's time to get to business asking the hard questions and finding the answers you've been looking for all along.

I started out by asking, "People will remember a doctor saying that you had a thyroid condition. Have any problems with that?" Some had reported that if his thyroid wasn't properly functioning, he could appear dazed and punch-drunk.

"No more," Ali said plainly. "I had that checked."

"When you try to put the pieces of the puzzle together, the picture is still unclear, flawed, because it's only natural that the people around him tend to protect him, flawed because the people who aren't around him tend to believe the worst. Ali will tell you as your eyes will tell you that he's not the man he used to be."

"I've taken about 175,000 hard punches," Ali returned. "I think that would affect anybody some."

I then asked Herbert the question that had been on everyone's mind, point blank: "Do you think Ali has brain damage?"

"No. I sent him to the Mayo Clinic, and they did an examination; they did a brain scan, and they said he didn't have no brain damage."

Ali chimed in, "I went to UCLA Medical Clinic, and those are white doctors . . ."

"And they said he didn't have no brain damage," Herbert finished.

I then went to the source. In an interview with Dr. Harry Gamololous, who ran CAT scans and other neurological tests on Ali, I asked, "How serious was Muhammad Ali's CAT scan?"

"Well, I think it was mildly to moderately abnormal. The ventricles are mildly to moderately enlarged."

Again, I had to get to the heart of it: "Is Muhammad Ali brain damaged?"

"Not at all," Dr. Gamololous replied confidently. "There's not any indication by any parameters, CAT scans, brain chemistries, neurological exams, complex tests of logic and function and motor skills—there's no evidence of any kind of brain damage in Muhammad Ali, not at all."

The story was all coming together, but I wanted to get at the truth from every possible angle. Sometimes those angles are closed off. I tried to talk with Ali's personal physician, Dr. Dennis Cope, at UCLA. He would not speak with us until he had a note signed by Ali releasing him from any doctor-patient confidentiality. While the letter came through, Ali said not to tell us anything too private. So on the advice of his attorney, the doctor declined the interview.

Hitting dead ends or bad leads is just part of the job. You just keep looking for new angles, searching for new questions.

As my three days with Ali were coming to an end, it dawned on me that we were looking for something that no longer existed, and our judgement may have been false. We still wanted to see Muhammad Ali the boxer, but that man no longer existed. He was now a prayerful figure in a quiet world. A stark comparison to a previous life, twenty-seven years of the most celebrated career in the ring.

Herbert told me that he knew Ali had changed when exposed to various situations, not filling his head with adrenaline as in the old days. So, after a three-hour drive from Berrien Springs, we pulled up to a gym in Kalamazoo, Michigan. Herbert had scheduled an exhibition match in the ring to promote a friend's gymnasium. But I think he was hoping we'd see the old Ali, free of talk of brain damage, spouting the poetry and bragging he'd always used to promote his fights.

Herbert was right. Suddenly it was the old Ali.

As we entered the gym, the wide-eyed gym rats stood alongside, waiting to see their messiah. And the young fighters just stood there in disbelief.

Ali picked up the moment with his standard phrase: "I am the greatest of all time, three-time world champ, no conditions!"

The smell of liniment filled the huge room as we walked toward a boxing ring in the middle. Ali excused himself to change in the locker room. I could tell he was rising to the occasion, even excited. It was all there in an authentic boxing venue, not staged for the cameras but equipped with hanging body bags and punching bags swinging so fast you couldn't count the hits. In another corner, a young boxer was skipping rope. The *thwack* each time it hit the floor echoed throughout the room.

Ali's opponent was K. P. Porter, who billed himself as the heavyweight champ of Michigan. He was fit and ready to go. But I couldn't help but feel sorry for him, even though he was twenty years younger and maybe faster than the champ, who had just come off three hours on the road.

It didn't matter. Ali came from the locker room and was nearly unrecognizable. He saw me and patted his belly, saying, "Overweight, three years out of training. But watch me put a whupping on. I announce it first."

Both fighters were in the ring. I knew that since the match was essentially scheduled for me, I was free to even climb into the enclosure. But once in there, it was like being trapped with the bull inside the bullfight arena. I got out quickly.

It was just an exhibition match, but K. P. Porter began to take it very seriously. I thought it was more a matter of survival than putting up a good fight for his friends at the edges of the canvas.

Ali landed a couple of jabs, then followed with a right cross. At the sound of the bell, he walked back to my corner as I leaned over the ropes to comment on the blow, "That's where those fifty pounds help."

Ali was focused on the fight, almost lost in the competition. He said, "I've got to warm up. I haven't opened up yet. Wait till I put somethin' on him."

Porter came at him in the corner, exchanging a left and a right to the body. Then Ali knocked him back on his heels with a hard right to his chest.

Herbert had planned for three rounds, but Ali would have gone further. His concentration was absolute.

While the sparring continued, I asked the obvious question: "Do you sometimes worry about what all the blows to the head may have done?"

It was a thoughtful answer: "People go to war for this country and come back with one leg. That's what he's done for something he values. And look at all my world fame, and I look at all I've done, physical and nonphysical; add it all up and I'd do it all over again."

One more series of blows ended with Ali delivering a hard right, rocking his opponent into an upright stance. There was no mentoring, no kindly instruction to a young boxer just starting out. Ali was boxing again with no sign of brain damage. I saw boxing greatness in those few minutes. Some people call it a killer instinct.

As producer Maurice Murad and I were completing this piece, we faced a dilemma. I had just spent three of the most interesting days of my career with the most charismatic character in the world in a variety of situations in which he appeared as normal as the "old Ali," but I still didn't have an answer to the brain-damage question.

We had doctors' statements of "no brain damage," including CAT scans, rare moments with Ali in the ring again, explanations that slow speech was part of his family genetics.

In many ways, Herbert was right. Ali could appear normal. Veronica said so. Friends said so. I saw it clearly.

But I was right too in continuing to question what I saw between the Ali "onstage" and the moments when the camera wasn't rolling.

There was still trembling of the left hand—the thumb—and other obvious clues that something was wrong. So I went back to Herbert and presented my case several times, saying, "If you don't provide an adequate explanation, at least some alternative to brain damage, the reaction will be worse than before. Being asked to accept that Ali could take all those 175,000 blows over his career without lasting damage is a rope-a-dope on the public."

Finally, Herbert Muhammad allowed Ali's doctor to say, "OK, you can say that Ali suffers from Parkinson's syndrome."

That announcement in our report in 1984 was the first official admission of the slow deterioration of Ali over the next forty years. Herbert may have thought he was avoiding a more serious-sounding diagnosis of Parkinson's disease, but most people ignored the word "syndrome."

That episode of *American Parade* on CBS-TV aired in March 1984. In September, a group of doctors in New York City confirmed that Muhammad Ali suffered from Parkinson's disease.

A definition of Parkinson's fit all the symptoms we had observed during our time with Ali. Mayo Clinic defines Parkinson's as a progressive nervous disorder that affects movement. A tremor or shaking usually begins in the hand or thumb when it's at rest.

The rest of the definition could easily have Ali's name on the symptoms. And most important, the disease can be causes by blows to the head.

A world of fans took the news stoically, as if learning that a family member had an incurable disease, knowing that it meant they were destined to watch his public appearances over forty years get worse. And yet they continued to accept any sight of him with a mix of nostalgia and admiration.

Muhammad Ali died on June 3, 2016, without argument that he was indeed the Greatest.

# TWENTY-FOUR

# Back to Chernobyl

After three years in New York, I had built quite the résumé. I was a morning anchor, which was the launchpad for many of the most storied careers in broadcasting. Sitting next to the singular talent of Diane Sawyer every day was an added bonus. At the same time, my work with CBS Reports had led to a groundbreaking exclusive with Muhammad Ali and, with the magic of Paul and Holly Fine, helped win the network a Peabody Award. On paper, it looked like my network career was off to a roaring success. In reality, it was anything but.

Ratings suffered for *CBS Morning News* and CBS Reports. The *Morning News* had perennially been in third place throughout its CBS history. The many careers that had been tested in the early-morning hours, from Walter Cronkite to Charlie Kuralt to Mike Wallace, had ranked high in journalistic effort but shared our pain of third place. For a while, the network took pride in producing a news program that excelled in daily coverage. But once the standard became ratings, we were outspent and outpromoted by the competition. Diane Sawyer and I did inch up to second place when the NBC *Today Show* became embroiled in some on-air replacements, but as soon as Diane took the offer to become the first woman correspondent at *60 Minutes*, *CBS Morning News* slid back to third.

CBS Reports gave me a remarkable opportunity, and I will always be proud of the work we did there. But traditional long-form documentaries were not a growth industry for the network in 1985. *60 Minutes* had found the perfect combination of packaging three twenty-minute segments, short enough to hold the audience and long enough to tell a good story, so that was where the network executives focused their attention and their money.

Even though CBS Reports never became the next big thing in broadcast journalism, it was a pivotal moment in my career. As my time in Kansas had shown me, dreams can change. In New York, my dream of being a network anchor was fading at the same time that I realized what I was most passionate about—chasing down a story, capturing it on film, writing it, and presenting it all to the public. It's an art to find the truth and then figure out how to combine audio and visual to best tell it. Every once in a while, an anchor will face the thrill of a live situation—like a tornado approaching—and get to gather, organize, write, and report the facts all on the fly. But live situations don't happen very often. For my colleagues who still get pleasure from bathing in the warm glow of klieg lights and feel the adrenaline starting to flow when the floor director points his finger, signaling "Go," God bless you. To each their own. But I loved to be out on the road, not behind an anchor desk. I wanted to investigate stories and write voice-over scripts and cut it all together in the production booth. I was obsessed with it all, and I was ready for more.

In hindsight, it was the next step in my path from field reporting in Chicago to CBS's West Coast Bureau to the first international correspondent at a local station.

So I left New York City and chased my dream back to Chicago, back to the girl who had brought me, back to the 'BBM. I was taking a step back to set up two steps forward. Johnathan Rodgers, the general manager at WBBM-TV, devised an attractive compromise that would give him what he wanted, a full-time anchor, and me what I wanted, a contract that allowed me to produce five-hour-long documentaries every year for five years. In the transition from national to local, I also started working with the documentary division at PBS, with NOVA and PBS Specials. The final piece of my documentarian puzzle was in a clause I inserted into my new contract to return to WBBM—I wanted the option to start my own company while working for CBS. This seed, buried in pages of legalese, eventually grew into Kurtis Productions, the second act of my career in journalism. But that's a story for another time.

What is important in *this* story is one of the first projects I covered after my documentarian turn. I led an American team for PBS NOVA to the Chernobyl Nuclear Power Plant less than two years after the infamous explosion in April 1986. The Cold War had not ended, the Berlin Wall was still standing, and I was the first American (and among the first journalists in the world) to go to ground zero of one of the Soviet Union's greatest failures. Another close encounter with history as it was unfolding.

We landed in Moscow around midnight, my first time in the Soviet Union. The airport was gloomy and unswept. The faces were what I expected at that hour, reflecting a miserable existence. The clothing was not exactly designer friendly. Everything was dark, which wouldn't change when morning came. It was as if communism had sucked the color from life to fit the morose mood of the always-present talk of "revolution." It was like waking every morning with the mental burden of having a serious disease.

On our way from the airport to the cars, we passed a collection of taxi drivers. While irrelevant to our journey, I was struck by their size, like NFL linebackers, square and muscular. I imagined them as the worker class of the Bolshevik revolution, here on the streets waiting for fares. As a former Marine, I thought, *Thank God we don't have to fight Russians*.

Our hotel was empty, and we stopped in the restaurant before going to bed. The kitchen was closed, but we took a beer and went up. In my room, I got a call from a young woman who wanted to talk to me. Never mind how she knew my room number. I was green enough to not even think she might be a KGB plant and didn't check with Jim Gallagher, a *Chicago Tribune* correspondent for several years who was part of the team. He would have known the drill inside and out.

So I went to her room.

I had seen her in the restaurant, eating alone. She opened the door, invited me in, and asked what we had come for. I explained the Chernobyl trip. She didn't seem impressed and began talking about her life there. She lived with her parents in their apartment and wouldn't be eligible for her own apartment for several years. A car was out of question and would come much later. That was life in Moscow, she said. Dreary, without much hope for change. Men wanted sex for advancement at every level. Did she want help to get out? If the room was bugged, as Gallagher later suggested with great certainty, was she trying to get some incriminating statement or admission that could be used against me or to prove that I wasn't really a documentary producer but had more political motives?

Jim explained later that she was definitely KGB. They often used women to "turn" visitors and obtain blackmail material for later. I thought it sounded like a ridiculous spy novel.

I'd like to say I outsmarted Russian intelligence, but frankly, it was my midwestern naivete that paid off. I left her hotel room clean of anything incriminating; otherwise I could be writing this from a Siberian labor camp.

The team slept for one night and day before catching the famous midnight train to Kyiv. We'd heard that foreigners were steered to the midnight train so the overnight travel would prevent them from seeing the poor living standards between Moscow and Kyiv. They needn't have bothered. Muscovites were already living along the tracks. They seemed universally afraid and unhappy, wrapped in permanent colors of beige and gray. Maybe this was what the "revolution" looked like before communism was hauled down like a hammer-and-sickle flag at sunset. I'm glad I saw "before" and "after."

Moscow *cold* could be one frigid block of the Chicago hawk, the wet-to-the bone kind. As we loaded our extensive gear onto the sleeping car, it was more like a black-and-white movie than reality, the kind where Humphrey Bogart turns the corner in a raincoat with collar turned up.

Rime crusted on the windows, from clouds of steam pouring from between railroad cars and around the wheel sets as the air brakes hissed impatiently, creating that never-melting look.

Soon the wood-paneled corridors were moving in rhythm to the click of wheels on rails and made everyone look like drunken sailors, grabbing for a handrail with every step.

By morning, we were in a different country, Ukraine, where we prepared to drive the ninety miles to the reactor.

Kyiv was beautiful even with only skeleton profiles for trees. Onion-topped churches showed off the attractive paint colors that were scarce in Moscow. A crowded streetcar defied the recent radiation scare as it pulled up a short hill. The countryside was flat as a tabletop, and it seemed as if every foot of ground was plowed, waiting for spring and an early planting of wheat. This was the breadbasket of the Soviet Union and highly treasured by every occupier since the Cossacks. Before that, peasant farmers, like my grandparents, worked the land with traditional tools and horses and lived in unpainted wooden shacks with chickens and goats ruling the small yards.

I said to the group in our van, "This looks very familiar to me." My grandmother was part Ukrainian and traveled to Kansas, as many Eastern Europeans did because of the wheat fields. I could see my distant immigrant family landing at Ellis Island, catching one train after another until they reached land that looked exactly like the farms they had left—in Ukraine. It was a Kansas postcard.

We were traveling in a white Volkswagen van, cold inside, but we didn't care. We were journalists on the track of a story, with access to the site of what could be, if the scare stories were true, the biggest story ever: "How the Soviets Destroyed the World."

Foolhardy, since we didn't know or trust the radiation readings of the Soviets running the rescue operation more than a year after the explosion? Well, you take chances when you're young.

We tried to minimize the risk by asking a well-known professor of physics at Harvard University to accompany us—with his Geiger counter, of course. Dr. Richard Wilson specialized in experimental particle physics, studying the nature of the smallest particles that constitute matter as they collide at very high velocities. He was perfect as one of the first American academics to lay eyes upon ground zero.

My cameraman was Tom Vlodek, a veteran CBS News shooter. As I've mentioned, Jim Gallagher, who qualified as an old Soviet hand from several years as correspondent for the *Chicago Tribune* living in Moscow, provided the running commentary on changes he could recognize as results of the explosion.

One other safeguard: we received a full-body scan for radiation as a baseline at Argonne National Laboratory near Chicago. Everyone has a certain amount of background radiation. We would report again for another scan after the trip to Chernobyl to measure radiation we may have picked up.

We were stopped by soldiers thirty miles from ground zero. Only official workers and visitors were allowed to pass.

There were two "zones" of safety. After the thirty-mile zone was a ten-mile inner zone that nothing would leave: buses, cars, work clothing, anything that might have been exposed to radiation. Everything would be there forever. When it was useless, it was buried.

Before entering the ten-mile zone by bus, we were invited to meet a tableful of reactor officials, both as a courtesy and indoctrination, an opportunity to ask questions.

Upon sitting down, the tradition is to throw back a shot glass of vodka as a toast to our trip. In one movement, the glasses went up with the authority of a salute, then down with a resounding finality.

Could anything be more Russian? I expected to see the men doing the gopak, the Ukrainian squat dance. But there was no celebration in this place, no robust reaction to having guests who brought an excuse for a daytime shot. I was growing aware that these men, all the men, looked like battle-scarred veterans who didn't want to talk about it. They'd clearly been through some dreadful experience that had taken them deep within their souls to find help.

This could not be explained away as communism. It was far beyond that. It was more like the realization that the foundation of their mother country was shattered. Like they had seen the edge of the world—really.

It was a good meeting in that it sobered us up for the final stage of our journey. No more tourist adventures. We felt like we were headed to a funeral.

We boarded the bus for the ten-mile drive to ground zero.

Professor Wilson sat next to me in the regular bus seats while Tom began taping. From this point on, every second of tape counted. I told Tom, "You probably should turn the camera on and don't turn it off till we leave." It was that rare and important.

About five miles in, I got up to talk with Tom near the driver, and Professor Wilson laid his Geiger counter on the seat where I'd been sitting. It pegged the needle and set off an alarm. We all looked at the professor.

"Do the volunteer workers take this bus?" he asked our guide.

"*Da*," was the answer.

"So when they sit down after working near the sarcophagus all day, their clothes must have radiation on them. A lot."

The Russian assigned to us just looked at him and the Geiger counter without comment.

The professor turned to us and said, "The important thing is not to ingest dust or particles that are radioactive. We don't want it inside us."

I thought of how day after day for a year, the volunteers had sat here, going back and forth from scraping six inches of topsoil away from the entire ten-mile safety zone—as a start. They came from all over the Soviet Union, responding to the desperate call from the central committee. Five hundred thousand volunteers would be regarded as heroes who would live here for six months at a time in barracks within the zone.

And then, there it was! A beast of a structure in gray, like a giant hive with working bees passing in and out. There was heavy equipment at the base, men running, still running so they wouldn't have to stay too long in a radiation area, always with an eye looking back over their shoulder at the sarcophagus that contained the remains of the reactor #4.

Our bus stopped at the entrance to the building containing four nuclear reactors, RBMK style, more military design than commercial.

Professor Wilson was studying his counter in the entrance plaza. It was deceptive because once we got past the big view, the rest looked quite normal. No signs of a disaster, more like a suburban corporate headquarters in New Jersey.

The director met us at the entrance with his hand extended, smiling. He spoke English and invited us to lunch in his office. On the way up the stairs, he leaned over to me and in confidence said, "We have the most beautiful women in Ukraine working here. You'll see; they'll be serving us lunch."

"I'm hungry already. And our visit to the control room of reactor #4?"
He said, "Yes, yes, after lunch."

With pride, the director ushered us into a room looking out to the western forest view of the grounds, where a long table was set for at least a dozen people. No vodka toast was needed to start the meal. The director was anxious to present his harem.

They came in with dishes piled high with chicken Kyiv, borscht, and *salo. Varenyky* with mashed-potato filling; *holubtsi* cooked with boiled cabbage; and *deruny*, potato pancakes. And walnut-stuffed prunes.

It was enough to make me forget about the Miss Universe servers who strategically brushed the director's back as they swung around the table and arranged the various dishes while the director, an obvious gourmet, described them.

I know this account is a little unorthodox, but if you want the science, there are many studies of the cause of the accident or the long-term childhood thyroid cancer cases. I'd advise googling "Chernobyl."

What you have just read is how journalism is made. It's a journey to get on-site, gather facts from interviews, and reach some conclusions with the facts available at the particular time. You don't accomplish much with a sterile, unsmiling, bullying approach demanding a story. You have to listen and observe. Well-timed questions that are nonconfrontational will give you more accurate answers. If you need to push, be ready, be prepared, and challenge in a matter-of-fact way as if you are so interested that you want to help by helping other people understand their story.

And once on the scene, compare what you *see* with what you are *told*—for consistency.

For example, I was going to interview the second-largest drug lord in the world, with 200,000 acres of opium poppies ready for harvest. We were in his stronghold in Myanmar (formerly Burma). His assistants were begging me not to ask him about being the largest drug dealer. I thought, *What's the point of our coming?* So midway through the interview, when we were getting along well, I asked, "How do you feel when the newspapers in Chiang Mai call you a drug lord?" He jumped at it as if he'd wanted to answer such a question all along.

It was nonconfrontational and, I suggest, more truthful than if I had "wrestled" him over the question. Very often that approach is an attempt to make the interviewer look "tough" by asking hard questions with a stare. You don't have to abandon the hard question that follows the first one; just do it in a way that shows you're genuinely interested in what your interviewee has to say.

After the interview, his assistants thanked me for not creating a scene and being such a smart interviewer.

After lunch, the Chernobyl director led us to a control room exactly like the one where the accident had happened. On the other side of the wall was the sarcophagus, or nuclear reactor "hall," where the core was still open. We would later see inside through photographs, a death zone that truly looked like the end of the world where a deadly force, as invisible as air itself, waited to burn any living thing that was exposed to it. It would be that way for a thousand lifetimes, which means it will be sealed forever.

As we stood in white lab coats looking at the controls and meters with their gauges bouncing, I asked the director to tell me (on camera) what had happened.

More than anyone else whom we had encountered to that point, the director was careful with his statements and I thought fell short of the truth. He was of the central communist regime, trying to hold his world together by perpetuating a lie about what had happened. The truth would soon escape to the people of the Soviet Union and the rest of the world. But not in this interview. I'd have to work harder.

For the NOVA program, I described it in my own words based on the other interviews I'd done there.

One thing I've learned in more than fifty years on the job is that most major human-caused accidents are combinations of untimely bad luck and stupid mistakes. Some call such situations a "perfect storm." That's one way to put it.

The Chernobyl disaster started, ironically, with a "safety" test that was scheduled in the early-morning hours in reactor #4. It was routine, to see how long the turbines would spin and supply power to the main circulating pumps following a loss of main electrical power.

In other words, it was to find out how the reactor would function if the control rods were pulled out of their graphite tubes. Those "safety" rods kept the fission under control by absorbing the radioactivity when the reactor was not in use or being used at low power. When the rods are slowly pulled out, the reaction gets hotter and more power is transferred to the turbines that generate the electricity. The goal was to see how low the energy could go and still keep the turbines spinning.

*Mistake #1* was scheduling the test at 1:23 a.m. There was a postponement of the test for nine hours earlier in the day, which required a new team of operators to run the test. Statistics have shown that many mistakes are caused by sleep deprivation. One's reasoning abilities are slower. Some believe the new operators had been awake beyond acceptable limits, like an airline pilot or truck driver in danger from lack of sleep. They were also terribly, inadequately trained. Some had been at their reactor jobs for only four months.

*Mistake #2* was the mistaken belief that the RBMK reactor was foolproof. In reality, there had been thirteen such reactor accidents in three years. That fact had been kept from the primary operators in charge of the nuclear reactors. Some believe the KGB redacted the information from a report that should have gone to the reactor personnel and scientists. But the report had to protect the reputation of the Soviet Union as infallible.

One report said, "As far as people in the Soviet Union know, the nuclear reactors are flawless. Nothing ever goes wrong. Nothing can go wrong."

Believing they couldn't make a mistake, the operators continued the test, even over warnings, believing they would always be able to stop the reactor's heat building up by reinserting the safety rods or shutting down the reactor.

*Mistake #3* was allowing the rods to be pulled completely out, thus shutting down all the safety features. When they needed them to stop the fission buildup, they could get the rods only halfway back into the core. The heat continued building, and the reactor was heating up out of control.

The tips of the safety rods—some two hundred of them—were made of graphite, which when heated excessively reacts badly with water, as in—it explodes. Now exposed to both air and the heat from the reactor core, the graphite moderator reached water intended to cool the reactor and caused a massive steam explosion that blew the top off the reactor and with it the roof of the containment building, releasing massive amounts of radioactivity across one-third of Europe.

The operators were blamed for the accident.

Valery Legasov was the leading scientist in charge of the cleanup. In August 1986, he presented a report of the Soviet delegation to a special meeting of the International Atomic Energy Agency. He felt that he had to cut through the Communist Party's cover-up and speak some truth: that the accident could potentially wipe out much of the European continent. He was devastated at the censorship applied by the Soviet nuclear agency. It would eventually come out that the plant supervisors had known of previous accidents and shortcomings with the design of the RBMK reactor but failed to pass this information along to the hands-on operators. Legasov had reached a point where he believed that the whole communist system was rotten, favoring lies to protect party officials' status and keep their jobs rather than telling the truth even when thousands, maybe millions of lives were at risk.

He told Gorbachev as much. On April 27, 1988, two years after the accident. Within a few days, Legasov hanged himself in his Moscow apartment.

On our way out of the ten-mile safety zone, the bus turned into Pripyat, the village of apartment buildings only seven miles from the reactors. Workers on the original reactors had lived there. We saw where the children had played, the seesaws and swings and slides. There was a small Ferris wheel outside the school decorated with children's drawings. It was empty, abandoned.

All forty-nine thousand residents had been bused out within hours of the explosion, never to return, perhaps the most important measure the officials took to protect them from radiation.

We walked down the empty streets of Pripyat, watching the wind blow curtains out the open windows of vacant apartments. The red berries were out on hawthorn trees. An orphaned dog meandered through the streets, looking for scraps. Block after block of abandoned apartment buildings were still filled with personal belongings left as they were being used just seconds before the evacuation.

Many institutions have wanted to know the effect of radiation on humans and the environment. Those who lived in Pripyat were lucky. Most left quickly enough on buses to avoid coming in contact with radiation. And lucky again because the cloud that went straight up from the reactor blew the other way and missed Pripyat.

According to a 2018 report by the United Nations Scientific Committee on the Effects of Atomic Radiation (UNSCEAR), about twenty thousand cases of thyroid cancer were diagnosed from 1991 to 2015 in patients who were eighteen and under at the time of the accident. The report stated that one-quarter of the cases (five thousand) were "probably" due to high doses of radiation and that this fraction was likely to have been higher in earlier years after the accident and lower in later years. Leukemia was also a feared result of the accident.

Before we left the Chernobyl site, the assistant director and I hit it off well enough for him to invite me for a quick visit the next day to the second-largest film studio in the Soviet Union. It was in Kyiv. He led me into the screening room, which was large enough to seat a symphony orchestra to sync a soundtrack with a 35-mm film on a thirty-five-foot screen above the musicians. As we sat alone in the auditorium-sized room, he motioned to the operator above us to roll the film. Up came black-and-white 35-mm footage from the first camera on the scene of the explosion.

"Watch the helicopter," he said.

The Russian chopper was flying over the reactor, trying to get a sight line into the core to see if it was on fire. Suddenly it flipped on its side and plunged into the hole above reactor #4. No survivors. He wanted a hefty price for what was indeed a shocking piece of film. I turned it down. We had our show in the can.

But there was more. Another helicopter turned on its side, and the camera was looking straight down into the nuclear core at a red spot. It was the graphite on fire, at 2,000 degrees. I asked my friend, "Was there a moment when you thought you wouldn't be able to put it out? I mean, the graphite metal was on fire."

He said, "No, no. we were in control."

That was not true. They were scared from spine to toes. None of them had seen a metal core on fire. There was no instruction book on how to put it out.

We looked at more footage. The most dramatic was footage of firefighters running exposed on the roof of the nuclear reactor to remove the pieces of the core that had landed there. They could be exposed for ninety seconds only and took turns.

At a conference in Kyiv in May 1988, the impacts were summarized as thirty-one deaths. Most of those deaths were of firefighters who exposed themselves to radiation in order to do their jobs. They were true firefighters in every inch of their being, believing at the time that they were the last chance to save the country. One firefighter referred to them as "kamikazes."

As we were over the Atlantic headed back to the US, now the first American documentary team to have visited the site of the worst nuclear disaster in history, I reflected on what I had seen, the officials I'd met, and the normal conversations with Russians. I'll call them Russians because even then I could see that they were ready to say goodbye to the Soviet system.

I predicted that Chernobyl would be the straw that broke the "bear's back." The Communist Party and all its members were more interested in keeping their positions than in telling the truth. My prediction turned out to be right.

Twenty years after Chernobyl, Mikhail Gorbachev wrote in an article for the magazine *Project Syndicate*, "The Chernobyl disaster, more than anything else, opened the possibility of much greater freedom of expression, to the point that the system as we knew it could no longer continue. It made absolutely clear how important it was to continue the policy of glasnost, and I must say that I started to think about time in terms of pre-Chernobyl and post-Chernobyl."

In the back of my mind, I wondered if my team and I would start to feel the effects of radiation poisoning. Upon returning to the US, we visited Argonne for a follow-up scan for radiation we might have picked up. We were all negative. But why take the risk? To learn what went wrong and how to prevent it from happening again. It's that simple. It's journalism.

In the most dramatic example possible, we had seen the consequences of failing to tell the truth.

# TWENTY-FIVE

# The Anchorman

There's a well-known axiom in news that serious journalists don't do movies. We've chosen to be trusted with truth and are given access in order to find the truth where others would not be permitted. Participating in movies was crossing the line between information and entertainment. It blurred the boundary between fact and fiction. The press corps feared that once a journalist went to Hollywood, the audience might start to ask, *So when you're on TV reading the news, is that the truth, or is that just another script?*

So in the early 2000s, when I received a script from first-time director Adam McKay asking if I'd be interested in being the narrator in a film called *Anchorman,* my first inclination was a firm no, thank you—next! It was the answer he expected, but he thought he'd give it a try anyway.

But then the little gremlin on my shoulder began to whisper, "Who do you think you are, Edward R. Murrow? Sure, you call yourself a journalist, but you're a long way from Agent Orange. At least read the script!" Okay, fine.

I agreed to audition with the script blind. I read it for the first time in front of McKay and the other two producers, Will Ferrell and Judd Apatow. I stood in the narration booth at Kurtis Productions in Chicago and started reading for the *Anchorman* team gathered in the sound booth at Universal Studios in California. I cleared my throat and got ready to give it the classic Bill Kurtis treatment. I had thousands of hours on camera and hundreds more in the narration booth, most recently for *Cold Case Files*. Reading this would be no problem.

But a few lines in, something happened. I was laughing. The hard professionalism broke, and I couldn't help myself. Each line was so funny, I had to take a pause to get my breath back and get back into character of Bill Kurtis, serious journalist, before moving on to the next.

I got a "Thank you, we'll call you" from the West Coast. I thought I had blown my audition. That was fine. Little did I know that my small audience of producers and studio executives was thrilled to hear that their worked-over words were funny to fresh eyes. McKay and Ferrell had been working over these jokes for so long that they couldn't tell what was funny anymore. When they heard me laugh, they knew the script was good. And they thought I was the perfect voice to introduce the movie and be the professional straight man, contrasted against the larger-than-life chaos of Ron Burgundy.

I left the booth and got ready to fly home to my ranch in Kansas. But I decided to take another look at the script while sitting in the squeezed-down tube of a fuselage in the regional jet. It was a laugh-out-loud experience and rather embarrassing among the other passengers.

I called Donna LaPietra, my life partner who would become my wife after forty-three years together. We had met when she was a producer at WBBM-TV. When I landed and asked her to phone our good friend and well-known Hollywood producer Harold Ramis, she was even more nervous than I was, wondering if signing up for a comedy movie would flush my forty-year career in journalism. Harold pleaded the Fifth, explaining that no one can predict the success or failure of anything that comes out of Hollywood. I'd be rolling the dice either way. But he said, "They're good people doing it, even though it's Adam's first film, and Will Ferrell has a good track record. Most of them come out of *Saturday Night Live*, so they know how to be funny. But it's still a crapshoot."

It was not an easy call. Did I want my name attached to a movie where local news teams meet in a deadly gangland-style alley fight? I must admit it was funny and creative. And it conjured up memories from my own days in the ratings wars.

But I couldn't get the opening image out of my head. A helicopter flying over San Diego: "There was a time . . . a time before cable . . . when the local anchorman reigned supreme. When people believed everything they heard on TV ... This was an age when only men were allowed to read the news. And in San Diego, one anchorman was more man than the rest. His name was Ron Burgundy."

The helicopter lands in the middle of a busy intersection, and loafers step down in the middle of a crowded street. The man has a commanding presence, an affable smile, and perfectly parted hair. All of San Diego seems to embrace him.

Back to the narration: "He was like a god walking amongst mere mortals. He had a voice that could make a wolverine purr. And suits so fine they made Sinatra look like a hobo. In other words, Ron Burgundy was the balls."

I couldn't fight the temptation to drop my voice to its lowest register to scorch the word "balls" with every ounce of gravitas I could muster. I must admit that I hesitated before reading the word.

I was hooked. Reading words that evoked laughter was intoxicating, and I wanted more. As they say, it was transformational. I was a small part of a comedic dream team. An older member, of course, and a stranger in a wonderful new land. Who cared if the movie was a hit or embarrassing? The process was thrilling.

So, like Ron Burgundy cannonballing into the swimming pool with a tumbler of Scotch, I decided to take the leap into the unknown. Forty years in journalism? I saw a danger if I might be associated with the comic character of Will Ferrell, the composite anchorman with all the quirks and shortcomings of typical anchor readers around the country. I was *not* the title character in the film. Rather, I played the network anchor, someone to play against, to remind the audience what a *real* anchorman should be, leaving the showcase to Will.

I still had some narration to record, so on my way to Universal City, I wondered about how Adam and Will had come up with the idea. Did they think *I* was their model for *Anchorman*? I would find out that the answer was yes and no. When Adam McKay was starting his career in improvisational comedy at Chicago's famous Second City, Walter Jacobson and I were riding high in local television news. With our emphasis on breaking our own stories and lifted by heavy promotion both in newspapers and on air, our local anchorman roles were, as my narration said, "supreme." From our seats at the newsroom anchor desk, our emphasis was serious. Our mission was an extension of the mission of CBS News: to introduce real journalism to television and hope the ratings would follow. We wanted to break stories, not just read the newspaper for a definition of news. Coming from three years in the West Coast Bureau of CBS News, with Walter Cronkite as a model, I was maniacal about straight-down-the-middle reporting.

But Adam McKay and Will Ferrell saw something in our anchormen personas, and in local anchormen in markets across the country, that they knew could be a platform for comedy. They would face years of questions, especially from journalists, about who the real anchorman was. After as many years of observing, it's my feeling that their Ron Burgundy is a composite of the hundreds of people who travel over the airwaves into homes on a nightly basis to read the news.

I was invited to Los Angeles and to the Universal lot, where the film crew was in the final days of shooting. It was the scene at the bear pit, where Christina Applegate, as leading woman Veronica Corningstone, was reporting on a new arrival—a large grizzly bear at the San Diego Zoo. In the scene, Veronica was in the pit doing a live report. The shot was quite safe and consisted of a mechanical head of a bear to be shot from a perspective behind the ears. Leading to the close-up was a real grizzly bear in the pit to make the audience think that the whole scene was real.

But unexpectedly, during the filming of the establishing scene, the authentic grizzly made a move toward Veronica, or at least appeared to. He took one look at Veronica and did what we would expect a red-blooded griz to do: he emitted a low, guttural communication and leaned toward her. It was totally unplanned.

The trainer leaped forward to get control, and the crew ushered Veronica up a ladder and out of the pit, quite disturbed at the brush with a carnivorous beast looking for a meal ticket.

That was when I arrived. Much like the bear, I felt the reporter's instinct move me toward the bear pit, anxious to put pencil to paper. Alas, I realized that all was under control, and although the incident was legitimate, it had happened on a fictional movie set.

Anxious to finish the shot in the pit that had been expensively dressed (in movie terms) overnight, the production team quieted the extras and sent Veronica back down to the lair. As they say in the business, she showed spunk.

My one trip to Universal Studios and a couple of hours in the recording booth was the closest I got to the actual production. But I was privileged to play at the edge of a cauldron of creativity. As an added bonus, I was included in the New York premiere and qualified for SAG residuals.

Was I worried about being identified as an egotistical boob for the rest of my life? No worry. *Anchorman* turned out to be a classic hit that earned $90 million from domestic and international sales. It launched the film careers of a generation of comedians who would dominate the big screen for years to come. If they weren't already, Will Ferrell, Steve Carrell, Paul Rudd, and director Adam McKay became household names in comedy.

To my even greater surprise, *Anchorman* captured the hearts of television journalists everywhere. Every anchorman and anchorwoman in America wanted to have the title role in *Anchorman*, and many proudly claimed to have been the model for the part. In Jacksonville, the local stations staged mock "alley fights" for charity. I was invited almost yearly to appear on San Diego television just to recite the signature line "Stay classy, San Diego."

My reputation as a serious newsman was saved and maybe even slightly improved. And when I was asked to come back for the sequel, it was a no-brainer.

Twenty years later, *Anchorman* stood as the launch point of many careers and could claim to have given birth to a comedy ensemble that would rule this genre of cinema for the next ten years, maybe twenty—spanning the end of the twentieth century into the twenty-first.

Ron Burgundy himself, Will Ferrell, led the way with multiple movie platforms for his pratfalls. It's one thing to have a studio hire a talent to repeat certain antics in one or two movies. It's quite another to create their own moneymaker. When you write and produce your first hit, it's easier to get funding for the next. The studio is along for the ride.

*Anchorman* producer Judd Apatow did the same thing. He brought his own style of humor to life with hits like *The 40-Year-Old Virgin*.

The *Anchorman* script commented, "Brian Fantana went on to have great success as the host of the hit reality TV show *Intercourse Island* on the Fox Network." Actually, Paul Rudd used his investigative-reporter role to become a leading male movie star in *The 40-Year-Old Virgin*, *Ghostbusters: Afterlife*, *Avengers Endgame*, and his own action flick, *Ant-Man*. That's also called leverage.

Perhaps the biggest leap forward was for the Weatherman, Steve Carell, who made the difficult turn from comedy to drama, parlaying his ditzy role in *Anchorman* into a wide range of serious and funny characters in productions like *The 40-Year-Old Virgin*, *Little Miss Sunshine*, the television hit *The Office*, and the breakthrough quasi-comic documentary *The Big Short*. And they just keep piling up. In the *Anchorman* script, I laughed loudest at the recap for Steve's mentally challenged character: "Brick Tamland is married with eleven children and is one of the top political advisers to the Bush White House."

Will Ferrell's name is in lights in Hollywood lore, as he has honored the great comedians like Abbott and Costello, Jerry Lewis, Robin Williams, Bob Newhart, and Bob Hope with a list of motion pictures that could keep a theater open for a year. The final answer to the question "Who is the real anchorman?" is Will Ferrell!

Finally, who would believe that out of a silly, slapstick directorial debut, there would arise a genius who found his God-given talent as a storyteller? Ironically, just as I was worried about losing a journalistic identity by crossing the line into fictional entertainment, Adam McKay was going the other way, using the instruments of moviemaking with all its creative visuals to tell complex journalistic stories. He chose subject matter that was difficult if not impossible to understand in print and television, using the nontraditional tools as a new language that had not been seen before in serious moviemaking. He tackled climate change on the big screen with major stars acting out the risk of humankind becoming extinct when a meteor hit Earth and followed with an array of television triumphs.

He also created a cinematic dissection of what had caused the near collapse of the economy in 2008, explaining it so simply that a high school student could understand. That takes guts because it goes against the "safe" path—the corporate way, the studio way.

And sound the trumpets—Adam McKay was rewarded with moviemaking's highest honor, an Oscar for best director in *The Big Short*.

Yes, the world was waiting for a sequel under the title *Anchorman 2: The Legend Continues*. As I entered the theater for the premiere on Broadway, Adam handed me a page of narration that he and Will had written and asked me to read it for the audience. I think it reveals the not-so-subtle workings of a comic mind that can't pass up an opportunity:

> Welcome to the premiere of *Anchorman 2: The Legend Continues*. We'll get started in a minute, but first, Adam McKay, the director, and Will would like for me to thank a few people. They would like to thank their wives for their support and patience. They would like to thank the president of Paramount Pictures. They would like to thank the men who raised the flag at Iwo Jima. Without them, we would be fighting a guerrilla war in our basement against men on skis with Uzis. They'd like to thank Metta World Peace [basketball player] for his defensive work, for his mental attitude on the court. And they would like to thank all the courageous and brave anchormen and -women who nightly read everything that is put in front of them. Without them, we would have to read the news ourselves, and that would be a drag.

In recording my lines for the sequel, I came upon an ending in the script that was ultimately cut. It's too bad because I'm still laughing. It read, "In 1980, Ron Burgundy died. I'm sorry, I misread that. I should have said he cried."

Is there a lesson here? Philosopher and cocreator of the Great Books series for Encyclopedia Britannica Mortimer Adler told me he would define achieving "success" as hard work and luck. Yes, it threw me too.

If there is one driving theme from my nearly ninety-year lifespan, it is *Do what you love, and you'll love what you do.* That also sums up my brush with Hollywood and my life as an anchorman.

# TWENTY-SIX

# Wait Wait . . . Don't Tell Me!

After decades of reporting in the field, sitting behind the anchor desk, and working in the production studio, I've learned that perspective matters. It's an old adage in the news business that the deeper you go, the more angles to a story you'll find. The first priority is getting your facts straight and reporting the truth. But you also have to decide what angle to approach those facts from, what to give the most attention, what tone to use to describe it all. There are wrong ways to do this, of course, but there's almost always more than one right way to do it too. When I joined the team at National Public Radio's *Wait Wait . . . Don't Tell Me!* in 2014, I discovered a new angle to get at the news—humor. And I was surprised and delighted to see the healing powers that this fresh perspective can offer.

*Wait Wait* is described as NPR's hour-long news quiz based on the weekly headlines. An interesting if somewhat mundane premise. But the magic is in the comedy. Peter Sagal and his panel of nationally known comedians, mirth makers, cutups, wise crackers, smart alecks, and jokesters find the humor in the week's news and riff on the absurdity of current events, all in front of a live studio audience. The show gives us all permission to laugh at the news. It puts out in the open what everyone is thinking but is too nervous to say. It's always deviously clever, somewhat shocking, and very intelligent. Beginning at a time when radio was still quasi-king and podcasts had not yet entered the scene, NPR found something special with *Wait Wait.* And our little news quiz is still going strong, with five million weekly listeners and writers who could go toe-to-toe with Stephen Colbert's, Jimmy Kimmel's, and Jimmy Fallon's late-night teams.

But every comedy needs a straight man, and that's how I fit in. In order to give the program some gravitas, *Wait Wait* has always been co-hosted by a straight journalist, a real live newsman. In the beginning, it was Carl Kasell, the Walter Cronkite of NPR, who left his ivory tower at *Morning Edition* once a week to provide a serious counterweight to the program. But when Karl slipped into retirement for health reasons, the show was left with a quandary—how do you replace someone who's irreplaceable?

My good friend and *Wait Wait* host Peter Sagal reached out, asking if I'd fill in. I'm still not sure why I got the call in the first place. Was it my journalistic bona fides? My voice? (You want gravitas? Listen to this!) Or maybe it was that I was conveniently living a short commute from the show's home theater. Regardless, I got the call not knowing that Peter and company expected me to last for a single show. But, like Carl, I found it so delightful that I shocked everyone by accepting the offer to become the permanent official judge and scorekeeper. Never let someone who's been reading about murders and disasters all his life taste the sound of laughter.

Even though I'm the serious newsman on-stage with a bunch of co-medians, I can still be part of the fun. As the straight man with the deep voice and anchorman persona, I help turn the satire up to eleven. As an audience member once said, "It sounds funnier when coming from the mouth of your banker."

Every week I glide through the broadcast reading limericks, announc-ing winners, reading sponsorship blurbs, and occasionally injecting a strategic humorous comment. Over time, the writers started to give me more and more jokes, still delivered with the same newsman persona. It first came in the form of my self-introduction at the top of the show. One of my favorite lines has become famous within the *Wait Wait* archives: "I'm Bill Kurtis, the voice that inspired your aunt's sexual awakening." And when Congress is in session: "I'm Bill Kurtis, the only bill that can't be vetoed in Washington." Over twelve years and four hundred shows, our writing team went to town on this short blast of a joke, received at first as a surprise, but then the audience expected it and waited for it.

How about "Crack open a cold one, it's *Bill*er-time"?

And when I returned from a few weeks off, my welcome-home statement was "I'm back, bitches!"

My twelve years on the *Wait Wait* stage has also allowed me, always the reporter, a glimpse into the world of the stand-up comic.

One of my first discoveries was that stand-up comics don't laugh easily or often. They appreciate humor as a surgeon admires a clean stitch. Whether it's a clever combination of words you might not expect or the association with another thought altogether, if it produces humor, it goes into the treasure chest.

Second, they are smart, maybe even exceedingly smart, constantly on the hunt for something that everyone is familiar with—a news report; a wife's comment when you're late for dinner; or a child's natural, authentic observation not yet filtered by an adult world—something recognizable they can turn on its head. At the best of times, our trio panel hits on a subject they can't let go of, like Paula Poundstone riffing on someone trying to get into an occupied bathroom. "Are you in there?" she pleads. Then Adam Felber, tired of the wait: "Shall I call 911? The firemen can get in through the window."

Some comics rise above the rest to become true observers of life around us. Using the kind of insight expected to be found on the opinion page of the *New York Times*, they become chroniclers of the times, jesters for the king, an antidote for calamity. They work close to the edge, like a matador flipping the cape from nose to ears until the bull gets tired of it and turns its horns into the soft belly."

Then there is the comedian's passion. The essence of any success that drives souls beyond human capacity. As an outsider, I was captivated from the beginning by the sacrifice it takes to "make it." There's no vaudeville tour scheduled by a fat, cigar-smoking agent in a dreary office overlooking Times Square. The most likely venue is a small firetrap in a shopping mall where the sticky floor measures success in spilled beer. I watched *Wait Wait* panelists hurry to the exit after a show to catch a plane to a far-off basement comedy club for the "privilege" of trying out material for ten minutes in front of an audience of judgmental, take-no-prisoners test groups daring the young upstart to make them laugh.

From behind my *Wait Wait*-branded podium, with decades upon decades of experience in the news business, I was surprised to see such a familiar sight. Ambitious, talented professionals chasing a dream in a punishing, cutthroat business, fueled by passion.

*Wait Wait* panelist Negin Farsad's observation about the job's sacrifice wrings tears instead of laughter: "My daughter doesn't have a mom that can tuck her in every night." She remembered one of the first "hell-gigs" that make you grow hair on your chest: "I was hired by the University of Chicago to do stand-up for the students. For some reason, a large population of elderly Iranian people from the community showed up and criticized me [Negin is Iranian] within earshot about how I sounded like 'a prostitute.' Turns out elderly Iranians are not my best audience."

Every stand-up comedian has to wear these calluses like medals. That's why the friendly and enthusiastic *Wait Wait* family offers such great validation and exposure for a comic. How many appearances at far-flung comedy clubs with fewer than twenty-five seats would it take to equate with five million listeners? Panelist Brian Babylon has done his time on the circuit and ranks *Wait Wait* as a near equivalent to doing *The Tonight Show*. And while Brian's club scene has transformed into Netflix specials, European tours, and fashion pop-ups on North Michigan Avenue, he always has time to come back to the Studebaker Theater in downtown Chicago and riff on the news for an hour. He'll be the one wearing black calfskin pants.

Even the talent that's been honed in Hollywood and on Broadway bows to *Wait Wait* as having remarkable value for a rookie to find the secret formula to survival. Peter Sagal's stage is a serious testing ground because of his speed and his intellect. The reigning queen of *Wait Wait*, Paula Poundstone, credits Sagal with being the wizard of creativity: "Peter is so good. . . . I don't think most people realize how difficult that role is. . . . Peter Sagal has done the job for so long, he doesn't appear to have any uncertainty."

Peter fires off a question, and it's up to the panelists to understand the news and jump on the setup with a brilliant, hilarious response. Mo Rocca is one of those veterans who thought he could use a style perfected on another show, *The Daily Show*, with prepared jokes. It didn't work. "Anytime I came in with a prepared joke, the audience didn't respond. . . . The audience is smart. It can sniff out a phony, maybe even more so when it's audio only."

A *Wait Wait* listener is an old-fashioned radio-centric loyalist who echoes the great Chicago radio days of the thirties. As Mo said, among the radio audience, "public radio is still a pretty big chunk. I'm recognized as much for *Wait Wait* as for anything else I've done."

Paula once told me, "I love doing *Wait Wait*. In my wildest dreams, I would never have thought I'd be on an NPR show nor that I would have NPR listeners for fans . . . but they're a great audience, although some come to my stand-up shows and wonder why I am not answering questions about the week's news." In much the same way, I love being a part of *Wait Wait* every week.

At any given point in my career as a broadcaster and a journalist, I never would have guessed that I'd end up as cohost of public radio's comedy news hour. But over a decade in, I'm so glad I'm here. It's given me new friendships, a peek into entirely new worlds, and a fresh perspective on my craft of telling the news. And just like everything else I've done, it's a lot of fun.

For me, the gig has been a fascinating portal into yet another phase of the news business. Truth and humor can go hand in hand and can make a potent, healing combination. Since I joined *Wait Wait*, we've lived through several crisis moments. Of course, the word "crisis" means "opportunity" to a bunch of comedians.

The endless news cycles about Donald Trump's campaigns, elections, and presidencies have given the show nearly endless satirical fodder, especially for the typical NPR listener. During Trump's first term, our permanent running gag about the "orange creature" was always good for a laugh. But eventually, political antics created real harm, and by the 2024 presidential election, many of the Trump jokes had gone stale. Our audience was shocked, depressed, and burned out with the endless quagmire of news. But still, week after week, they tuned in to *Wait Wait*. We had to change the jokes, find the right stories to riff on, and adjust the tone, but folks still come to us to escape the news by laughing at it.

The second crisis during my tenure was more serious: the COVID-19 pandemic. In only a few short years, more than a million Americans died and countless more were left with lasting side effects and emotional trauma. Not exactly fertile ground for harvesting a weekly laugh, right?

And yet that's where we were wrong. At the end of one show, Peter Sagal was answering questions from the audience. A woman stood up and offered her thanks for providing a humorous break from the bad news. Others chimed in that they looked forward to the weekly show as a respite of normalcy when the world was unraveling around them. Even after the pandemic subsided, the news continued to be difficult for many. And *Wait Wait* is there as a release valve, letting even the most depressed news-obsessed listeners find something in the world to laugh at. After decades in the business, I am still finding new angles, and I'm always delighted.

# TWENTY-SEVEN

# The Journey Continues

Whenever I return to Topeka, Kansas, I drive to Burnett's Mound and climb to the top. Looking toward the northeast, I can still make out the twenty-two-mile path of the tornado, clear as the day it happened that evening in June 1966. Just as clearly, I can see the journey of my life. A whirlwind of events, a dizzying collection of stories, given clarity by the passage of time and the warm, soothing wind as it comes up the west side of Burnett's Mound, having traveled across miles of cultivated crops and native prairie.

Looking at all the stories I've gathered here, a whirlwind career that's pushed me into history more than enough times for one person, it may be surprising to know that there's even more adventures to share. I've learned by now that there's always another question to ask, always another side to the story.

For me, the other side to my story appeared when I stepped into a different part of the news business and threw everything I had behind what I had come to love the most—documentaries. In my mind, true journalism was four things: find the story, record it, write it, present it. And I wanted to do it all. So while I was at WBBM-TV (the third time), I started Kurtis Productions. And again, armed with a combination of experience, skill, and luck, I was up and running. PBS, WTTW-TV, and I brought the world of scientific discovery to kids across the country with *The New Explorers*. I helped usher in the golden age of cable documentaries with

*Cold Case Files* and *Investigative Reports* on A&E and *American Greed* on CNBC. I traveled the world again, telling stories. Over five hundred documentaries and many narrations later, I'm still going strong.

But that's all a story for another time.


The wind keeps blowing, and the journey continues.

# Acknowledgments

Every person who appears in these pages deserves my thanks. While writing it I could see their faces again, as they were sixty years ago. They all linger in my memory with the clarity of a sunny morning. Writing this book has offered me the chance to relive my memories and revisit these old friends. I felt the backwash of a jet engine at Tan Son Nhut and the warm lagoon water in Marquette Park. I tasted the chili rellenos during the lunch break at the Manson trial and smelled the sweet curing tobacco in North Carolina barns. I shuddered in the chill October night running from Lincoln Park protests and saw clearly the young man lighting a stoop in the fires along Madison Street. I felt the honest friendship of Iva Toguri D'Aquino, the kindness of Muhammad Ali, and the pure joy of radio listeners. With the passage of time, friends and colleagues have become characters in a lifetime of stories, all gathered as a marvelous cast of characters, arranged like it was always meant to be. Nothing is lost nor forgotten in a life's journey.

The few who made this book possible deserve special thanks, and this is as good an occasion as any.

Joyce Harrison, editor in chief at the University Press of Kansas, was the first to believe in this book.

Alec Loganbill, my editor, provided a talented eye and steady hand when judging *Whirlwind* from inside the vortex of my life.

Kelly Chrisman Jacques, my production editor, offered her kind guidance and skill as she turned a manuscript into a book.

Justin Henning and the rest of the marketing staff at the UPK shared my excitement for these stories as they introduced this book to the world.

Nick Carswell, Feloniz Lovato-Winston, and the whole team at Audio-Reader and Kansas Public Radio brought this story to life as an audiobook.

No memoir of mine would be complete without an acknowledgment of my wife, Donna La Pietra. She has been my daily partner in a life of fulfilling journalistic work and a private life of committed volunteerism. I could not have wished for a more creative producer to walk together on the long road of my career or a more caring woman who often took me down paths I would never have traveled alone. She is herself a whirlwind of creative storms, but also the calm where we reside.

For my daughter, Mary Kristin Kurtis, who shared a whirlwind life that started in the tornado. She now manages her own bison ranch and the Red Buffalo gift shop in Sedan, Kansas.

We remember my son, Scott, diagnosed with schizophrenia, who passed away at the age of thirty-eight in 2009. He never had a chance.

The writing of this book has been nearly as much of a whirlwind as the stories it contains. Everyone mentioned here and so many others have my deepest gratitude and thanks.

# About the Author

**Bill Kurtis** is currently the president of Kurtis Productions and has also authored *Bill Kurtis: On Assignment* and *The Death Penalty on Trial: Crisis in American Justice*. He founded the Red Buffalo Ranch in southeast Kansas, where his daughter, Mary Kristin Kurtis, raises grass-fed bison, and he works to restore small-town America in Sedan, Kansas. He and his wife, Donna, conserve gardens, woods, and prairie north of Chicago, where they live.

# Plainspoken Books

Born in Kansas, Plainspoken Books is a boutique publisher of nonfiction books that explore the politics, cultures, and environments of the Midwest.

The Midwest is culturally complex, politically relevant, and environmentally essential to understanding where the United States is at and where we are going. We at Plainspoken Books are committed to discovering and nurturing talented writers who share this vision and are eager to share their stories with the rest of the country.

Plainspoken Books is an imprint of the University Press of Kansas.

www.ingramcontent.com/pod-product-compliance
Lightning Source LLC
LaVergne TN
LVHW090848210925
821584LV00010B/151/J